Explore

Explore

Vocational Discovery in Ministry

Edited by Kristina Lizardy-Hajbi
and Matthew Floding

AN ALBAN INSTITUTE BOOK
ROWMAN & LITTLEFIELD
Lanham • Boulder • New York • London

Published by Rowman & Littlefield
An imprint of The Rowman & Littlefield Publishing Group, Inc.
4501 Forbes Boulevard, Suite 200, Lanham, Maryland 20706

www.rowman.com

86-90 Paul Street, London EC2A 4NE

Copyright © 2022 by The Rowman & Littlefield Publishing Group, Inc.

All rights reserved. No part of this book may be reproduced in any form or by any electronic or mechanical means, including information storage and retrieval systems, without written permission from the publisher, except by a reviewer who may quote passages in a review.

British Library Cataloguing in Publication Information Available

Library of Congress Cataloging-in-Publication Data

Names: Lizardy-Hajbi, Kristina, editor. | Floding, Matthew, 1955- editor.
Title: Explore : vocational discovery in ministry / edited by Kristina Lizardy-Hajbi and Matthew Floding.
Description: Lanham, Maryland : Alban, an Alban Institue Books/Rowman & Littlefield [2021] | Series: Explorations in theological field education | Includes bibliographical references and index.
Identifiers: LCCN 2022021951 (print) | LCCN 2022021952 (ebook) | ISBN 9781538167632 (cloth) | ISBN 9781538167649 (paperback) | ISBN 9781538167656 (ebook)
Subjects: LCSH: Pastoral theology--Fieldwork. | Clergy--Training of. | Clergy--Office.
Classification: LCC BV4164.5 .E975 2021 (print) | LCC BV4164.5 (ebook) | DDC 253--dc23/eng/20220706
LC record available at https://lccn.loc.gov/2022021951
LC ebook record available at https://lccn.loc.gov/2022021952

Contents

Introduction *Kristina Lizardy-Hajbi and Matthew Floding*	ix
A Community Said Yes *Matthew Floding*	1
Callings Shaped by Purpose *Kristina Lizardy-Hajbi*	5
What Are Pastors For? *Will Willimon*	11
A Priest of Priests *Melissa Florer-Bixler*	17
Hear. See. Tell. Walk Through the Unlocked Door *William H. Lamar IV*	21
A Calling Worthy of My Life *Brian Keepers*	25
Chaplaincy: Ministry that Ferments and Seasons *Nancy Elizabeth Wood*	29
Engaging, Embracing, and Expressing Self in Callings *Tammerie Day*	35
What is Your Thing? Discerning "It" and Doing "It" Scared! *Danielle J. Buhuro*	39
A Call to Serve *Ruth Naomi Segres*	43
A Calling to the Academy *David Emmanuel Goatley*	47

Vocation as Communal 53
Christine J. Hong

Learning To Be Carried 57
Keith Starkenburg

Rags to Riches to Rags 61
Miguel A. De La Torre

Participating in God's Wide Welcome: The Ministry of Camps,
Conference, and Retreat Centers 65
Theresa F. Latini

It Started with Trees 71
Kent Busman

In Such a Season 75
Elivette Mendez Angulo

Becoming the Clay 79
Megan Shepherd

A Calling to Campus 83
Trygve D. Johnson

Doing Campus Ministry Latinamente 87
Eddie De León

Unfolding 91
Kate Holbrook

Called by Name for Engagement with the World 95
Mary Schaller Blaufuss

So, You're the Bishop 99
James Hazelwood

To Say Yes, Again and Again and Again 103
Karen Oliveto

Ministry in the Public Square 107
Traci Blackmon

The Inward and Outward Journey of Ministry 111
Wesley Granberg-Michaelson

The Communion Table as Vocational Pathway in Nonprofit
Leadership 115
David Harrison and John Senior

Discovering God's Call in Prayer and Community 119
  greg little

Ministry Connecting Faith and Health 123
  Kathie Bender Schwich

Called by Community 127
  Marilyn Pagán-Banks

Spiritual Entrepreneurship 131
  Patrick G. Duggan

A Way Out of No Way 135
  Tawana Davis

A (Non) Sacramental (Non) Ministry of Food 139
  Mariah Hayden

A Thread You Follow 143
  Nathan E. Kirkpatrick

Holy Friendships: Ecumenical and Interfaith Connections 147
  Katie Crowe

An Unexpected Way 153
  Liddy Barlow

The Unexpected within a Call 157
  Michael Bos

Just Keep Walking 161
  Amanda Henderson

Starting New Faith Communities: What's the Point? 165
  Chris S. Davies

On Starting New Things While the World Is Burning 169
  Tyler Sit

Mi Camino 173
  Rhina Ramos

Farm Church 177
  Allen C. Brimer

Introducing Bivocational Ministry 181
  Darryl W. Stephens

Thank God for Friends 187
  Scott Cameron

Jarena's Daughter *Faye Taylor*	191
Cobbling a Mosaic in Vocation *Rebecca Jeney Park-Hearn*	195
Conclusion *Matthew Floding and Kristina Lizardy-Hajbi*	199
Notes	201
Index	209
About the Contributors	219

Introduction

Kristina Lizardy-Hajbi and Matthew Floding

"Now there are varieties of gifts, but the same Spirit; and there are varieties of services, but the same Lord; and there are varieties of activities, but it is the same God who activates all of them in everyone" (1 Cor. 12:4–6).

Clearly, when it comes to gifts and service, a spirit of openness and a rich theological imagination are needed. The Explorations in Theological Field Education series, of which *Explore: Vocational Discovery in Ministry* is the latest installment, aims to catalyze the kind of growth that can take place in a highly experiential and relational learning environment. The books in the series—*Engage, Empower,* and *Enlighten*—each address a different facet of this lived learning experience: supporting the student and the supervisor-mentor, and providing theories of learning that create lenses for both to reflect more deeply on their experiences.

Our observation (confirmed by ATS research) is that MDiv graduates follow diverse vocational pathways.[1] It is also our observation that many of our MDiv students, while confident that they are in the right degree program, are less confident about discerning the particulars of where it will lead them. Confirmed in our conversations with both students and colleagues is that many of these gifted students are not aware of the multiple vocational pathways for which the MDiv prepares students.

Explore: Vocational Discovery in Ministry aims to encourage and equip you in your vocational discernment by informing and enlarging your imagination. We hope to ignite your passion for service by providing plausible pathways by way of inspiring examples. We've chosen for *Explore* eleven common vocational pathways followed by MDiv graduates. For each, a framing chapter informs by describing what is at the core of that particular service and provides personal examples. To inspire and enlarge imaginations, three practitioners then tell their personal stories of discerning their way to this calling. Encountering these stories might be the spark that ignites the passionate desire you have for performing acts of love, mercy, justice, and witness through that vocational pathway. That is our hope.

Our journey together in *Explore* begins with our own stories. We (Kristina and Matt) have each lived the discernment process. We also represent not only personal difference in terms of gender and race, but also generational difference. We hope that these, too, might encourage you on your unique vocational journey.

For theological field educators, supervisor-mentors, and instructors who utilize *Explore* with students, we invite you to share the chapters that might resonate the most depending on individual journeys and contexts. Perhaps a student is just beginning to discern the possibilities for their field education experience, or maybe someone is currently serving in a role that is not aligned with their passions and gifts in ministry and wants to imagine other prospects. Perhaps an individual is wanting to be inspired by another's unique or even unconventional path to their current ministry, or maybe a student wants to gain a firsthand account of the joys and challenges of a particular vocational path. This book contains wisdom for each of these individuals, as well as for classes, cohorts, and other groups that would benefit from diving more deeply into the range of reflections and ministry options herein.

We are grateful to each of the contributors for sharing such deeply personal reflections. We hope that reliving the journey has been a source of joy and renewal for their service. We are grateful for the support and encouragement that Natalie Mandziuk from Rowman & Littlefield provided throughout the process. We also wish to thank Hilary McKane for her careful work as copy editor.

A Community Said Yes

Matthew Floding

A Community said "yes" to Jesus first.

Something like this was asked of the congregation: "Do you promise to nurture Matthew in the Christian faith as you are empowered by God's Spirit and help him to live in the covenant of baptism and in communion with the church?"[1] I can't recall—I was two months old—but I'm pretty sure they responded with conviction, "We will!"

Later, I said "yes" to Jesus in making public profession of faith as part of my confirmation experience. I hope that it encouraged the congregation that had kept their baptismal promises. They collectively had instilled in me the notion that saying "yes" to Jesus meant following him in a way that included acts of love, mercy, justice, and witness. I wanted to follow Jesus.

I found a special joy in living this commitment at summer camp. Seeing the winsome leaders at work as a camper led me to aspire to be *just like them*. So, from fourteen years of age on I spent the summers at camp in Minnesota and later, while in college, in Colorado. Most important for my formation was the intentional mentoring, training, support, and being given what felt like huge amounts of responsibility—with opportunities to reflect on exercising that leadership regularly, and then being given more responsibility. It fed my passion for growth and service.

I began to see that I had some leadership skills emerging that were affirmed by other leaders. Given that these environments were specifically Christian in orientation, I began to wonder how that leadership transferred to a church context. I shared my wonderings with my pastor and some other church leaders during my sophomore year in college. Their response was to provide additional service opportunities at church and to keep in touch with me. Then just before my senior year they provided some critical guidance. They suggested that I check out the "Jobs Board" at college and see if a church was looking for a part-time youth minister for the year. This would, they assured me, provide another context in which to gain perspective on using my gifts for service and discerning direction. I checked it out. There were opportunities, and as it turned out a small urban church took me on as youth minister for the year. I taught Sunday School, organized socials, preached my first sermon, attended student sports and theater events, took the group on a weekend retreat—and had a blast! More than forty years later I'm still in touch with some of the "kids." As I headed back to camp in Colorado at the end of the school year, that Community seemed to be saying, "yes" to my gifts and encouraging me to consider next steps in discernment.

Parenthesis. This may seem like a seamless experience, but I assure you that I was a pretty normal 1970s teenager with all of the mishaps, misadventures, successes and spectacular failures, emotional highs and lows, fears and self-doubt. Luther's saint/sinner would be a pretty accurate description of me. For this chapter, however, I'm focusing on pulling on the thread that is the Communities that encouraged me and the experiences that led me to attend seminary and enter ordained ministry.

What I was feeling *internally* while serving at camp and in church contexts encouraged me to explore more. Learning from the Bible that God could use flawed people—that in fact that's the only kind available to God—was also reassuring! Add to that the *external* affirmation of camp leaders, home church, my experiment church, and quietly supportive parents, there seemed to be only one direction to go—seminary to prepare for the future of which I had been given a glimmer.

I was given an additional gift. A pastor from a church in neighboring Minneapolis approached me as I headed out to Colorado for summer camp with an invitation to work with their high school group and coach the local high school's soccer team (I played soccer in college, and it turned out to be Prince's high school—but that's another story). They had a two-year grant. It seemed like a great opportunity, and it gave two additional years to discern. During that time, I got married—another story—received more mentoring, had amazing opportunities, learned more about my gifts, and importantly, about myself. Another Community said "yes." Then, it was off to Chicago to attend McCormick Theological Seminary.

The church where I was able to do my theological field education invited me to extend that experience with a part-time position while I finished seminary. I had a tremendous mentor and a generous and forgiving congregation that took its mentoring role seriously. I continued to grow into my ministerial identity. With a newly minted MDiv in my hand, that Community said "yes" by extending a call, and having completed denominational requirements, I was ordained and installed as associate pastor.

I'm thinking about where you are in your journey of saying "yes" to Jesus. I haven't described the financial strains of those years, the joy of our first child coming into the world and being stretched tremendously by the range of demands (and skills) expected of pastors. I'm not taking time to tell you about being coached by the pastor from another church when my senior pastor asked me to conduct his father's funeral two weeks after being ordained. I wish I could take pages to tell you about how members of the congregation continued to lovingly mentor me. The Community kept saying "yes." And I haven't shared stories of transformation, answers to prayer, seeing the Word at work in a congregation as it became more inclusive, and two more children arriving in our family! What all of it underscores for me, and I hope you have already come to understand, is that call is about discernment—yours and a Community's—and not merely a decision. I also need to acknowledge that the vocational pathway I traveled as a cisgender white male Protestant fairly corresponded to the expectations of the church and seminary systems of the 1970s and 1980s. I felt the ease and support of those constructs while some of my peers did not.

Matt Bloom, who has researched well-being at work for over two decades, considers clergy well-being specifically in his book, *Flourishing in Ministry: How to Cultivate Clergy Well-Being*.[2] I hope that your discernment will include considering how to incorporate his "wise 'small step' well-being practices" in your days of leading and serving.[3] In his work with clergy he also identifies three pathways to ministry.

The first pathway he identifies as *discernment*. This pathway Bloom discovered was true for many whose first career was pastoral ministry. It essentially describes the route I had taken. "Discernment unfolded over long periods of time, often years, and followed a process of self-discovery, mentorship, imagining possible futures, and an eventual and often powerful acknowledgement of the pastoral call."[4]

The second pathway he calls *exploration*. He found that many second-career pastors had traveled this route. "It was through trying out different jobs that explorers learned about not only their talents and aptitudes but also their deepest values and beliefs."[5]

The third path Bloom describes as the *thunderous calling*. "Thunderous callings were unexpected and powerful moments in which individuals experienced what they understood to be a divine revelation."[6] It's possible that someone could experience a combination of these pathways or all three!

Over my lifetime I have met persons in ministry who have traveled each of these pathways. I can only speak to my experience, which has been more like what Parker Palmer describes in *Let Your Life Speak*: that discernment should lead to growing into "the person one has always been."[7] I find this liberating because it spares the headache and heartache of trying to conform to the image of a personal hero or cultural stereotype.

I have found another thing to be true about ministry pathways by reflecting on my journey. Neither you nor I can see the end from the beginning. Who knows—thankfully God does—where the ministry journey will lead us? I could not have predicted that eight years of congregational ministry would be followed by ten years of college chaplaincy to be followed by twenty-three years serving in theological field education.

The other thing I have found to remain true is that while I (and my spouse) needed to discern carefully along this pathway, Communities did too. Their "yes" made these opportunities plausible and possible as we discerned our way. It was their "yes" that created joyful partnerships for collaborative service. For them and to God, I am grateful.

QUESTIONS FOR REFLECTION

1. What rings true about the author's experience as you reflect on your own?
2. Which of the three vocational pathways is most like your own?
3. What Communities have been involved in your discernment of vocation?

Callings Shaped by Purpose

Kristina Lizardy-Hajbi

I am a child of the liminal, of the betwixt and the between. As a result, my deepest vocational discernments have arisen from this aspect of self-knowledge and experience. In my childhood and younger adult years, I loathed always feeling caught between the both/and and the neither/nor of being Puerto Rican-Italian and raised in a primarily Mexican-Chicanx-Native context. In many ways, I resonated with the phrase *ni de aquí, ni de allá* (neither from here, nor from there). However, I came to realize later in life that these core aspects of my identity and formation birthed my most genuine God-breathed gifts and callings in the world. I, Kristina, am a bridge, a border crosser, and a misfit; and this has cultivated within me the ability to exist with resilience and courage in the tension between polarities, to create connections, to be the glue that can hold entities together, and to fit into (and be embraced by) a multiplicity of spaces and places throughout my life and ministry.

The work of discernment is a lifelong endeavor that arises from an assemblage of one's identities, experiences, and relationships. It is helpful to distinguish distinct aspects of this work in order to see the ways in which they converge to form this continual pattern of unfolding. Stephen Lewis, Matthew Wesley Williams, and Dori Grinenko Baker offer three such distinctions in their book *Another Way: Living and Leading Change on Purpose*:

Purpose is the *telos* or the ends toward which a life aims. Purpose is the answer to the question, "Why am I here? Toward what end is my life pointing?"

Call is the time-bound, episodic expression of purpose, as it bubbles up repeatedly over the course of a lifetime.

Vocation is the long arc of a life spent searching for purpose and acting out callings, and it applies to both communities and to their individual members. While vocation often appears more clearly as we look back on our lives, trying to figure out our next steps toward lives of meaning and purpose is the ongoing work of vocational discernment.[1]

Without a sense of purpose, calls can feel and become detached from meaning. For those who come to ministry calls later in their lives, they can often see threads of purpose being lived out in their previous employment and career paths or in other aspects of their lives.

All of my nudges related to call as part of the long arc of vocation have arisen from deeper explorations of purpose. As well as being connected with racial identity, my own sense of purpose cannot be separated from my familial legacy. "Each individual's life vocation emerges in the midst of a community's life and can even span generations," write Lewis, Williams, and Baker.[2] Both of my parents (as well as their parents) were in-between people too. My father was the younger of two children who were born and raised and whose families spent generations in Puerto Rico. He journeyed with his mother and older brother to the mainland United States in the early twentieth century and settled in the Bronx. My mother was the child of Italian immigrants who also arrived in the United States in the early part of the twentieth century. They spoke no English and worked hard to make sure their children were as fully assimilated into American/white culture as possible.

As the bridge generation, my parents never really felt that they were fully Puerto Rican, Italian, or American/white; they were continually caught between their parents' respective cultures and traditions and the overarching American/white culture, which also offered divergent socioeconomic opportunities based on how well they assimilated. Both of them also ended up leaving the Catholic faith of their childhoods and embracing the peace and love movement of the 1960s. They moved from the urban center of the East Coast, the only home they had ever known, to the rural, mountainous region of southern Colorado in order to start a family. *Ni de aquí, ni de allá.*

Culturally, my parents spoke with a New York accent. Socioeconomically, we were poor and could often barely scrape up enough money to pay bills and keep ourselves fed and warm. We were separated by great distances both geographically and contextually from our families of origin, so I did not have the chance to know aunts, uncles, and cousins. I never truly fit in at school either, or within any of the clubs I joined as extracurricular activities (especially 4-H because my parents knew nothing about farming or ranching!). *Ni de aquí, ni de allá.*

We also did not fit in religiously; nevertheless, from an early age, I felt the spark of the Divine. When I was six months old, my father attended a local revival event and gave his life to Christ. The evangelical-Pentecostal tradition in which I was raised impacted me in profound ways; while there were many aspects that were problematic for me, in retrospect, it solidified my faith commitments and nurtured an early sense of my vocation in ministry. My father's passion for embodying his faith in every aspect of his life—which often included full-on dancing during worship each Sunday and handing out cloth patches with the words "It's Hell without Jesus" to acquaintances, much to my embarrassment—ignited my own passion for all things related to faith.

I couldn't wait for Sunday School each week to learn about stories in the Bible and how they applied to my life. Vacation Bible School every summer was my favorite time of the year; and I worked hard to win the Bible verse memorization contests, often besting competitors much older than I was. Lent, Easter, Advent, and Christmas times in our church were also special occasions for embodied rituals that I found to be particularly salient for my burgeoning faith (particularly the Maundy Thursday meals and washing of one another's feet). Most summers, I also attended a weeklong Baptist camp in the foothills of the Rocky Mountains, the sights and sounds of which I can still recall vividly (including "Onward, Christian Soldiers" blaring through the camp's loudspeakers at 7:00 a.m.). Combined with church retreats, early morning baptisms at the lake, and attending Christian and Catholic schools for junior high and part of high school, the sense of belonging I felt—not within these communities, but rather in my faith and relationship with the sacred—offered the one "space" in which I could express my full self, liminal identities and all.

I attended college and participated in an evangelical campus ministry that continued to nurture my faith and some of my first real ministry experiences. However, even while I began to sense this calling, the leaders at the time discouraged my pursuit of pastoral leadership beyond college, largely because I was a woman and did not quite fit their archetype of a ministry leader (which was gendered and somewhat raced in terms of certain charismatic leadership qualities). I could lead Bible studies and mission trips among my peers, but I could not be a *real* minister. *Ni de aquí, ni de allá.*

Nevertheless, I couldn't ignore the stirring within me. After college, I served on staff at a small, bilingual congregation in the poorest neighborhood in Denver for a year and quickly realized that I needed additional skills to pursue ministry as a lifelong series of callings. The pastor of the church was doing his doctoral studies at Iliff School of Theology; I decided to apply. In short, seminary changed me in profound ways—theologically, vocationally, and academically. It was truly the first space in which I was affirmed as my liminal, multiplicitous self. It was also the first time that others identified out-in-the-real-world gifts of ministry leadership in me, as well as gifts for advanced theological study. Moreover, I found my theological place of belonging—one that included many misfits like me—within the United Church of Christ (UCC).

Slowly, I began to see my in-betweenness as a strength—and perhaps even a gift—from which my callings could be expressed in the world. Granted, there were still ways in which my theological studies exposed this in-betweenness in quite painful ways, but rather than burying these parts of me and my experience in order to belong, I was exposing and expressing them to others and to myself because they provided space from which deeper creativities and connections could be cultivated. My abilities to be both this *and* that, to develop connections between people and entities and gain trust in spaces of difference, to speak the various codes and "languages" of particular groups and institutions reflected a life spent in existence within and yet just beyond multiple worlds.

Since seminary and ordination, I have served in a variety of settings and roles, each one reflective of this deeper vocational calling as a *connector-creator-misfit of multiplicities* (CCMM for short). Even more surprising is that my roles have often involved supporting and nurturing other in-betweeners—first as a hospital chaplain, then as a professional at a private undergraduate school supporting minoritized students, then as a denominational leader overseeing Christian formation and research, and now as a faculty member at the very theological school that fostered my vocational formation nearly twenty years ago. In that time, my liminal identities and connections have taken on different characteristics, most notably in the form of a hyphenated last name resulting from marrying Ali, my Moroccan Muslim spouse of fifteen years.

In retrospect, I see the ways that my parents also embraced their roles as CCMMs and the courage, resilience, joy, and, at times, burden that this thrust-upon purpose entailed. But knowing that part of my purpose is connected with theirs, and their parents before them, ties me to a sense of intergenerational legacy and beyond me-ness that can only be of/from God. In her description of evangélica faith—the unique Latina religious expression born from the convergence of our particular historical and cultural histories—theologian Loida I. Martell says, "God, then, is the source of [our] call. God is the reason for [our] being. Because [we] love God and recognize God as the source of all life, the very expression of that love must be in service in the world. [Ours] is an embodied witness, *un testimonio encarnado*, of spirituality."[3]

Any call should originate from who one is, what one's gifts are that arise from who one is, and how those gifts can be brought forth for the good of the community. Of course, identities, gifts, and purpose over the course of a life can change; and they often do. Regardless, God-breathed callings shaped by purpose allow one to live a *testimonio encarnado* that wholly enfolds and nurtures the complexities of who we are—in-betweennesses included—so that all may be known as beloved.

QUESTIONS FOR REFLECTION

1. What is your purpose? Has this changed, or become more nuanced, over the course of your life? How does your sense of purpose relate to your sense of call?
2. How have your identities, experiences, and family legacies shaped understandings of your purpose and call as part of the long arc of vocation?
3. How might you strive to be *un testimonio encarnado* (an embodied witness) in ministry? In your life?

What Are Pastors For?

Will Willimon

Glad to hear that you are wondering whether God may be summoning you to pastoral ministry. Hope I can be helpful in your deliberation.

Let's start by asking "What are pastors for?"

From the first, leadership is not optional for Christian mission. Whatever Jesus wants to be done in the world, he chooses not to do it alone. Ever the great delegator, Jesus begins his work by calling twelve none-too-talented, untrained, often inept disciples and sends them out to do the very same work that he does (Luke 9:1–16). Even though The Twelve soon show that they are not the brightest candles in the box, Jesus then calls them to himself and sends out seventy more (Luke 10:1–14).[1] When the Acts of the Apostles tells the story of the early church in action, Acts does so mainly by telling of the leadership of people like Peter, Paul, Dorcas, and Mary. The way that Christ leads is by summoning a few to lead the many.

The mission Christ gives to his church is too difficult for the church to wait to get in gear when we feel like it. The wiles of the world are so daunting that somebody has to step up and take responsibility for equipping and motivating God's people for participation in Jesus's mission in the world (Ephesians 4:12) and for forgiving them when they don't. So, drawing from the ranks of the baptized, the church invented clergy. Despite fancy vestments, arcane language, and ceremonial claptrap, pastors have mainly functional rather than sacerdotal significance. Pastors are a function of what needs to happen in the church so that the church can be part of what God wants to happen in the world.

We clergy are frail, finite, flawed human beings, whose specialness lies almost exclusively in our having been chosen by Christ to work with frail, finite, flawed people whom Christ has chosen to work with him. The church has always believed that clergy are a gift of God to the church, a means of keeping Christ's Body in motion, an essential component of Christ's determination to use ordinary people in his extraordinary, vast reclamation of his world.

One cannot aspire to Christian leadership; one must be summoned, commissioned, called. Unlike many jobs, you can't choose your way into this line of work. I'm a pastor on the basis of God's choice of me rather than because of any of my innate virtues, talents, wise choices, or (sometimes) pleasing personality. My being summoned for Christian service was God's idea before it was mine.[2]

Around my sophomore year of college, I overheard some young pastors talking about their ministry (in my native South Carolina, the 1960s, in the midst of the civil rights movement). One had a brick thrown through his car window after a church meeting. Another's spouse had been verbally abused in a grocery store because of a sermon he had preached. I thought, in my low, sophomoric imagination, "This sounds great! I thought preachers were old guys who wore suits and ties. Where do I sign up for seminary?"

Thus, I got the crazy notion that God was enlisting me to prepare to be a pastor. Although I didn't know as much as I know now about my weaknesses and lack of talent, I did know enough to say to the Lord, "Who, me? You must be kidding!"

A romp through scripture's many renditions of vocation, the call of Abraham and Sarah, Jacob, Moses, most of the prophets, and Jesus's twelve disciples will quickly disabuse you of the notion that God calls people to do God's work because they are good, pious, wonderful people. God's choice of someone like me (or you?) to be a pastor says more about the gracious, forgiving, forbearing, surprising, outrageous love of God than the good qualities of the one being called.

The summons into ministry comes both from above (the Holy Spirit) and below (the church). Pastors cannot be adequately paid for what's routinely expected of them; you've got to be pushed, shoved, prodded, that is, *called*, into this way of life. Although few pastors can adequately explain how or why God has called them, most believe they are in ministry because God wants them to be.[3] That means that although pastors are paid (usually not very well) by a congregation, they are accountable to and authorized by more than the congregation's opinion of them and their work. While we try to love the people whom God has committed to our care, even more we must love the God who summoned us.

At the same time, the pastoral ministry is an act of the church. Leadership is not optional for the church. The work of witnessing, evangelizing, protesting injustice, acting up in Jesus's name, healing, and truth-telling is given to all the baptized but in order to do such difficult, demanding work, someone must lead. All Christians are baptized to share in Christ's ministry. For each of us to live out our ministries, someone must be minister to the ministers.

Pastors are a function of what needs to happen in the church in order for the church to be the church.

I predict that one of your challenges, in deciding whether God and the church are calling you to ordained leadership, is to discern whether you're being called to be an active, committed disciple (every Christian's call by baptism) or if you are called to the specialized ministry of being a pastor—someone who helps the baptized live out their baptisms. Sadly, some of the baptized are misguided toward seminary; their call is not to be Christian leaders but rather to be more faithful Christians. Seminaries (literally, "seed beds") have as their mission to plant and to nurture leaders for Christ's church, to give budding pastors the theological resources, biblical knowledge, and self-understanding they will need to sustain ministry over the long haul.

Pastors are "ordained." They are under orders, from God and God's church, to worry about keeping the church faithful as the church, to teach the church's faith to new generations of Christians, to help the church test its faith to be sure that we're believing in and in service to the God of Israel and the church rather than some more congenial, pliable God-substitute of our own concoction.

Before the altar of God, at the bedside of the sick, daring to enter the pain of troubled souls, sharing befuddlement before an obscure biblical text, insisting—from the pulpit—that God's people have difficult conversations about matters folks would rather avoid, there you'll find the pastor. Each Sunday the pastor rises out of the fateful, sometimes comforting, often contentious conversation between God and God's people and dares to speak a word from God so that the colloquy can continue and deepen.

The church ordains a few from the ranks of the baptized to be the priest who mediates between God and God's suffering, sinful, loving, obdurate, rebellious, and faithful people, the prophet who risks voicing truth we would as soon avoid, the pastor who walks with folks through some of the best and worst times of their lives, assuring them that Christ walks with them.

A pastor can't be hired; a pastor must be called, sent, that is, coerced by God to serve God's people so they can serve God in the world. Because a pastor's care for the flock is in the name of Jesus, pastoral care is more than mere hand-holding and ruffled feathers soothing. It's vocational care that patches up laity who have been damaged while working with Jesus so that they can be sent back to the front lines in the world where the battle rages.

Clerical sin by demagogic, unaccountable, big-headed clergy has been church at its worst. I hope you haven't been the victim of clergy behaving badly. It's my conviction that overbearing clergy get that way, not by a power grab by priests but rather because the laity have been all too willing to dump their baptismally assigned ministry upon surrogate clergy.

Therefore, most clergy find that they must discipline themselves not to rob the laity of their baptismally bestowed ministry. "Preacher, you be the Super Christian so the rest of us don't have to be." No. All the baptized have responsibility to witness, serve, give, and to speak truth. As far as God is concerned, everybody in Israel or the church, even without an MDiv from an accredited seminary, is a priest, someone who works with Christ as priest to a hurting world. A harried, stressed-out, overworked pastor is usually a cleric with an inadequate theology of baptism.

Yet in spite of the dangers within the malpractice of Christian leadership, somebody has to convene, orchestrate, organize, be blamed for congregational gaffes, teach, and tell the truth in order to equip the saints (all the baptized) for the work of ministry. Thus, the church lays hands upon the heads of regular Christians, making them pastors, priests, deacons, elders, bishops, telling them to care for Christ's people and his world in Christ's name. Is that you?

By whatever names the church calls its clergy, however the church organizes itself—including how the church vets, chooses, and authorizes its leaders—is a matter of taste and tradition rather than biblical warrant. A few utterly human, vocationally reckless, called by God and the church from the ranks of the faithful say, "Okay, okay, Lord. I give in. I hope you know what you are doing. In spite of my self-doubts, I'll take responsibility for helping the church stay the church."

CLERGY: ONE OF CHRIST'S SLY STRATAGEMS FOR GETTING WHAT HE WANTS FROM HIS CHURCH

Although service in the name of a crucified Savior is a risk-filled challenge, after decades of ministry I can testify that it's a joy to have one's life expended in a vocation that's greater than oneself. You'd have to be a pastor to know how living a life tethered, yoked to Christ and his mission through the people of God is true freedom. It's great grace to have your life wrenched out of your control and caught up in Christ's great pageant of salvation. The life you are living is not your own. You are rescued from the conventional American, "What do I want to do with me?" and thrust into asking the more countercultural, "Which God am I worshiping and how is that God having God's way with me?" In a world where too many people are answerable to little more than their own ill-formed desires, what a joy to be enlisted by the One who says, "I'm reclaiming my world. Guess who's going to help me?"

And if the time is not right for you to be called, if you have grave reservations about your ability to do God's work, don't want God to mess with your life plans, are beset by personal doubts or insecurities, not in the best of health, or burdened by cares and worries, God doesn't care. Christ's mission takes precedence over your reservations and doubts.

I don't know whether Christ is indeed calling you to offer yourself for Christian leadership. However, I can say after decades of being a pastor, pray that he is. Being a pastor is so much more interesting than being chief of Microsoft or general manager of the Carolina Panthers. Sure, the pastoral ministry is a risk, but what a joyful adventure as well.

QUESTIONS FOR REFLECTION

1. Bishop Willimon writes, "Jesus begins his work by calling twelve none-too-talented, untrained, often inept disciples." How have you felt about your qualifications for congregational ministry? How does what he writes in that section encourage or even liberate you? Or raise further questions?
2. Bishop Willimon describes being energized when his assumptions about clergy were called into question: "I thought preachers were old guys who wore suits and ties." Where have your assumptions been challenged? How does that energize you?
3. "Somebody has to convene, orchestrate, organize, be blamed for congregational gaffes, teach, and tell the truth in order to equip the saints (all the baptized) for the work of ministry." What draws you to this position description? How has Christ been calling you, or not, to this work?

A Priest of Priests

Melissa Florer-Bixler

"You can't be what you can't see." Those words return to me as I recall Sunday afternoons, surrounded by a congregation of stuffed animals. I raised a Ritz Cracker above my head as I sang the Great Thanksgiving to my play-church. Despite growing up in the Episcopal Church, a tradition that opened the priesthood to women in 1976, I have no memories of women standing behind the altar or preaching from the raised dais. I was welcomed here, among my toys, but there were no priests in the church who looked like me.

The body of a priest was male and, I assumed, so must be the body of God. Older men, set apart by robes and collars, distanced further by their gender and their age, were the priests of my youth. I found my way near to the altar that was their domain, first as an acolyte and then in the altar guild, able to touch the holy things that animated our life of worship. But I was different, and my body didn't belong there.

It would take nineteen years before I heard a woman preach for the first time. Mother Martha was the priest of the Episcopal church that welcomed me in college. I can still hear the sound of her voice, a voice like mine, echoing off the soft stone walls of the New England sanctuary. I remember the first time I saw hands like mine hold the host, as she said the words of Jesus, "This is my body for you." Martha's body was also for me, sliding the first whisper of a pastoral call through the cracks of gendered exclusion built around me.

But there were other barriers. The priesthood was set apart and I wanted to be *with*—with the people, with the broken, with the despised. They, too, were holy, and who was I but one of them, another pilgrim? I did not feel particularly righteous or moral. I recoiled at the idea that I possessed gifts or talents that specially positioned me to intercede for God. I'd already experienced an ontological change in baptism. That was enough. When I saw my future, I saw it among the ordinary people of God's church. They were, to my observation, as holy and good as any priest, as gifted and wondrous as any cleric.

I didn't know how to reconcile my conviction of worship among the people with the growing recognition that my gifts were pastoral. I found myself drawn to teaching and preaching, but not to the theological academy. I believed in worship as the central form of life that shaped a body politic called the church. I felt at home in the work of worship.

Reconciling my gifts and my commitment to the priesthood of all believers came by way of the Mennonite church. It took several weeks of attending worship with the Mennonites to figure out who the pastor was. Everyone had a role in worship, people getting up from their seats to lead prayers, preach, read Scripture, and sing, then returning to sit with everyone else. There was no raised platform, no pulpit erected above the people. The architecture communicated something new—all the people here were priests.

A year later I was far from North Carolina, living among the people of L'Arche Portland, Oregon. I began each day in the routines set by the people in our homes who had intellectual disabilities. We shared what we had in common. We ate together and went on walks, visited the park and celebrated birthdays. I learned not to take the quotidian for granted. For many of the people with intellectual or developmental disabilities (IDD) who called L'Arche home, this ordinariness was hard earned by advocacy and organizing. Their lives, choices, and desires were significant, and each of us was necessary for the community to function, for us to be whole.

The life we cultivated had little to do with hierarchical power or intellectual prowess. Instead, being a part of this community meant paying attention to gifts that are often underappreciated and at times despised. Those gifts included taking time, slowing down, seeing the world differently, and asking questions in new ways. It was a gift to overcome the stereotype that people with IDD are saintly or "angels," allowing me to also be fully myself without the weighted expectations that followed in the wake of my identity. We were people, sharing the complicated terrain of daily life, and finding Jesus along the way.

In those years living among the people of L'Arche, I came to realize this is what church could look like. The language we used in the Mennonite church to describe something like this is "the priesthood of all believers." By baptism we are priests. But what did it mean to take up the awkward distinction of being a priest of priests, a priest among priests?

In the Mennonite church, I learned, pastoral identity is fragile. There's nothing the pastor does that couldn't be done by another baptized member of the church. As a priesthood of all believer's tradition, each of us can preside over Communion or baptize someone. I'm a good preacher, but so are others. We have loving and thoughtful church people who offer one another pastoral care, people who show up in times of struggle, and hold one another through the messiest times of life.

Instead of offering an exclusive and necessary role, something only I could do or be, I learned that it was my job to pay attention. As a pastor, I was tasked with paying attention to worship, so that our praise of God made space for all of our bodies in the fullness of our lives. I was tasked with paying attention to our gifts, that none were overlooked or taken for granted. I was tasked with paying attention to our community as we looked for the eruption of the good news beyond the walls of our church and learned how to link our lives with those who bore that good news in their bodies.

The better I paid attention, the less necessary my role became. More people were invited to lead and preach, teach, and pray. If I lived into my gift of pastoring, people would love one another well, showing up in the difficult and beautiful moments of life's journey.

When people ask me about this strange work of being a priest among priests, I tell them my pastoral vocation looks a lot like being a farmer of a community supported agriculture farm, a CSA. Volunteers invest their time and labor in our farm. It belongs to us—to all of us. The people who work this farm don't need me to plant all the seeds, water the ground, and harvest the crops. But it's good to have someone who can remember what didn't grow in the past and what will thrive in this ground. We need someone who knows who can do the heavy lifting and who is better suited for the tender work of replanting seedlings. It's helpful to have a farmer who can offer wisdom and reminders of difficult times, knows how to manage drought and disease, and can offer hope that food that will nourish us is already coming to life.

QUESTIONS FOR REFLECTION

1. How does the author's reflections on the nature of ordained ministry compare with your own?
2. Who modeled pastoral ministry for you? Whose body was absent or present that made it more or less challenging for you?
3. What of Florer-Bixler's description of active ministry engages your imagination around what ministry is about?

Hear. See. Tell. Walk Through the Unlocked Door

William H. Lamar IV

I heard Someone. I saw something. This was my call.

I told others that I heard Someone and saw something. I keep telling them. This is my vocation.

Without having heard and seen there is nothing to tell. My ancestors put it this way: "If you ain't heard nothing and you ain't seen nothing, then you ain't got nothing."

I told my daddy that I had heard Someone and seen something. His counsel yet sticks to my ribs and to my soul. Ribs and soul, you ask? This call is corporeal; this call is spiritual. A call to gospel ministry that does not reside in your bones is not to be trusted.

"Son," he said, "Go back and pray. Make sure that if it is indeed God calling, you are being called to preach and not to plow. There are too many farmers in the pulpit and too many preachers in the field."

You are reading this because you heard *a* voice. Led by Spirit in community, you must discern whether you heard *the* Voice. Of utmost importance is that you are seeing something. Many clergy hear the Voice and talk to God's people *ad nauseam*—without ever showing them God at work in the world and bidding them to follow.

Don't think that you must search for God as you discern sound and sight. God is not lost. Your feeling of dislocation is not about finding an elusive, evasive God; it is about clearing space in your soul, in your being, where you can commune with Spirit. She waits for you there.

Spirit, like a fire gasping for air, wants to burn brightly within us. Things, theologies, loyalties, politics, people, definitions, and desires inhibit the possibility of this blessed conflagration. To hear and to see we must wrestle with these inhibitors. They ever press upon us to diminish Spirit's flame to flicker. Our spiritual work, our bodily work is to become bellows—blowing with, not against Spirit.

If after doing this work you determine that the call to ordained ministry is not for you, you are among the brave. Continue your interrogation of self and the Divine. There is something that you are being drawn to that will move us all closer to God's dream for creation. Go forward in the beautiful struggle.

If you are conscripted into ordained ministry, you will need ancestors from among the great cloud of witnesses to guide you along the joyful, terrifying, and costly path that Spirit is unfolding before you.

John is such an ancestor.

John was in Spirit. Spirit was in John. You are in Spirit. Spirit is in you. Embrace and fall into this mystery.

Like you, he was the recipient of a revelation of Jesus Christ. This revelation disclosed God's activity in the world. Faithfulness to this revelation landed John in prison. Prepare now for the promise, peril, and pain of your vocation.

John heard a loud voice. A blaring trumpet of a voice. What is the voice that you cannot not hear saying to you? This voice follows you, finds you, and frustrates you. For John, this voice was the Voice. The Voice could not be ignored and gave John clear instructions.

Write what you see. Send it to the seven churches. Tell them that they have not been abandoned. You have seen the Human One amid them. Christ is leading them, defeating the power and merchants of death, and enlisting them in the same work.

You may not always be the beneficiary of the divine clarity that John describes here. I do not read Revelation linearly, so I imagine that this clarity was the result of wrestling with God over time. But John emerges with the mystery of faith that sustains and saves us. He heard and saw it. He wrote and told it to Ephesus, Smyrna, Pergamum, Thyatira, Sardis, Philadelphia, and Laodicea.

John employs vibrant, visual language and images that compel God's people inward to commune with Spirit and outward to join God in the creation of a new heaven and a new earth. People living under the cruelties of the American Empire today need poetry as badly as people living under the cruelties of the Roman Empire did in John's day. We need something more than three-point sermons. Please don't flatten the marvelous three-dimensionality of the gospel. We need something more than alliterative lessons. We are being swallowed by death!

After hearing and seeing, be bold enough to show us golden lampstands and the Human One arrayed in a long robe with a golden sash across the Divine chest, woolly hair, flaming eyes, and burnished feet—walking among us. In Congress, the Supreme Court, oval offices, banks, classrooms, executive suites, pulpits—the Incarnate One walks among us holding seven stars with a sharp, two-edged sword dancing from the Holy mouth. The Divine face shines like the sun and death withers in the light and heat of holiness.

We are afraid. Hearing and seeing this is hard. Telling it is damn near impossible. We are seized by fear. So was John. But the Human One places the Divine right hand upon us and says, "Do not be afraid; I am the first and the last, and the living one. I was dead, and see, I am alive forever and ever; and I have the keys of Death and of Hades" (Revelation 1:17b–18).

If you are still reading, you have known and will know locked doors. The door to your own soul. The doors of churches. The doors of justice and equity. The door behind which may cower your yes to God's call to ordained ministry.

What Howard Washington Thurman called the hounds of hell specialize in guarding these doors. One hound is fear, the other death. They never cease to bark. But the One whose Voice you hear, whose face you have seen, has the keys.

Hear. See. Tell. Walk through the unlocked door.

QUESTIONS FOR REFLECTION

1. What are the spiritual disciplines that help you to hear and to see?
2. Name the ancestors who have accompanied you on your journey.

A Calling Worthy of My Life

Brian Keepers

When I was seven years old, I asked my grandmother for a Bible for Christmas. I can still remember unwrapping it on Christmas morning and carefully flipping through its pages, mesmerized by the glossy full-color maps at the back. Eighteen years later, on the night of my ordination as a minister, my grandmother hugged me and whispered in my ear, "I always knew you'd be a pastor, ever since that Christmas you asked for a Bible. I just knew it!" God let Grandma in on this secret long before me.

While I have always had a genuine curiosity about God, God seemed so distant and elusive, so unknowable. Even though both of my parents believed in God, church and faith didn't play a primary role in my family's life. We were sporadic in our church attendance; typically, my parents would drop me off for Sunday School (where I got "religious teaching") and then return later to pick me up. We prayed rote prayers like "God is great, God is good, and we thank you for this food," at meals. My parents loved us unconditionally, but there wasn't any sort of measurable personal faith that really shaped the way we lived.

This started to change in the eighth grade when I began attending youth group at the church with which we were loosely connected. Soon the annual "Youth Sunday" rolled around, where the youth were given (mostly) free rein to design and lead the worship service. We performed a drama based on the call of Samuel for the sermon. I was cast in the role of young Samuel. Afterward, Mr. and Mrs. Scuttinga, a couple in their early fifties, pulled me aside and said, "Brian, have you ever thought about being a pastor?" Their question caught me off guard. *Me, a pastor? Seriously? How can I teach people about God when I'm still trying to figure out who God is?* No, the thought had never crossed my mind. It struck me as absurd. I politely thanked them for their affirmation and tucked it away. But something started to stir within me; a quiet ember was set aglow.

During my freshman year of high school, I got involved with an evangelical parachurch ministry. One blustery January night, Kent Prescott, my English teacher, spoke at our monthly gathering and gave an invitation to respond to Jesus's call to follow him. Something inside me awakened. This God, for whom my heart was restless, revealed himself. Along with seven other students, I committed to following Jesus.

Mr. Prescott urged us to find a local church and get involved, saying, "You can't follow Jesus without being a part of a local expression of his body." He recognized that as wonderful as this parachurch ministry was, it wasn't the church.

So, I started showing up regularly on Sunday mornings for worship. I often went alone, although occasionally members of my family joined me. I went through a membership class with my mother, joined the church, and stepped into leadership roles in youth group and in the parachurch ministry. I started meeting regularly with my pastor on Saturday mornings for breakfast and we developed an authentic and beautiful "Paul and Timothy" relationship. Mr. and Mrs. Scuttinga's question stayed with me. I was not convinced that I had what it takes to be a pastor, but I couldn't shake their question.

Art had always been an important part of my life, and I had my heart set on going to the state university to become a graphic designer. A turning point came my sophomore year of high school when my parents divorced. It remains one of the most painful experiences of my life. Although my parents had always had a strained relationship, I just assumed they would find a way to make it work. When they announced they would be getting a divorce, my world suddenly turned upside down.

I recall the feeling of walking around our small town with a "D" on my forehead, marked with failure and shame. Divorce makes hidden pain and brokenness so public and visible. I felt very anxious about showing up at church, so I stayed away for several weeks. But then one Sunday, I screwed up the courage and went by myself. I walked into the lobby, and a fierce rush of shame caused me to nearly turn around and walk out. Suddenly I felt a hand on my shoulder. It was Ray Meyer, one of the elders who sat in on the meeting when my mother and I joined the church.

Without hesitation, Ray embraced me. I buried my face in his chest and just sobbed. All the grief and anger and confusion that was bottled up got uncorked in that moment. Then he looked me in the eyes and spoke words I will never forget: "Brian, I'm so sorry about what you're going through. I want you to know how much you are loved. Loved by God. Loved by your church family. You don't have to do this alone. We're going to help you get through it."

Many experience the church as a community that is judgmental, hypocritical, and unwelcoming, which deeply grieves me. This was not my experience.

When my nuclear family was unraveling, the church became my family. The congregation loved my family and me *in* our pain. And they loved us *through* our pain.

My experience of the church as a place of healing, embrace, and belonging had a profound impact. I wanted to give my life in service to Christ and lead this kind of community. By my senior year of high school, that quiet glowing ember had slowly grown to an intense burning of the heart. The internal call caught up to the external call. I couldn't deny it: *God was calling me to be a pastor*. As much as I loved art, this passion would need to be integrated into the calling to pastor a local church.

I had enrolled at the state university to pursue a degree in graphic design but during the second semester of my senior year in high school, I withdrew and enrolled instead at a Christian liberal arts college with the intent of going on to seminary. It was there, through relationships and my studies, that my call to be a pastor was confirmed and deepened. This would be my experience in seminary as well.

The two most significant factors in discerning my call have been *people* and experiences of *pain*. It's remarkable, going all the way back to my grandmother and so many others since, how God has "peopled" my journey with those who saw in me what I didn't see in myself. And they named it. They called it out. Vocation is always discerned in community.

God also used my most profound experiences of pain to shape my calling. The way the body of Christ loved me in and through the pain of the fracturing of my family led me to vocational ministry. Since then, there have been other experiences of pain, including my wife and my journey with infertility and adoption, a teenage daughter who became pregnant in high school, and struggles in our family with mental health. The writer Frederick Buechner insists that our pain can be *a gift*; and instead of hiding or burying our pain, God calls us to *steward* our pain.[1] So much of my call to be a pastor arose from and has been deepened by pain and heartache. I'm convinced that our best ministry arises from our deepest pain.

I have now been an ordained pastor for twenty years, having served three different congregations in the Midwest. There have been challenging seasons along the way—the past two years with the global pandemic being among the hardest. There have been moments of fatigue, when I've nearly lost heart. But when I look back and trace the way my history bears the fingerprints of grace, I'm reminded that this call is so much bigger than I am. I can honestly say I have never regretted the decision to become a pastor. In the words of the late Eugene Peterson, "being a pastor is the best life there is," if you are called to it.[2] It's a calling worthy of your life. Even with seasons of adversity and loss, I can only whisper, "Thank you."

QUESTIONS FOR REFLECTION

1. In what ways has God "peopled" your own journey? Who are the men and women, along the way, who saw in you something that you didn't see in yourself and called it out? What role has community played in your own discernment of call? What role might community play now?
2. Reflect on some of your experiences of pain and loss. How might you, in God's healing grace, steward this pain for God's glory and the benefit of others? C. S. Lewis wrote, "God whispers to us in our pleasures . . . but shouts in our pains: it is his megaphone to rouse a deaf world."[3] In what ways might God be speaking through your pain to help you discern his call on your life?

Chaplaincy: Ministry that Ferments and Seasons

Nancy Elizabeth Wood

When I met "Monica" I knew very little about her, save her age (twenty-seven years old), her religion (Muslim), and her location in our hospital (psychiatry). It's standard practice to prepare for a spiritual care visit by spending a few minutes reading a patient's chart in order to know a little bit about who she is and why she's been admitted. But, in Monica's case, I didn't delve into her electronic medical record (EMR).

I changed my usual preparation for a patient visit because I thought it unlikely Monica wanted to see a chaplain. There are several nurses on the psychiatry unit who routinely consult spiritual care services for their patients because they, the nurses, deeply value religion. Often, the patients themselves don't share the nurses' enthusiasm for chaplaincy. Even if Monica had requested the spiritual care, given that the EMR order simply read, "Muslim," I thought it likely Monica wished to see an imam, and my care for her would be making a few phone calls to the Islamic Society to arrange that. And, there was the strong possibility that Monica's name had automatically appeared in our chaplaincy consult list because she followed Muslim dietary practices. (More on that in a minute.) I had three good reasons why I was prepared for Monica to tell me she wasn't interested in talking with me.

We can all see where this is headed. Monica, of course, did want a spiritual care visit. In the forty-five minutes I spent with her, I learned much from and with her. This is not unusual. I often change for the better because of my patients. Relational Cultural Theory, one of the theories that most informs my work as a spiritual care provider and educator, believes the caregiver and the care receiver both grow through the relationship they create together. In other words, transformation is a two-way street.[1]

That was certainly true of my visit with Monica. What follows are a few essential aspects of chaplaincy that I love and came to better understand through my relationship with Monica. For those of you considering chaplaincy as a vocation, I invite you to consider whether you would like to learn and relearn these key components of spiritual care throughout your life in ministry.

EXAMINE YOUR ASSUMPTIONS (AGAIN)

Monica knew what she was up to when she asked to see a chaplain. Raised in a very religious family that believed all of life was preordained by God, Monica was having difficulty integrating her study of science with her childhood faith. She wanted a chaplain to accompany her in her questions. Chief among them were, "Can I remain Muslim, treasuring the pieces of the tradition I love and that make sense to me, while believing I have the free will to decide how to live my life? And, if so, how do I handle the immense responsibility of determining how to live well?"

Like most faith leaders I know, I love existential questions; I became a minister because I wanted to think about them every day. In hospital chaplaincy, I found a setting where the pace and depth of those questions matched my energy and temperament. Monica and I met one another in her questions and quickly established a trusting pastoral relationship. While she did more of the talking and I more of the listening (a good chaplaincy ratio), the spiritual care encounter contained mutuality and authenticity. Despite the incorrect assumptions about Monica I brought to our encounter, our spiritual care visit was zesty.[2]

Let me be clear, experience matters. I'm a better chaplain now than I was when I started, due in large measure to the hundreds of people I've ministered to in hospice and hospital settings. They've shown me the power of being present to people who are in pain. They've taught me that there are few words that can make an experience of suffering better but there are plenty that might make it more painful. My interdisciplinary colleagues have also helped me grow. I now know more disease diagnosis, symptoms, and progression than I did at the start of my career. I'm better able to adjust my approach and timing to align with the patient's experience. When meeting a new patient and family, we chaplains use all the learning we have at our disposal, including theology, behavioral science, and our past experience, to create a pastoral plan.

But it's important to hold that plan loosely and always be ready to examine the assumptions I carry with me. One of the things I love about chaplaincy is how often I'm surprised by people. The Evangelical Christian woman I was sure would never want a Reiki volunteer gratefully accepted that service when I offered it. The agnostic corporate lawyer with ALS loved the prayer bracelet I brought him and needed to be wearing it on the day he died. My patients continually defy my expectations, reminding me of how complicated and complex we all are, and how much I don't know.

BE WILLING TO WORK WITHIN COMPLICATED ORGANIZATIONS AND MINISTER TO THE PEOPLE IN THEM

While I need to learn from the assumptions I brought to the spiritual care visit, our EMR systems likely didn't help matters. I could try to explain all the idiosyncrasies of our charting system here, but I wouldn't be able to do justice to how confusing it is, and you'd be bored. The bottom line: in the EMR, our patients' spiritual, religious, and cultural information isn't always well communicated.

In Monica's case, I didn't know if the one-word referral of "Muslim" was intended for nutrition services because Monica needed Halal food or for chaplaincy because Monica needed spiritual support. For a couple of years now, several able chaplain colleagues have been working to fix this and other problems with our EMR, but we still have plenty to improve. No one is trying to be obstructionist. It is simply that our medical center is large and complex.

I've been the pastor of two congregations and, while I ultimately found the work to be too solitary, I liked being able to make change in fairly direct and immediate ways. If I wanted to create a new program, I'd call up the church council chair and we'd put it on the agenda for the next leadership meeting. My voice mattered; congregational members didn't always agree with me, but they always listened to what I had to say.

In chaplaincy, I don't have a great deal of institutional power. Very few people are going to listen to what I say based on my status as an ordained minister. My experience in health-care chaplaincy has involved a fair amount of negotiating around and through complicated systems. At times, I feel excited and invigorated to be part of a large medical center community, in which all of us are working together in a common goal of providing excellent patient care. At other times, I feel insubstantial and disempowered in the very same work environment.

Chaplains aren't alone in this. Our interdisciplinary colleagues also negotiate complex systems as they provide care. This can often be an entry point for chaplains to provide spiritual care to staff. As I write this, our medical center is consistently operating at or above capacity. Every day I'm out on the floors, while I'm checking in with colleagues about our shared patients, I am also fostering a deeper connection with them, one in which they can choose to talk with me about their fears, anxieties, hopes, and worries. I think of my relationships with staff as akin to those I had with parishioners when I was in the congregational context.

Before I went to see Monica, I spent a few minutes talking to staff in the nurses' station. I asked how everyone was dealing with the stress of a full census and patients waiting in the Emergency Department for a bed on the unit, what people were doing for Halloween, and what bad TV we were bingeing. In other words, I checked in about how they were, spiritually—to whom and to what they were connected, and all the small and large ways they were making meaning in their lives. Just as I was about to do with Monica.

BE READY TO BE CHANGED, TOO

Monica appeared to relax visibly as the spiritual care visit unfolded. She told me she felt better knowing that she wasn't wrong or bad for wanting to remain close to her family while needing to grow beyond the religious framework they had given her. She spoke of how much she was holding in tension—she grieved letting go of her childhood belief that her whole life was predetermined and felt excited to choose for herself the direction her life would take. She loved how precious each moment felt to her and feared never doing justice to the potential each moment held. When she shared that "the only thing I can be certain of is this very moment," I felt very connected to her words and her experience.

But it went deeper than that. I have a daughter just a few years younger than Monica. Like Monica, my daughter seeks to live justly. Like Monica, she is curious and bright and makes beautiful connections between literature and life. Like Monica, she has struggled with depression.

One of the things I've most feared is that my daughter might one day need to be admitted to an inpatient facility for mental health care. Monica's situation was the very one that has kept me up at night. In addition to all the other reasons I gave for not reading Monica's chart before seeing her, there's likely another one, too: I wanted to protect myself from discovering that there were very few differences between Monica and my daughter.

In my role as a chaplain, I met a thoughtful, capable young woman receiving the treatment she needed. Soon after we began talking, I knew, fundamentally, Monica was going to be okay. Through my relationship with her, I learned to be a little less afraid of what the future might hold for my daughter. My intention in and motivation for providing spiritual care to Monica wasn't that I should receive some healing of my own. By God's grace, I did.

EMBRACE YOUR PASTORAL IMAGINATION

After Monica thought through how she would talk with her parents about what she was discovering about herself, she formulated a plan to find Muslim teachers to grow more fully into her faith. She stated she felt a little clearer and more hopeful than she had before we met.

The visit was naturally coming to a close. I asked Monica if I could offer her some sort of blessing to end our time together and prepare her for her journey home. I told her I was no expert on Islam. She laughed and said she wasn't either. That's why she'd needed a chaplain in the first place.

People often think that chaplains need to be experts in every spiritual and religious tradition in order to give good care. Even if it were possible to know everything about each world religion, which it's not, people from different communities and cultures express the same faith in very different ways. For sure, chaplains need to know major tenants of many traditions. But cultivating their pastoral imaginations—making connections between songs, images, poems, and Scripture stories and the patient's experience—is also important. The poem or song that comes to mind while talking with a patient may be the creative expression that helps her understand her circumstances in a new way.

As I had listened to Monica, I been reminded of a poem by Hafiz I had once had on my living room wall. Monica had never heard of Hafiz. I knew only that he was a Sufi poet and his poem had helped me through a very dark time. We closed our eyes and the Muslim mystic's ancient words became a blessing we shared in that moment, in the only moment any of us is ever sure of.

> Don't surrender your loneliness
> So quickly.
> Let it cut more deep.
> Let it ferment and season you
> As few human
> Or even divine ingredients can.
> Something missing in my heart tonight
> Has made my eyes so soft
> My voice
> So tender,
> My need of God
> Absolutely
> Clear.[3]

QUESTIONS FOR REFLECTION

1. A chaplain's workday is quite variable, and often fast-paced and stressful. What is your preferred work environment like? How might you respond to rapidly evolving emotional situations?
2. Chaplains often provide spiritual care to people who have a faith or spiritual tradition different from their own. How might your ministerial call flourish in such settings?
3. Depending on your chaplaincy context, you may be witnessing and providing care to people experiencing significant suffering. What theological and emotional resources would sustain you in this ministry?

Engaging, Embracing, and Expressing Self in Callings

Tammerie Day

My current context is chaplaincy education in a Level 1 trauma center in Chapel Hill, North Carolina. This was never my plan.

I grew up in the Rio Grande Valley in south Texas, the child of a farmer and a PE teacher who became a coach after Title IX. Dad taught me faith in seeds and to fight for love, and Mom taught me to evade the limits on my life. Julia was another mother, the Latina housekeeper who stayed on after Dad married Mom and my brother and I came along. Julia taught me to dance to norteño music, to eat tortillas with butter and salt, how to write my name, and literally saved my life when my brother's roughhousing got too rough. My childhood playmates were Carlos and Idolina, the children of my father's farm foreman. The dictate when I turned ten that I could no longer play with them—"because it just doesn't look good for an Anglo girl"—was the first time racism broke my heart, although I did not have language for it then.

My spiritual life began before language, too. The swaying treetops around our house were my first spiritual sanctuary; I could hide from my brother's predations and feel the kiss of the wind on my cheeks. I learned later, in a Southern Baptist church Sunday School class, about a Spirit that blows where it will, and my body felt a mystical knowing my heart and mind raced to catch. I read voraciously, wrote creatively, and rode horses, motorcycles, and trucks away, away, away.

As I grew up and out of stifling south Texas environs and that Southern Baptist church, I spent twenty years free ranging from college to early marriage to journalism to corporate communications to motherhood. The gravity of pregnancy and pause of maternal leave gave the Small Voice a chance to whisper more insistent invitations. I found myself not only leaving the corporate life but also church-shopping with a toddler, a baby, and an agnostic spouse. Finding cold shoulders in the mainline churches, I stumbled into a warm-hearted Mennonite church at the invitation of my neighbors, cradle Mennonites (although that's more than a bit of a non-sequitur).

A fire was lit in my bones: hearing words like "social justice" and "anti-racism" *at church* swept me from Sunday school to seminary, and on a deep dive into both theology and church planting. Peace Mennonite Church was a mostly white English-speaking congregation in community with four or five Spanish-speaking congregations in Dallas, Texas. This group of churches and the conference of which they were a part had a vision for planting an intentionally anti-racist, multicultural new church start. After trying for several years to find someone to plant this church (why was that so hard in the late 1990s?!), a few of us women who had begun with a Bible study decided to do it ourselves, and the Church of Many Peoples was born. Why is it so often "a few of us women decided to do it ourselves"?

We described our little church as equal-opportunity-discomfort: a Latina and a white woman in leadership, soon joined by an older African American female pastor from the Methodist tradition, all focusing on dismantling racism in the church and doing justice in the south Dallas neighborhood around us, *part-time*. Only God makes folks that kind of crazy.

Studying for an MDiv at Brite Divinity School while working to plant an anti-racist church was a lot; figuring out being gay was a whole lot more. I spent my last year of seminary wrestling with what to do about that realization. Prayer and fasting led to studying Greek and Hebrew and German so I could pass the language exams for a PhD program, because being a gay minister in the Mennonite Church was not going to work out, and neither was being a queer wife to a straight man.

My heart broke into so many pieces: I did not want to be divorced; I did not want to be a single parent; I did not want to leave my dream anti-racist church, even though it was struggling to stay born. And yet—

I did want to be a person who lived the truth. And the truth was, before I made the promises of my marriage or entered the covenant of my ordination, I had failed to keep a promise to myself: to *be myself*, the self God made me to be.

And so that year I graduated with my MDiv degree from Brite, left the Mennonite Church, separated from my spouse, set up house with my two kids in a shared custody arrangement, and entered a PhD program at SMU in Dallas. Running and dancing kept me sane while I poured everything I had learned from anti-racist education, organizing, and the Church of Many Peoples into a white anti-racist theology called *Constructing Solidarity*. While in my PhD program, I met the woman who became my partner, and after completing my degree moved with the kids to North Carolina to begin a new chapter in my life with her: adjuncting part-time and parenting full-time.

Somehow in the late oughts, no one was looking to hire a queer white anti-racist female professor; nor were pastor gigs on the horizon, once I realized how much I missed being in ministry. My partner, a hospital administrator, suggested chaplaincy. "Hell no," was the immediate reply. "What part of 'I'm an introvert' don't you understand?" I might have been slightly more polite. I might not have been.

Finally, wearily, opening to the possibility of something I did not know was an opportunity, I applied for a CPE internship, trying not to let my PhD get in the way of my next U-turn (terminal degrees are not terminal diagnoses, after all). I dusted off the spiritual care training I'd received back at Brite, willing to meet strangers in order to be present to suffering, and tried again to not be so damned *directive*.

I dreaded the effort to go in people's rooms and meet strangers; but I loved what sometimes happened once I was in the room. Something sacred. Something deep. Something I eventually chose, especially when I realized I could bring all my selves into the work. In deciding to train to become a chaplain educator, I could integrate my loving self, my learning self, my theological self, my mystical self, my queer self, and—most importantly—my anti-racist self.

In the years since, I have found my theological home with the Alliance of Baptists, and my vocational home as a certified educator with ACPE, serving as the associate director for Clinical Pastoral Education at UNC Hospitals. As I have moved into leadership roles in all three settings, I have been able to educate and organize around anti-racism and racial justice efforts, with the clear sense that human well-being and spiritual health *require* racially just formation and treatment. Through the twin pandemics of 2020—the racial reckoning and the first waves of COVID—the traction I had developed in all three of these organizations gave me tremendous opportunities to learn and teach and organize with colleagues seeking to learn and build more racially just and resilient ways of facing into the challenges surrounding us.

In 2022, I will celebrate the twentieth anniversary of my ordination in the Mennonite Church *and* recognize twenty-five years of anti-racist organizing, education, and activism. I will continue to engage the struggle of caring for myself, my family, my colleagues, and my hospital through the continuing evolutions and harms of COVID—and the warping effects of white supremacy.

One of the graces of the U-turn into chaplaincy education has been studying and applying trauma theory to both learning and care. This has helped me personally and has helped me help others to learn and heal. And I have found deep meaning, strength, and insight in Buddhist and religious naturalist contemplative practices, and astonishing coherence of these fields of study with anti-racist practice in personal becoming and systemic belonging.

I'll be honest; the last couple of years have been more than a lot. I am tired some days. Paraphrasing the Sweet Honey in the Rock song, we who believe in freedom sometimes have to rest, so that we can run and work and sing and fight and dance and struggle another day—whether things go according to plan or not!

QUESTIONS FOR REFLECTION

1. When have you experienced a divine interruption or redirection of your plans? How did that feel? What came of it? What is helping you through it?
2. How do you understand the relationship between love and justice?
3. How (and what) has working across lines of difference taught you about love? About God? About vocation?

What is Your Thing? Discerning "It" and Doing "It" Scared!

Danielle J. Buhuro

"So you know you're going to hell when you die, right?" I looked confused and dismayed. I couldn't understand these heinous words coming from the mouth of one of my favorite relatives. This was my favorite relative with whom I spent endless summer nights staying up late bingeing hot television shows. This was my favorite relative who would effortlessly sneak me a folded twenty-dollar bill when no one was looking. This was my favorite relative whose phone calls were always answered. I absolutely adored her and thought she could do no wrong. She was an angel in my eyes. I placed her on the highest pedestal one could ever craft. Now, this beloved relative was damning me to hell because of my sexuality. How could this same loving and affirming mouth when I was a child now spew hate in my adult years?

"Welp, I guess God couldn't call me into ministry then; that would be divine hypocrisy." These were the thoughts that filled my fearful, ashamed, unworthy mind. Thus, I didn't fully accept a call to ministry until I arrived on the doorsteps of clinical pastoral education. This was intended to be an experience that would teach me pastoral care skills, but this experience transformed into so much more in my life. This experience gave space for me to address both the spoken and unspoken voices in my life that sabotaged my pastoral identity and functioning. Thus, I believe that no matter how many pastoral care classes one takes in seminary or other continuing education opportunities one attends, one cannot be "taught" to provide pastoral care because the essence of how persons function as chaplains or spiritual care providers is less about academic acumen and instead more about those inner voices, thoughts, and perceptions (implanted by others) that persons wrestle with and that subsequently influence the trajectory of their ministry calling.

I believe that influential family members impart most persons' theological ideas and beliefs to them during childhood. As persons journey through life and discern pastoral calls to ministry, these theological views can both help and hinder persons' pastoral identities and pastoral competence. Clinical pastoral education (CPE) is an educational resource that offers care to help students remythologize their theological construct to deepen their understanding of their pastoral identity and enhance pastoral competence. *Remythologizing* is a strategy highlighted by Katie Cannon in womanist theology by which persons can redefine or reinterpret their theological dogma to expand their relationship with the Divine. In CPE, the peer group and supervisor assist students in remythologizing their views of God through empathy, education, and empowerment. This leads to students experiencing personal, professional, and spiritual transformation.

Not only has CPE supervision been rewarding in a sense of affirming students' authentic genuine being through their personal, professional, and spiritual transformation, but I have a deep love for clinical pastoral education because it creates an exciting and new experience every time I meet and journey with a new student. Chaplaincy seems boring and mundane to me. How many times will I have to work long hours on call, working holidays, being away from my family, carrying and responding to a pager, and asking patients and families to complete health-care power of attorney forms? As I age, chaplaincy seems harder and harder on one's body physically. Chaplaincy also seems to foster compassion fatigue and psychological burnout, especially when one must deal with traumatic patient cases continuously. Aside from the joy of teaching and educating, CPE supervision provides a career that is less physically demanding on one's body and emotionally draining on one's mind. Add to these dynamics that CPE supervision is less physically demanding and emotional draining a career path than health-care chaplaincy, yet CPE supervision financially pays more in salary compensation than chaplaincy. Who wouldn't love that? Thus, my life has found extreme joy in CPE supervision during the last eleven years since I first began this ministry. All of this joy took a turn in 2020, however, when COVID-19 and police brutality against African Americans took center stage in this country and around the world.

Can I share something with you for a moment? Can I be open and transparent for a second? This time a year ago I was feeling defeated, depleted, and depressed, longing to move up the ladder in my career and serve as a director or manager of CPE at this stage of my personal and professional development. I worked so hard to desire a seat at other people's tables, to no avail. It's only so many times one can hear "No." One morning, after I spent the whole previous night crying, my partner said, "It's time to do your own thing." I called Rev. Ardella Gibson. She had been doing her own thing as executive director of her own online CPE center, Serenity Enterprises, for a few years and doing it well. I asked her to help me. She did without any hesitation. When one believes in you, he or she will always support you no matter what. She helped me create and birth Sankofa CPE Center, LLC.

The term "Sankofa" represents three distinct meanings that influence the objectives of Sankofa CPE Center. First, Sankofa represents the belief that it is important to "learn from the past." Sankofa is a word in the Twi language of Ghana that translates to "Go back." The symbol of Sankofa is referenced by the Asante Adinkra symbol, which is an image of a bird with its head turned backward while its feet face forward. With this meaning of Sankofa in mind, students are invited to "go back" and reflect on encounters with their "patients" in their unique site learning contexts, which also speaks to the pastoral reflection learning goal of ACPE's Level I and Level II programs. This notion of "going back" and reflecting on my own family history has been helpful in my discernment process. For example, when I reflected on whether I had the capacity to spearhead my own CPE center and subsequently run a business, I was nervous and scared. I had never operated a business before. Then, in my personal reflection time, I remembered my paternal grandmother, Ruby Duncan, and how she had founded her own real estate company when I was a teenager. I can vividly remember her teaching me about the importance of one owning their own company. I remember the times when she would train me as her eager protege on useful tips for operating her business, hoping one day I'd take the mantle of her real estate company after her demise. Reflecting on this once-forgotten detail of my life and recalling this story from my unconsciousness to my consciousness (as Edward Wimberly would highlight), gave me a sense of pastoral confidence to start my own ministerial business—a CPE center.

My grandmother would make frequent trips to the bank where her business account for the real estate company was held. I can remember accompanying my grandmother to the bank and sitting in the waiting room awaiting her meetings with the bank's savvy business accountant to end so that we could move on to a fun activity like eating ice cream or shopping. I held on to this memory as a golden nugget, unaware of how it would later serve me. Reflecting on my grandmother's visits to the savvy business accountant reminded me of the importance of selecting a proper, professional, and savvy staff (a reputable accountant and lawyer) to help me navigate the operations of my CPE center. This golden nugget from my grandmother has been invaluable. The image of the Sankofa bird looking backward also features the bird holding on to a golden nugget in its mouth. With this meaning of Sankofa in mind, students are invited to retrieve "golden nuggets" from their personal history that will help them to develop or further enhance their pastoral identity, which also speaks to the pastoral formation learning goal of ACPE's Level I and Level II programs.

I became fully certified as a CPE supervisor in 2014. I had been utilizing CPE theories that were prominent when I began the supervision certification process in 2010. However, starting my own CPE center in 2021 has pushed me to continue growing and developing my supervisory theories, moving forward in the latest chaplaincy and chaplaincy education trends and theories. Starting my own CPE center has pushed me to resist getting stuck in old ways of thinking and doing from roughly ten years ago. This speaks to the third meaning of Sankofa, which symbolizes an understanding that in the process of looking back and retrieving golden nuggets from one's history, one's feet are still planted firmly in the direction of moving forward. Thus, students are invited to ever evolve and continue growing in the provision and demonstration of meaningful interreligious spiritual care skills, which also speaks to the pastoral competence learning goal of ACPE's Level I and Level II programs.

My life has taken a dramatic turn in the last year. I no longer have to contain my voice, whisper, and wait. I simply had to begin taking just one step beyond the limits of my own imagination. The Divine can do more than what we simply ask for or imagine. For so long we beg for seats at oppressive tables, beg to be recognized by oppressive persons, beg to be affirmed by oppressive entities instead of creating our own progressive tables, embodying progressive mindsets that care for and empower others. My favorite Kwanzaa principle is called "Ujamma," which means *cooperative economics*.

What is your unique calling? What is your thing? Have you discerned your thing? After you discern it, now is the time to do it! Do your thing! If need be, do it scared!

QUESTIONS FOR REFLECTION

1. What is your unique call to ministry? Is there a ministerial business you've thought about starting?
2. Is there a pastoral dream that you have that you're nervous about putting into action? Why or why not?

A Call to Serve

Ruth Naomi Segres

In 1998, I was a seminarian at the Samuel DeWitt Proctor School of Theology at Virginia Union University in Richmond, Virginia. While in class, Rev. Dr. Patricia A. Gould Champ, my field education professor and my pastor at Faith Community Baptist Church, posed a question to twenty-one students; six were women. "How many of you feel called to pastor?" she asked. It appeared that every male hand shot up fully extended without hesitation. In what felt like hours, but in essence were seconds, with a bowed head my hand slipped up just above my shoulder. When I got the courage to lift my head, my eyes locked with my professor-pastor who offered an affirming smile and approving nod.

Most of the men stated that they were going to get a "big house," the euphemistic term for a church. I said, "I don't know where I'll serve, but it won't be traditional." There was a lingering silence before the next man enthusiastically offered the same stanza as the others. In that lingering silence, looking at my professor-pastor, she again gave that affirming smile and approving nod. I felt empowered even though I had no idea what nontraditional pastoral opportunities were available for this Pentecostal-Holiness turned American Baptist Black clergywoman. But my professor-pastor, through her sagacious silence, aided me in overcoming the greatest hurdle: myself.

In November of that same year, I attended the annual Ellison-Jones Convocation, an event in which alumni returned to their alma mater to share ministerial stories, network, and encourage students. At this convocation, my nontraditional pastoral probability became a possibility. Outside of Coburn Hall, two chaplains, Majors Willie Marshall and Reginald Cleveland (wearing what I later discovered were US Air Force uniforms), approached me. Willie asked about my plans after seminary. I said, "I don't have any, but I need to be gainfully employed." Then he asked if I had considered becoming a military chaplain. I said "No" but thought to myself, "If a military chaplain is like a hospital chaplain, he could do the opposite of the hymn 'Pass Me Not' and pass me right by!" I wasn't called to hospital ministry. Knowing where you are *not* called is equally important as knowing where you *are* called.

As he spoke, however, I realized that military ministry sounded adventurous and as nontraditional as it came. It would satisfy my desire to travel the world, and the pay and benefits were attractive. I talked with my professor-pastor and she supported my decision to pursue military ministry.

To be endorsed by my denomination as a military chaplain, I had to be interviewed by an American Baptist Church (ABC) endorsed military chaplain. The closest one was a Navy chaplain. In February 1999, I drove from North Carolina to Virginia and was interviewed by an ABC Navy chaplain. During the interview he told me about the first Black woman Navy chaplain, Vivian McFadden. I said, "Patricia McFadden?" He responded, "Yes, do you know her?" "She's a distant cousin!" I exclaimed. He said, "God is telling you to follow in your cousin's footsteps." He said that I'd make a great chaplain, but I knew that the Navy was not for me.

After the interview and submitting a mountain of paperwork, Ms. Dottie called to inform me that I was accepted into the chaplain candidate program (CCP) and would attend commissioned officer training (COT) the next summer. I said, "Oh, no, ma'am. I am going this summer." She said that all the slots were filled, and I was seventh on the waiting list. I repeated, "Ms. Dottie, I'm going this summer." About a week later, Ms. Dottie called saying, "Ruth, someone 'upstairs' already likes you. We had a cancellation, and the others have something missing from their package. Your package is complete, and you'll be attending COT this summer."

That Christmas, my uncle, US Army Major (Retired) Richard "Buck" Segres, called me. Uncle is high-spirited; and on this particular day, he had had spirited drinks. For what seemed like hours and with very vibrant language, he proceeded to tell me why I wasn't going be become an Army chaplain. Uncle had witnessed Army chaplains in the rain, cold, mud, snow, and ditches shivering and trying to share encouraging words that nobody gave a damn about in the moment. His narrative was harsh, and he was emphatic that I wasn't going to live like that. When he finally paused, I said, "Unc, I'm going into the air force." He said, "Oh, God bless you," and hung up.

Before I knew it, I was in Montgomery, Alabama, for COT at Maxwell Air Force Base. While in-processing, I discovered that I had no orders to report for duty. COT officers contacted another office to fax my orders, which took twenty-four hours, but no one had told me. I was placed in a room for eight hours, only leaving to get food and for bio breaks. Periodically, people came by; but no one had meaningful conversation with me. I was nervous and scared. I returned to my room, discouraged, wondering what was going to happen to me.

About two o'clock in the morning, sitting in bed praying and crying, God showed up. I happened to be watching Bishop T. D. Jakes interview Rev. Dr. Claudette Anderson Copeland. During her interview, she looked into the camera, as if she was looking directly at me, and said something like, "I don't know who this is for, but I am speaking to women called to ministry. I once served as an Air Force chaplain and that field is ready for harvest." At that moment, I started bawling. God used Dr. Copeland to confirm that I was exactly where God ordained. My orders came through; and twenty years later, I am still serving as an Air Force chaplain. Seven years after that night, I met Dr. Copeland and shared with her how she confirmed my call.

My first ten years, at different locations, I was the senior pastor for gospel services (GS), the name for predominantly Black/African American style church services in the air force, doing all the responsibilities of a civilian pastor while simultaneously serving as a chaplain. As a flight line chaplain, I took ministry to the people who flew and cared for aircraft. As the medical group chaplain, I did lunchtime brown bag Bible studies in military hospital breakrooms. As a chaplain at the Air Force Academy, I was a college campus pastor.

In twenty years, I've had eleven assignments and two deployments: from Alabama to Afghanistan; from Enid, Oklahoma, to England; and many locations in between. I concur with Bishop Vashti McKenzie that leadership for Black women in ministry is "not without a struggle."[1] My initial struggle started when I sensed the call to serve on active duty instead of remaining in the reserve and pastoring in a church. I was preparing to be ordained, serving as the assistant to Pastor Gould Champ at Faith (the field education professor and church I mentioned earlier). I felt that she was grooming me to become her successor, and many members said that I was their next pastor.

Sitting on the floor in my apartment, I tearfully called and told pastor that I was called to active duty. She said, "Daughter, there is a strong call on your life, and I'd love for you to stay at Faith. However, more than that, I want you where God is calling you. Your ordination isn't dependent on location." Once again, as she had done years earlier, she affirmed my call.

The motto for my life and air force ministry is the amalgamation of quotes, one by an anonymous author, the other by the late Rev. Dr. Katie G. Cannon, paraphrased, "She who kneels before God can stand before anyone to do the work her soul requires."[2] The work my soul requires as an Air Force chaplain at times is challenging.

At my first duty station, a senior ranking chaplain stated that he would never share the pulpit with me because I was a woman. I responded, "Sir, why do you think I'd invite you to share the pulpit with *me*?" He walked away. When I served at the Air Force Academy, I was intentionally left out of the preaching rotation. I confronted the scheduler, who responded, "As a preaching machine in the community, I don't see the need to put you on the schedule." I documented that and other conversations, eventually going to his supervisor. His supervisor told him that it did not matter how often I preached in the community; I worked here and should never have to fight to be included. When I served as the senior chaplain at a base with a predominantly white male staff, one of the white men shook my hand on my first day and said, "You're not my boss, and I'll not answer to you." He was prophetic. I documented that and other conduct unbecoming an officer; in four months, he was fired.

The air force has enriched my life. As with any profession, there are not-so-pleasant moments; but in the grand scheme of my call to serve in the air force, I say:

> My call to serve is an adventure of ups and downs;
> For thorns and thistles made up a crown.
> Peaks and valleys—twists and turns,
> All provided lessons from which I learned.
> To glean and grow—become refined;
> Sharpen my skills—the choice is always mine.
> My call to serve is a mixture of highs and lows,
> Gladness, sadness, and yes, some woes.
> I have gained and I have lost;
> But all keeps me bowing at the foot of the cross.
> There, I will always gain more than I will ever lose.
> So, I'd do it all again—for the sake of the cross, I choose.

QUESTIONS FOR REFLECTION

1. Are you your primary obstacle to your call? If yes, in what ways? If no, who or what is?
2. Will you disappoint anyone by accepting a nontraditional ministry vocation? If so, who and why?
3. How do you presently navigate challenges? How might they be preparing you for future roles? What, if any, character traits are being developed through challenges?
4. I believe that God develops us where we are to prepare us for where we are headed. In what ways are you presently being developed? For what do you think you are being prepared?

A Calling to the Academy

David Emmanuel Goatley

"Dean Goatley, I know I'm called to be here at divinity school, and I want to prepare for serving the Lord, but I'm still not clear where that is. Tell me, what exactly does a professor do?" I love to hear this kind of question from theological students for a couple of reasons.

EXPLORATION

First, a question like this shows an openness to answer God's call. This indicates more than choosing something to do with life that one believes oneself to be good at, or interested in, or suited for, or passionate about. Those are commendable motivations but calling needs more. While ministry as vocation can take various forms, it is ultimately about God's call and our answer.

Ministry as vocation is worthwhile work. I get a little nervous about people who seem eager to pursue ministry out of desires to help people, or be fulfilled, or do good work in the world. All of that is admirable, but ministry demands something extra. While ministry can be tremendously fulfilling, it can also be terribly draining. When the winds blow, the rains fall, and the waters rise, you need somewhere to stand for strength and sustenance until the Lord can restore your soul—literally to give you back yourself.

Ministry as vocation has to do with accepting an invitation—in the words of Yvonne Delk, the first African American woman ordained in the United Church of Christ in 1974, acknowledging that "God's 'Yes' was louder than my 'No.'"[1] Or in the words of an old spiritual song that was popular in the African American Baptist churches of my youth:

> When he calls me
> I will answer.
> I'll be somewhere
> Listening for my name.

Second, that great question shows a desire for discernment. Students who pause long enough to ask this question have decided not to plunge headfirst or have concluded that leaping before looking has not turned out too well. What does God want me to do with the gifts entrusted to my care? Where is the Spirit drawing me? Where is Jesus leading me? Discernment takes time and emerges from within and without. Sensing the hand of the Lord nudging, guiding, preventing, and providing is part of the process. Learning from previous experiences and exposures along our journeys are part of the course.

Discernment also comes through community and in conversation. The philosophy of Ubuntu teaches: "We are who we are through other people." Put another way, "I am because we are." This acknowledgement of communal participation in shaping our identities is so embedded that it is sometimes obscured by certain North Atlantic Western fallacies of independence. There are no self-made people. We are interdependent. All of us stand on the shoulders of others, drink from wells we did not dig, and sit in the shade of trees we did not plant. Habits and rhythms of formative years, observations of influential people, aspirations aroused by those we admire, and people who create opportunities for us without our awareness all help to form who we are, what we attempt, and how we function in the world. Intentionally asking someone who is doing something that you might be interested in is a wise part of the discernment process.

LOCATION AND REPRESENTATION

It is a blessing for faculty and administrators to function in ways that make students comfortable to ask, "What does a professor do?" Our responses should be offered with wisdom and care. We need to take seriously our responses and use good judgement in order to be helpful rather than harmful. We should facilitate illumination rather than set up some trusting souls for disillusion.

One issue faculty advisors should take seriously is student location. Suppose the student is of a different social location than the faculty member consulted. One's response could be injurious or beneficial. Some faculty advisors assume that the path that has worked in their case and social location is normative and fail to consider whether the opportunities they have enjoyed are realistically or remotely plausible for their advisees. I assumed, for example, that doing well in my doctoral studies, securing a university teaching position, and publishing my first book in a highly respected series would position me for consideration at the theological institution from which I graduated. Was I wrong! The socio-theo-politico dynamics of the school prevented me from having a snowball's chance—at the equator—of being considered for a faculty position. I subconsciously harbored the hurt of this disappointment for years before the Lord showed me how blessed I was that the Spirit closed that door.

One's social location is not the sole factor to determine one's vocational opportunities. It must, however, be taken seriously in considering the path one seeks to follow in the answer to God's call. It is irresponsible for advisors to ignore the reality of discrimination from racism, sexism, classism, and more. A professor may assume that a student is not "academically superior" because the student does not get near perfect grades and is, therefore, not an ideal candidate for a vocation in higher theological education. Suppose, however, a woman student is only exposed to male teachers, male authors, and male models of intellectual excellence. She may not be inspired to be fully invested to master the subject matter when there are so many times and ways that texts and teachers minimize, stigmatize, or erroneously summarize wisdom as discerned and described by women. She may be perfectly able and willing to excel (whatever the guys assume that means) but not inspired because of the narrow normativity that she must endure. Faculty should be cautious about assessing students' potential in higher education, or other vocational options, and consider how one might be socialized to implicitly or explicitly value or devalue potential.

Social location matters and representation counts. Women students need exposure to women scholars, authors, mentors, and more. The same is true of various groups of people who have been implicitly and explicitly marginalized by the overly privileged who disproportionately enjoy unearned benefits. I recall Asian and Latinx doctoral students responding with deep emotion about my syllabi that included Black, Brown, Latinx, and White required texts. They had never taken classes with required texts by authors who shared their heritage in undergraduate studies or graduate theological educations. These omissions are untenable in twenty-first-century theological education. Institutions of higher theological education should attend to social location and identities in their faculties, staffs, and students. If they do not have adequate diversity for modeling and mentoring in their personnel, efforts need to be made to redress this deficit and augment this deficiency. Faculty should be expected to incorporate appropriate diversity of required texts across the curriculum and penalized or ostracized for failure to do so.

PREPARATION

So, what does a professor do? A professor seeks to curate learning experiences that help people acquire tools and the ability to use them well in the work the Lord has assigned. This can be approached in different ways, but the end should be similar. Our work is not to teach people how to do everything they may face. Theological educators and their schools get many complaints from pastors and leaders who say, "They didn't teach that in seminary." It is impossible to teach people what do in every potential predicament related to programs, people, possibilities, problems, politicization, and pandemics! However, we can teach people how to approach problems and discover or design solutions to complex situations. We do well when we equip leaders to draw on biblical texts, theological constructions, historical insights, practical responses, intellectual resources, relational networks, personal capacities, and more to find ways forward (or at least minimize the backward retreats).

While every theological educator or professor in a theological institution may not have the MDiv or pastoral experience as part of their preparation, I think it is very helpful. Most people who earn the MDiv are preparing for ministry as vocation, and most of those are pastoral expressions (pastors, pastoral staff, chaplains, etc.). While it is not impossible to be an excellent theological educator without ministry experience, colleagues without this experiential learning do well to be intentional about discerning what pastoral leaders might actually need rather than imposing theoretical or conceptual ideas. I sometimes wonder in what universe some theological propositions might be plausible or have a chance to succeed. The journey that has led me to my current expression of ministry as vocation through service in teaching and administration has been enriched by the MDiv and pastoral life. One of my colleagues notes that I am the rare academic dean who has actually done what we claim to prepare students to do. My journey is not normative, but it has been instructive.

My vocational path has included service as urban missionary, denominational staffer, congregational pastor, global missions executive, theological educator, and educational administrator. My MDiv coursework blended biblical, theological, philosophical, historical, clinical, and ministerial training. Building facility with the tools introduced through this preparation has helped me to think and act critically, constructively, faithfully, and with integrity as a leader. A consequence of this journey is my commitment to help students understand contexts of communities and congregations, build consciousness about factors affecting people's lives and resources available to support their exercising agency toward thriving, and constructing ministries that lead toward flourishing communities and sustainability for the most vulnerable. Leading students toward this kind of work is a positive contribution that professors can make.

CONCLUSION

"Dean Goatley, I know I'm called to be here at divinity school, and I want to prepare for serving the Lord, but I'm still not clear where that is. Tell me, what exactly does a professor do?" I think I might respond to the student inquiry something like this:

> I am glad that you are here, and that we are able to support your preparation for what God is calling you to do. A lack of clarity need not be anxiety producing. Very few of us know where we are going, but that is OK when we are sure that God is leading. Knowing who you are following is likely more important than knowing where you are going.
>
> Part of your work in theological school will be listening and learning. You will meet people, encounter ideas, explore experiences, and more through texts, conversations, projects, and relationships. Be open to the lessons you learn along the way. They will be useful as you discern more of what God is calling you to do and where the Spirit is leading you to be. You do not want to miss the journey because of a fixation on a destination.
>
> I rejoice that you are open to the possibility of being a professor. We need more teachers in institutions of higher education who have answered God's call to serve through teaching, writing, and mentoring. While different professors will answer variously, one way that I describe being a professor is mentoring and teaching leaders to serve faithfully and with integrity. They seek to learn continually and to help others grow in their capacities to inform and influence others as witnesses to Christ Jesus for the sake of the reign of God in the world. At our best, we help to discern and describe complex issues in ways that make them digestible to people at different stages of life and levels of comprehension. We do not show people how smart we are by speaking in ways that are complicated. We work to meet learners where they are and help them to draw from personal, spiritual, intellectual, and communal resources to move with the Spirit toward where they can be. This is a noble calling that you are considering. I look forward to supporting your answer to God's call.

I wonder, with great anticipation, what God is going to do.

QUESTIONS FOR REFLECTION

1. How have you been discerning your call to help students prepare for ministry leadership, and how do you fan the flame to sustain your vocation?

2. How do you continue to deepen your understanding about various locations and identities that shape your students so that you can be a more helpful companion in their preparation?
3. How do your previous ministry experiences equip you to help in student formation for leadership, and what continuing ministry engagements can equip you as a better guide?

Vocation as Communal

Christine J. Hong

As a child and adolescent, I didn't understand what people meant when discussing the difference between vocation and profession. Vocation and profession felt and sounded like one and the same thing to me. I was a child of Korean American immigrants; my parents raised me to prioritize dreaming about profession as vocation. My parents framed profession as a pathway for bringing others along. I made the immigrant bargain, as many children of immigrants do, to commit to choosing to live in such a way that honored what my parents gave up, and all they subsequently lost through the experience and trauma of immigration. In my parents' portrayal, my profession should become, by default, my vocation. My call should be the desire to adopt the dreams that came before mine as my own, just as my parents had adopted different dreams for the sake of their unborn children. Just as my grandparents had adopted different dreams as internally displaced people for the sake of my parents.

I know for many who don't identify as Asian American, Korean, immigrants, or the children of immigrants, stories like mine about growing up to fulfill someone else's dreams sound terrible and unfair. It sometimes felt that way to me, but most of the time, I was okay with it. It didn't feel like my parents were burdening me with things I didn't want. I didn't resent them. The sacrifices they made were apparent to me even before I could put words to what I witnessed about their lives. As a child, I watched them endure racism and dehumanization. I remember one incident when my mother and I were checking out at a grocery store. While a cashier was ringing us up, a bag of sliced bread tore open, scattering pieces of bread all over the bagging area. The cashier looked straight at my mother and said in a cold tone, "You. You pick it up. You clean it up." Another time, I watched my father ask someone for directions only to be brushed off with a wave of the hand and the words, "I don't understand a thing you're saying." Except my father had asked for directions in perfectly clear English. My childhood and adolescence were marked with this kind of brutal and episodic racism. Violent words and actions hurled in our direction, mostly because we dared to exist, were visible, and took up space. So, when my parents would tell me my college education or my chosen profession would become a fulfillment of their dreams, it made sense to me. It wasn't a burden. It was a way I could acknowledge what they had given up, the way they paved for me day to day. I understood from my parents, in the deepest way possible, that my vocation was somehow mixed up in how I was to interpret what it meant to grow up, work, and make a life.

I learned from my parents and from being a child of immigrants that vocation is not just about yourself. Vocation is communal. The question I ask myself as my vocation continues to refine itself as I age is, does my profession through my vocation give life both to me and to the people I claim and who claim me in return? It helps me to think about vocation as not only a divine calling, but also a calling from the collective voices of those who came before me. My parents were not wrong about the collective call to vocational life. We are someone's dreams fulfilled, even as we dream our own dreams about different futures. Our existence, our questions, our curiosities, our ability to laugh and possess joy, are a reverberation of someone's once-upon-a-time dream, embodied now through us. For many of us who are racially or otherwise minoritized in a white supremacist world, our very ability to choose different futures for ourselves is the fulfillment of that generational vocational call. It's true what people say: It takes a village to raise a child. Sometimes, it takes the power and tenacity of generations to get that child to adulthood and to continue to remind that adult of whose dream they are.

The understanding of vocation as both a divine and communal call brought me first to ministry in the Korean American immigrant church and then to the ministry of teaching. At first, fresh out of seminary, I knew I loved to teach but I didn't want to teach in ways I knew would only stifle the call of the generations behind me. Why would I want to teach in an academy that failed to see me or my people in any way except as caricatures of ourselves? Particularly, an academy that insisted on its whiteness and the understanding and teaching of Christianity through the white gaze. I heard instead the call of both the Divine and the Korean community back to the places that formed and shaped me.

I resisted the call to teaching and threw myself back into the Korean American immigrant church. My experience in the Korean American church in my childhood, adolescence, and young adulthood was as a place of nurture. It was a set-apart place for a kid in a world that continually othered her. It was the only space where, as a child of immigrants, I didn't have to explain myself. It was a place, like in my home, where I could speak "konglish" or the Korean English hybrid language many second-generation children use with their parents and one another. I didn't have to suffer through explaining what

I was eating and why I enjoyed it. I wasn't asked to perform an Orientalist interpretation of Asian-ness. I could exist in complexity rather than become essentialized. At church, I was just another kid working out what it meant to find growing up awkward, painful, and joyful, all at the same time.

The communal call of vocation deepened to nudge me again toward teaching, and I left pastoral ministry. As I continued to read, learn, and practice teaching, I began to see the ways my life experiences were coming to bear on what was important to me to pursue in teaching and learning. It was during this time that I noticed how many moments of joy in my life were tied to the experience of teaching and learning. My first teachers were my parents and grandparents. They taught me through stories. How I loved to hear them tell stories. I could listen to their voices talk about their lives, the beautiful and the painful, all day and never grow weary of the tenor of their voices shaping words into pictures in my head. Their stories and voices helped me learn my own voice and tell my own stories. I realized I had first started to share those stories in ministry with youth, then in classrooms, exchanging dialogues with colleagues and students, all the while growing my voice. Those stories knit me together in so many ways. I could see and feel the power of stories as threads between people, places, and generations, always connecting and pulling us closer to different truths and understandings.

The threads of story in my life were also threads of the same generational vocational pull of my parents, grandparents, great-grandparents, and my other ancestors. I felt the call to continue telling their stories, to retell them by weaving in my own, to teach toward BIPOC students who also understood what it meant to be and live as someone's fervent dream, who understood the deep and earnest call of generations into the communal vocation to thrive and be, fully. Today, I am a professor at a seminary, but I didn't always envision myself here. It was the people who came before me who could see it, who dreamed it, and who paved the way. We are, each of us, someone's dearest dreams come to life; and through our lives we tell the stories of those dreamers and weave them together with our own voices, a shared and communal vocation full of power and joy.

QUESTIONS FOR REFLECTION

1. Who are the people and what are the places that call you into being?
2. How do you understand vocation as communally wrought and shared?

Learning To Be Carried

Keith Starkenburg

I currently serve as professor of theology at Trinity Christian College, located in Palos Heights, Illinois, a suburb of Chicago. As of late, I've come to think of the Christian community as a vineyard, or forest. Trinity Christian College arose from a grove in that forest that nurtured me in my youth—the Reformed grove, but especially the part of the grove that produced various Dutch Reformed species. Among the faculty and staff, Trinity includes people from all kinds of Christian communions. Among the students, we strive to welcome all kinds of human beings, Christians or otherwise.

I came to do this work because of a series of experiences in college and seminary. At eighteen, I arrived at a Christian college with what I thought to be a distinct and settled goal for my post-college life. I was going to be a lawyer, and, after I made my way through the law, a politician who fought for certain political causes. God had awakened me in my last year of high school, and I wanted college to be a place where I could talk about the big questions of life and politics among those who thought mostly like I did. On the one hand, I was being opened to the presence of God in Christ. On the other hand, I wanted to become a more articulate leader of what I would now call a defensive and aggrieved Christian politics.

In that college environment, God kept waking me up. In my first-year philosophy course, for example, I remembered being taken aback by a professor who contrasted Plato's figuration of the material body as a prison for the soul's capacity for knowledge with the creation story in which human beings are created with, and even as, bodies. When he made that comment, I felt relief. At that time, I was in a relationship with a fellow student, and I felt guilty that I found her beautiful. My professor said nothing about sensual desire or beauty or dating, but the Spirit drove home the obvious. God had made her beautiful. I could love her for all that she was and is. Eventually, I married her!

In another class during my second year, Christ showed up in another way. One of my professors assigned *The Peaceable Kingdom* by Stanley Hauerwas, a book that my professor held somewhat in disdain. The professor, to his credit, wanted to expose us to the conversation in ethics even if he didn't approve of the book. But, to me, Hauerwas seemed to outmaneuver everything my professor had to say about the claims in the book. In part, Hauerwas helped me see that Jesus was the embodiment of a kingdom, a politics. More importantly, Hauerwas argued for a Christian political imagination informed by God's gift of peace. Until that time, peace was, for me, only a feeling. For me, peace wasn't a practice or a way of life for followers of Jesus. Peace was feeling good about being saved from God's judgment. And so, I began to desire to act in social and political contexts in ways that gave witness to the kingdom of Jesus Christ and the peace he brings. I started to vote differently, and to look for Christian communities that embodied this peace.

I had many other similar experiences in and around classrooms. However, being awakened in college courses does not mean that one will be a teacher in the academy. In that same introductory philosophy course, I noticed that I was able to explain ideas to my classmates in ways that helped them. Doing so wasn't a chore. I *enjoyed* understanding the material and helping them understand the concepts. One of my classmates remarked that he needed to study with somebody like me, someone who was passionate about these ideas. I believed I was taking a philosophy course in order to prepare myself for law school, but something else was happening. In dialogue with those who came before me, I was learning how to cast ideas that made sense of the whole world. I didn't have words for it at that time, but I was starting to experience, through my own rudimentary learning and teaching, that the world had a unity. I didn't much know what that unity was, other than it had something to do with God. Nonetheless, I was experiencing it as I learned with others.

Experiences like that continued. In a class during my junior year, I was invited to give a couple of short lectures on the history of Christianity in the United States in an interdisciplinary literature course. I had taken one course on US religious history and my professor challenged another student and me to distill that history for other students in the course. The first lecture went horribly. I thought I knew what I needed to say. As I spoke, I became overwhelmed by the events and connections and got lost. No one said anything to me about that session, but I knew it didn't go well.

The professor allowed me to take another shot at it, and I worked hard to create a focus and organization so that the other students could sense the context for the works we were reading. I practiced what I was going to say. Delivering the second presentation, from my perspective, was exhilarating. I adhered to my plan, but I also identified new links between events in American history that I did not see until the very moment I was speaking. I realized that teaching was itself a kind of learning, and it felt magical. In a way, I felt like I was being carried away by a current, even being poured over a waterfall of reality. After the presentation, my fellow students mentioned that they learned a lot during that talk. I have an old friend from that class who always references that moment. He likes to say that he knew I was meant to be a teacher after he saw me teach that day.

I couldn't say this at the time, but now I'm certain that those were uniquely joyful moments wrought by the Spirit as I gave myself over to God's world for the sake of others. I've experienced this many times over the years. Teaching, in my experience, is a place where I can participate in the emptying of God in the incarnation. It is a way I can give myself over to God's world as God gives God's self over to the world in Christ. It is a way I've found myself being carried into the life of God in Christ.

My seminary experience was significant as well. At first, I found myself quite disoriented in both seminaries I attended. I cannot tell the whole of that story, but part of my disorientation had to do with how church communities were taken to be so crucial to a life with God in Christ. My professors and fellow students kept talking about church, serving in churches, being frustrated with churches, etc. For me, at that point, it was hard to sense the Spirit at work outside of the academy. In college, my sense of the whole of reality refused to stop widening and deepening. Given that I wasn't connected significantly to congregations as an undergrad, I couldn't sense how that college environment was, in a way, an extension of the church (and vice versa, for that matter). Obviously, my spiritual senses were far too truncated at that time, but it was also a testimony to where God had continued to open me to the divine life.

When I've looked back at seminary experiences, I can see now that those communities, along with other communities I encountered later, invited me into a life of worship—a life of listening to God and participating in God's self-opening in Christ—with others. Bonhoeffer once remarked that he had to move from the phraseological to the real, and that was true for me. One of the seminaries I attended had daily worship services followed by an informal gathering in the seminary's dining area for coffee, announcements, and general chatter. Many of the seminarians also ate together in that same dining area with people from the larger community who were served free lunches. It took some time, but I was learning from those people that an academic life can and should arise from and support a community's life of worship and service. They encouraged me in my intellectual pursuits and gave me opportunities to continue some teaching appropriate to my learning. In the end, the best gift they offered was patiently nurturing me to take up a life lived with others before God that could not be boiled down to discussions about the latest academic fashions. Theology begins and ends in joyful worship and service because it is itself meant to be joyful worship and service.

Self-giving in the academy has its burdens, and I think it is important to mention a burden I've carried. One of my graduate professors, a Jewish philosopher, once remarked that learning involves suffering, the loss of something. For me, academic formation changed my relationship to the grove in the forest that nurtured me. I come from a restrictive, even fundamentalist, Reformed culture. In graduate school, I studied Christian traditions intensely alongside people with multiple kinds of faiths and refusals of faith. After learning in that context, my trust in the central realities encountered in Christ—such as God's triunity and the incarnation—became more profound. But, at the same time, I am taught too much from other cultures and traditions within and outside Christianity to think that the Christian church has all the truth there is to be had. Christ is Truth incarnate and the Christian community partakes in Christ. Yet the Christian community has much to learn about Christ across its own divisions and across the borders of other religious cultures. I know God in Christ more deeply not simply because I have read Scripture intensely in the Christian community, but also because of the relationships I have built in pluralistic academic contexts. That has meant that my belonging to my own grove within the forest of the Christian community can feel quite strained at times. I've been nurtured by other soils. That's a gift, but it is also a difficulty when my own ways of thinking cannot fully correspond to the community that I'm tasked with handing on to others.

I went into teaching in higher education contexts because the Spirit showed up for me in the academy. God opens human beings to the love of Christ wherever the creation is to be found. There are many other places where God finds us. All I can say is that the academy, too, is one such place. It has been for me. Perhaps it will be a place for you to participate in God's unveiling as well.

QUESTIONS FOR REFLECTION

1. The author writes that he found himself teaching "in higher education contexts because the Spirit showed up for me in the academy." To what extent can we find our vocation in service to the places or contexts in which *we ourselves* have been transformed? Does this help you find your way to your own vocation?
2. The author mentions that he experiences teaching as a participation in the kenosis of God, as giving himself over to God's world for the sake of others. In this essay, what confirmed for him that his joy in teaching was beneficial for others? In what ways does the essay hint that confirmation by others does not mean confirmation by everyone around you?

Rags to Riches to Rags

Miguel A. De La Torre

Growing up poor and knowing hunger can, at times, serve as a motivator to succeed. They say children growing up poor usually don't know how poor they really were. That was never my case. Living in a rat-and-roach-infested tenement apartment in the slums of New York City, sharing with all the residents of the floor the only available bathroom, seared the reality of poverty into the consciousness of a small Latino boy. The Catholic school I attended during the day, and the Santería rituals practiced in my apartment at night, provided little spiritual comfort to the violence experienced because my parents had the audacity to be among the first Latinxs to move into Jackson Heights, at the time a predominantly white neighborhood. Each punch that landed on me during elementary and high school, simply because I occupied a Latinx body, formed necessary calluses capable of enduring the harder knocks that were to be received in adulthood.

Living in Miami, I resolved to no longer be poor, to instead eat at fancy restaurants, to date models, to drive fast cars, to enjoy all that life had to offer. When I turned eighteen, I obtained my real estate license and became the youngest realtor in the state of Florida at the time. A year later, I passed my broker's exam and opened my own brokerage house. With time, I grew my company to more than one hundred sales associates. Besides eventually serving as the president of the Board of Realtors, I also ran political campaigns, even running for the Florida legislature as the most conservative Republican among the three candidates, endorsed by Pat Robertson, who was making his own bid that year for the Republican presidential nomination.

How did I become involved with conservative evangelicals? Originally it had more to do with matters of the heart than matters of the soul. I wanted to date one particular woman who would only go clubbing with me on Saturday nights if I went to church with her on Sunday mornings. And while our relationship did not last, I remained attracted to the wholesome message of the sermons, where the answers to all the mysteries of the universe were relatively available. I kept attending this church until, during one service, I walked down the aisle during the second chorus of *Just as I Am* and gave my life to Jesus as part of a born-again experience. At the time, I thought my conversion was to Christ; now, with the benefit of gray hair, I realize I was converted to ontological whiteness. Soon I was adopting political positions that I previously did not hold, positions that were—to say the least—misogynist and homophobic. And because I was embracing a Euro-Christian worldview that has historically provided spiritual cover for white supremacy, I began to see and define myself and my community through Eurocentric eyes.

I lost that election in 1988, but there would be another election for the Florida House in four years. Few ever win on their first attempt. That first run was to get my name in the public sphere so that I could win if I ran again—which I planned to do. But much changed during those years. The woman I married gave me a son, and now a daughter was on the way. We were not wealthy, but we were comfortable. We became more engaged with our church, and I became both a deacon and a pillar. The dreams and hopes of that barrio boy were fulfilled; and yet, something was missing. Self-actualization was not yet achieved. There was a particular scripture that gnawed at my soul. Found in the Gospel of Mark (10:17–27) is the story that has come to be known as the "rich young ruler." According to the story, a rich ruler asks Jesus what he must do to inherit eternal life. He has done everything religious people are supposed to do; nevertheless, according to Jesus, he was missing one thing: giving his riches to the poor and following Christ.

This story deeply touched me. And while I was committed to taking such radical steps, unfortunately, I was still enmeshed in Euro-Christianity. I decided to postpone my run for political office and instead attend seminary, become a minister, and then run for office with the vision of saving America for Christ. So, I sold my company at a loss, packed up a U-Haul, and drove to seminary with my wife, son, and day-old daughter. I enrolled at a conservative seminary that, during my tenure there, was taken over by fundamentalists. When we arrived at seminary housing, it became obvious that my rags to riches story had now become rags to riches back to rags. We were poor, in need of WIC coupons to eat. And to make matters worse, the theology I was learning did not resonate.

Eventually, I was given a pastorate in a rural town in western Kentucky. We moved into a trailer as I began my ministry. The town was so small, the population was counted in the tens, not the hundreds. I was told that I could preach about anything I wanted except tobacco since all of the parishioners were tobacco farmers. This did not bother me because I understood smoking to be more of a filthy habit than any type of sin. Then one day, the head deacon commented that he never understood how "them Colombians" could grow cocaine that was so destructive. That Sunday, I preached a sermon about cash crops and how growing cocaine had more to do with meeting international demands than whatever the Colombian farmer cared to do—"kinda like you tobacco farmers." The church did not appreciate me comparing them to Colombians; and before the week ended, I was asked to leave.

During my year as a pastor, my political and spiritual views began to change. I started moving in a different direction from others at my seminary. Besides pastoring, I also had two other jobs, one as a stereotypical janitor and the other as the seminary's night librarian. One night, after reading Karl Barth for one of my classes, I realized that I could not relate to this theology. At first, I thought it was because it was too obtuse. Now I realize that it was because it was too white. That night, I decided to read perspectives from my community. I walked over to the bookshelf and pulled every theology book I could find with a Latinx sounding name: Gustavo Gutiérrez, Ada María Isasi-Díaz, Justo González. Reading these books, and the works of other Latin American and US Latinx thinkers, led to another conversion. I became born-again-and-again.

That was the moment I realized that regardless of my love for preaching and my desire to return to politics, both dreams died in that seminary library. I could never again run for office, especially as a conservative. Also, I would never again be able to pastor a church, especially among Southern Baptist churches, which were quickly aligning themselves with fundamentalism. With graduation a few months away and the realization that my vocational options were limited, I did what any other unemployed graduate student would do: I continued my studies in higher education, focusing on obtaining a PhD in religion.

If the seminary I attended was fundamentalist, the university in Philadelphia was quite liberal. There I studied under womanist theologian Katie Cannon. There I became a liberation theologian. Rather than thinking that I simply pulled myself up by my bootstraps during my real estate years, I came to realize that my success probably had more to do with all the money flowing through the city, known at the time as the cocaine capital because it was the main entry point for the illicit narcotic. During my doctoral studies, I focused on Foucauldian power relationships and issues of marginalization and oppression. When I graduated, I was offered a tenure-track position at a Michigan four-year college. All went well until the day I decided to write an op-ed for the local town newspaper. I made fun of James Dobson for outing SpongeBob SquarePants. Within a week, Dobson, surprisingly, responded to my article and decried my professorship as a platform for advancing the so-called homosexual agenda. Unbeknownst to me at the time, the major financial backers of Focus on the Family were also major patrons to my college. A major controversy ensued (Google it!) that ended with me resigning my tenure. That is what has led me to my current position at one of the most left-leaning theological schools in the nation.

One can say that the contours of life have led me to this point. If it was a calling, I did not hear it. If it was preordained, then it truly was a very roundabout way of arriving. Who I am and what I do has more to do with the journey to get to this point than any preconceived idea that I would end up here. Who I am and what I do, in the final analysis, is the summation of difficult, joyful, and challenging hardships—and how I faced them. The physical abuse of poverty, the attempt to assimilate to Eurocentrism, and failures in politics and pastoring have made me the person I am today. Although I have not always lived up to my ideals, falling short more times than I'm willing to admit, I tried to maintain several guiding principles along this journey.

1. Be truthful with myself, not so much seeking answers, but questions.
2. Be not afraid.
3. Be bold in unmasking oppression and let the chips fall where they will.
4. Be not someone who communicates by what they say and write, but by what they do.
5. Be in solidarity with whatever community is relegated to the underside of society, regardless of my personal agreement or disagreement with them.

And here is the good news: so much more lies ahead! Opportunities to learn and grow abound. The story is not yet finished, or as Monty Python reminds us, "I'm not dead yet."

QUESTIONS FOR REFLECTION

1. How has your own vocational journey been influenced by Euro-Christianity? How might you engage potential vocational paths with different understandings and practices of faith?
2. In what ways might your calling be a "summation of difficult, joyful, and challenging hardships," at least in part? How can you work to reconcile, heal from, honor, and otherwise address these as part of your vocational preparation?

Participating in God's Wide Welcome

The Ministry of Camps, Conference, and Retreat Centers

Theresa F. Latini

I remember well the day a former colleague and longtime friend asked me if I'd consider applying for an open position as executive director of Mount Olivet Conference & Retreat Center. I was in the midst of significant transition, and I had long ago learned to open my heart and mind to conversations like these. Plus, the position was located near the Twin Cities, a place I had previously lived and loved (minus the cold winters). One conversation led to another, and I accepted the job offer, all the while wondering, "What am I doing?" I had visited retreat centers for educational events and team-building meetings, but I had no special relationship with any such place. I hadn't grown up attending church camps and, in fact, had often quipped to friends, "I camp at the Marriott." After nearly fifteen years working as a pastor and seminary professor and administrator, I knew little about the inner workings of outdoor ministries generally or conference and retreat centers specifically. "What is a retreat center director and how does that compare to other kinds of pastoral and educational work?" was a pressing personal question.

I have been reminded again and again that leading a retreat center is first and foremost ministry, and ministry is first and foremost God's work. Retreat center directors (and staff members) join, accompany, and witness to God's ministry of hospitality, justice, and care. The Spirit enlivens and empowers us to participate in God's wide welcome of all—a welcome that nurtures guests' well-being through inspiring programs, beautiful land, nourishing food, and comfortable accommodations and amenities.

Hospitality is the heart of ministry for camps and conference and retreat centers. Just as God receives us into a space not our own, that is, into relationship with God, so outdoor ministries welcome and receive guests with openness, warmth, and attentive care. This impacts not only our programming but also our indoor and outdoor spaces. As a retreat center director, I ask these questions with my staff: How can this building or this lounge invite people to rest, be still, collaborate, or reconnect with themselves? How does the land (in our case, prairie, woods, and marsh) beckon people home to God, to themselves, to their vocation? How can we facilitate our own retreats and resource other leaders so that guests are renewed, healed, and empowered in this place?

God's welcome is wide, and so is that of camps and retreat centers. These outdoor ministries exist on the margins of church life—a challenging but potentially generative place—and so they are well positioned to embrace those who have been excluded in other settings. It's not surprising that camps and retreat centers frequently welcome those who are marginalized. BIPOC leaders, LGBTQIA+ youth, those who are disabled or afflicted with mental illness experience acceptance, belonging, ease, and community at camps and retreat centers.[1]

Given all this, one of my most important responsibilities is to articulate and embody the mission and values of retreat centers (and other outdoor ministries) generally and that of Mount Olivet Conference & Retreat Center specifically. For well over a century, camps and conference and retreat centers have played an important role in the ecology of Christian education across a broad array of ecclesial traditions in the United States.[2] Along with hospitality, they cultivate spiritual practices, encourage care of creation, and educate persons for faith in daily life. They often rejuvenate church and nonprofit leaders, health-care and educational specialists, and others for works of compassion and justice. Camps, in particular, contribute powerfully to the identity and faith formation of youth and young adults, sometimes launching them into a lifetime of service.

Retreat center directors communicate this mission of hospitality, justice, and care to a diverse group of constituents: fellow staff members responsible for the daily operation of the retreat center, retreatants and program participants, volunteers and donors, board members (if applicable), affiliated churches and judicatories, umbrella organizations for outdoor ministry, and the larger public. In any given week, program staff and I might communicate the mission and events of our conference and retreat center to groups and individuals who receive our blog, to members who read our church newsletter, to those who follow us on social media, to individuals, families, and organizations inquiring about retreating with us, and more.

It's important to note here that camps and conference and retreat centers come in all shapes and sizes. They vary greatly in terms of accommodation size, geographical location, indoor and outdoor amenities, religious affiliation, and governance structure. Many are independent nonprofit organizations, and some are outreach ministries of a larger church or judicatory. And all that impacts the director's daily life. If you lead a stand-alone camp or conference center, you'll likely spend a lot of time fundraising. If you have a large staff, you may dedicate significant time to human resources (e.g., hiring, onboarding, and carrying out annual reviews). If you run your own events more than you host other groups on retreat, then you will devote considerable energy to creative programming and event planning.

Regardless of size, retreat center directors administrate—a lot. I remember telling my supervisor, after my first six months, that most of my work focused on "programs, personnel, and policies." Almost three years later, that's still true. The pandemic brought this home sharply. I stopped counting after writing a tenth version of our COVID-19 Preparedness Plan required by the state department of health. I reduced staff, a painfully necessary decision, and then hired new staff in an economically challenging time. With each surge, I supervised decisions about cancellations and rescheduling. Senior staff and I restructured departments and listened to and encouraged those whose personal and professional lives had been upended. Together we imagined new, creative programs to encourage others to "retreat where you are." This was some of my most rewarding work: launching virtual mini-retreats and curating a set of resources (contemplative prayers, mindfulness meditations, and a regular blog) to support people in learning to retreat at home.

Because Mount Olivet Conference & Retreat Center is embedded in a larger church, I have regular opportunities to teach, write, preach, and periodically administer the sacraments. A number of our programs (e.g., a summer midweek worship series and day-long Advent and Lent retreats) fall within the contours of congregational life and include worship services. But here's the distinction: *what* and *how* I teach are shaped by the aims of retreats and the needs of guests. People retreat for many reasons—to rest, to heal, to learn, to grow—individually and communally. We all need the kinds of spiritual renewal, emotional regulation, and quiet intellectual stimulation cultivated by gifted retreat facilitators. We need connection to nature, others, ourselves, and the Divine. The pandemic has reminded us that time apart in welcoming, picturesque landscapes restores our souls (and bodies). Experiencing solitude; taking time to meditate, pray, and write; and being present to life in its many forms bolster our resilience and renew our faith, hope, and love. For these reasons, when I teach or facilitate retreats, I often introduce retreatants to practices of mindfulness and contemplative prayer. Silence, reading poetry, *lectio divina*, and *visio divina* are part of my regular repertoire. Our site naturalist gives nature talks and leads guests on nature walks. Outside wellness experts offer massage therapy, yoga sessions, and forest bathing as well.

One of the more unique and vital responsibilities of leaders in outdoor ministries is stewardship of the land and care for God's creation. Camps and retreat centers are located in beautifully diverse "geographies of grace," as Dorothy Bass puts it. She defines geographies of grace as "place[s] infused with the grace of the Triune God," landscapes that, for a variety of reasons, have a sacramental quality.[3] Sacraments are visible signs of invisible grace, everyday items like water, bread, and wine that communicate to us the promises of God. Geographies of grace, then, remind us of God's everlasting love and convey beauty, truth, and goodness to us in ways that we can receive. Camps and retreat centers frequently function as geographies of grace, which may be the reason that persons and groups return to the same center year after year. In a particular landscape (mountains, forests, desert, oceans, or prairies), people find themselves upheld by love and renewed for daily life.

A generous grant from the Louisville Institute enabled me to interview a small group of camp and retreat center directors and to survey participants in our own programs at Mount Olivet Conference & Retreat Center. I heard again and again that retreats nurture guests' holistic well-being by inspiring, supporting, and curating their connection to nature. Encountering the land (and its many inhabitants) reorients our relationship to time and space, recalibrates biorhythms, enhances inner peace and calm, and grounds us in God's presence and provision.[4]

Camp and retreat center directors recognize that nature matters in and of itself, that our relationship to the land is reciprocal. We are creatures born from and returning to the earth. Mount Olivet Conference & Retreat Center sits amid 151 acres of woods, prairie, and marsh land. It has more than five miles of walking trails, twenty flower beds, raised vegetable gardens and fruit trees, an outdoor labyrinth, and a gazebo. Guests are invited to learn about and participate in our bluebird recovery program, monarch waystation, and green initiatives. Skilled staff members and volunteers tend this particular geography of grace with respect and humility. In short, caring for and being cared for by this particular part of God's creation impacts annual decisions about budgeting, staffing, and programming.

In recent years, outdoor ministry leaders have become more aware of the importance of land acknowledgements—statements that confess the indigenous history and stewardship of the land, on the one hand, and the destructive impacts of colonization, on the other. These statements should be preceded by educational processes: deep listening to local indigenous leaders; rigorous study of the history of indigenous peoples and unjust treaties or policies foisted upon them on retreat center lands; and commitments to empowerment and reparations. When embarking on this kind of work, camp and retreat center leaders face a number of challenges (i.e., the relative new awareness of land acknowledgement processes, the difficulty in engaging key constituents, such as board members, in this process, and socioeconomic stresses that stretch staff thin and pull directors in multiple directions simultaneously).

The call to retreat center ministry surprised me. I suspected that this might be God's way of sending me on retreat. Surrounded by a team of people who love the land, who embody hospitality, who serve cross-departmentally so that guests experience God's wide welcome: this has been restorative for me as a leader. The rhythms of retreat and lifegiving connection to nature have been integrated more deeply into my own life and faith journey. The prairies and marsh—diverse ecosystems home to a plethora of plants, animals, insects, and fungi—speak: here you belong in and with this exquisite array of creatures. As I roam through the "seas of grass," I am reminded how God's welcome elicits wonder, openness, and possibility for us all and inspires us to seek the flourishing of others.

QUESTIONS FOR REFLECTION

1. Where and when have you experienced God's wide welcome, receiving it yourself and extending it to others through hospitality and care? How significant are hospitable practices for your own faith and life?
2. What places have functioned as "geographies of grace" for you? How has your own faith been shaped by engagement with the land, plants, and animals in these places?

It Started with Trees

Kent Busman

It started with trees, or perhaps with my love of trees. In seventh grade walking around outside of school collecting leaves to be pressed in wax paper. I was shown a ginkgo (*ginkgo biloba*). This species of tree was around during the Jurassic Period, 170 million years ago. Such a marvel! What other strange and mysterious stories were contained in all the branches, roots, and stout beams carrying what Wendell Berry calls "weightless grace"?[1]

Forestry was to be my vocation. My first college course was "North American Conifers." We were to be able to identify forty species by needle, bark, cone, and Latin name. *Tsuga canadensis*, *Pinus strobus*, and *Larix laricina*: the deciduous conifer known locally as tamarack. Calling them trees was too broad. They were individuals. I could recognize them as I would my own family.

It was love of trees that made me challenge my understanding of Christianity. The version I was given twice on Sundays and once on Wednesday evening each week implied that accepting Jesus was the only goal and my ticket off this earth filled with sin and darkness. Trees became like Sirens to me: calling me away from that understanding. For with trees came rivers and streams, deer and fox, largemouth bass and birds—a world filled with birds just like Genesis 1 promised. If Jesus was my savior, wasn't he also the savior of these creatures that I so loved? A God who loved me wasn't enough. I needed a God who so loved the world.

That's what I set out to find. Switching majors to Religion and Philosophy, I pursued the possibility that this God who my native religion said became incarnate, lived among us, died on a cross, and was raised from the dead might also love trees. I was praying that my love for the world may be more a reflection of this God than a rejection of this One.

I was aided my mentors: One who didn't buy into the God talk but cared for others far better than the minister models my youth showed me. One who never feared my asking questions of well-established doctrines. And one who showed me that ministry could take place outside within the realm of trees. I was nurtured by an ecosystem of colleagues who challenged me but also gave me space to hear God's call in new ways.

I worked guiding youth groups on backpacking, canoeing, rafting, and rock-climbing trips during my college years. I had gone to a week-long Christian camp once as a kid and frankly thought very little of it. At the camp, we had to do what they said all week rather than be free to go out to the woods a mile from my house and camp on my own. My mentor and co-leader in college was a bit older and far wiser. He began to show me scripture that affirmed God's love for all creatures: Psalms, creation stories, bad translations of Greek that aligned with the interpreter's theology rather than what the original intent might have been.

And if God also loved and redeemed this world, then a faith focused on escaping this planet for a heavenly realm was not only folly, but antithetical to the way of Jesus. My studies began to include readings of liberation theologians, feminists, and those who would give voice to the voiceless ones, including my beloved trees. A ministry of status quo and comforting the comfortable (including myself) was not what I was going to be part of.

I found the Sanctuary of my ministry in a small overnight camp in 247 acres of *Pinus strobus, Tsuga canadensis,* and *Larix laricina* in the Adirondack Mountains of upstate New York. My congregation was comprised of the one hundred motley and laughing children who showed up each week. "Decently and in good order" were part of my ordination vows, although I can say that they are goals rarely achieved and even less rarely sought after. Neither trees nor children have much power, so my ministry has mostly been on the edges of denominational strife, goals, or conflicts.

For thirty-five years I've been tending trees, training young adults, and engaging children in the acts of awe and wonder. My hope is that they get as excited about the world as I was about a ginkgo tree as I share with them a God who is as awesome and wonder filled as the creation that God called into being. Unlike my earlier understanding of Christianity, whose only goal seemed to be a verbal assent to Jesus's role in my life, this ministry continues to engage, grow, morph, die, and be resurrected time and time again.

My call into ministry was preceded by a great love and is guided daily by that same love. The work has changed greatly since my arrival in this wooded mission. The forest has grown, faced disease, been wind blown and snow packed. New trees have grown taller than some buildings and a few old giants have died in order to nurture the next germination of seedlings. The children have grown, become parents, sent their children, and often share how their lives have been impacted by their time here.

Neither love nor ministry remain static but must be reincarnated every day. This ministry has taken root in me and has made me grow old so that perhaps someday it will make of me fodder within which new ministries may germinate. No longer is the need to escape with Jesus to some faraway heaven, but to be present with the Christ in the humus of this earthly home.

QUESTIONS FOR REFLECTION

1. Frederick Buechner wrote that vocation "is the place where your deep gladness and the world's deep hunger meet."[2] What are one or two things that bring you "deep gladness"?
2. This "call story" is less like Paul's Damascus Road story than a gradual awakening to God's presence all around. How does Busman's story relate to your own understanding of what it means to be "called"?
3. Busman writes, "Neither love nor ministry remain static but must be reincarnated every day." What do you think he means by that?

In Such a Season

Elivette Mendez Angulo

I always knew that the struggle for justice—in all the ways necessary—was a fight that Jesus would have joined. I knew it as a kid in early 1980s New York in the beginnings of the AIDS epidemic as I was meeting toddlers grieving the deaths of their parents. I saw the need for Jesus when walking through my neighborhood and watching panhandlers begging for thirst-quenching nourishment. I knew that Jesus would have been upset at the plight of all those who were not being welcomed into God's household—the "church"— because they wore makeup or jewelry, were too sweet, too bold—or loved too loudly. I knew that while the Spanish-speaking, immigrant/migrant, Holy Spirit welcoming, worshipping (raja table) Pentecostal tradition of my youth seemed to disagree with my assessment, I was learning the stories and ways in which Jesus walked with those who needed and required justice. And as a young person who was already fully embracing her sexual attraction to many different types of people, I was relieved. But I just knew that I could not lead in church.

As a kid, I learned to see church as personal nourishment for only a select few. On the other hand, around my mother's dining room table, I regularly saw the work of justice when she—like my grandmother before her—fed people from what little they had. My mother would invite queer friends over and welcome them into our family. I learned that teaching is sacred work, even outside the church.

In the midst of these dueling realities, I heard God's calling: To be authentic, to be true, and—most importantly—to love. For a long time, I thought that to be who God called me to be would require that I leave my faith, because the tradition had no room for the justice movements that seemed to call me to action. So, I did my best to ignore that calling and instead prepared for a life of secular work.

Outside the boundaries of my church tradition, I considered what it meant to do justice. To be just. To love God and their people in a way that was bigger than any building and more ethical than any business model I had ever considered. I began to study the different ways in which justice might be needed and discovered that God truly *is* justice. As the Black, Brown, and Indigenous church mommas say, "But, God!" I was able to find a new church home in the United Church of Christ that had space for the weirdly churched, and I began to serve as a lay leader ministering to youth and young adults.

Because my younger self felt unworthy of any degree in religious studies, I completed an undergraduate degree in business management. In the course of these studies, however, my passion for justice came through and was centered in a divine understanding of God's transformative power. My final project was the development of a new entity created by the merger of a predominantly white church with their ministry project, a Hispanic community of faith. And what were the issues or concerns that needed to be addressed in that process? Justice and reconciliation!

After I completed my project, I met with my advisor to discuss what I should do after graduation. His response was, "Have you considered how a degree in business is helping you to answer God's call?" We had never spoken "faith" before; but he said that in the current reality of church closings, a business degree with an understanding of ethics and morality and a deeper knowledge of the business realities of an organization might be useful for ministry. How could my five-year-old Pentecostal self, preaching to my *peluches* and anointing them in Vick's, ever imagine a world in which I would be worthy of a seminary education? *¡Pero Dios!* In 2015, I graduated from Andover Newton Theological School with a master of divinity degree. My local church, Manantial de Gracia (Spring of Grace) United Church of Christ in Connecticut, called me as their co-pastor and teacher.

In 2017, when I asked my church to pray for me as I considered accepting a position at Franklinton Center at Bricks (FCAB) in Whitaker, North Carolina, and when I expressed my concern that I would step outside my calling, it was my church board chair who sat with me in my discernment. After a time of deep prayer, she laughed and asked, "Can I remind you of something?" She said, "Pastora Elly, God did not call you to the building; God called you to the fields. That is where you have always been called."

When I think of FCAB, it is literally a field—a large field filled with rich soil and the ability to grow wonderous vegetation. This field has a unique, rich, and intersectional history as a former plantation that became a place for education of newly freed slaves in 1895. The community in which FCAB resides continues to be deeply impacted by its history of systemic oppression and racism. The three surrounding counties have the worst health outcomes in the state of North Carolina, and North Carolina has some of the poorest health outcomes in the nation. As a whole, rural eastern North Carolina is a food desert. Food insecurity, unjust systems, nonexistent public transportation, and underfunded libraries are all realities that our children have to navigate.

When people ask me about my current ministry setting, I laugh and tell them, "Life!" I am currently the interim executive director of the Franklinton Center at Bricks. Today, we exist as a site of restorative justice and healing of all God's people. Our mission is to provide a nurturing home to local, national, and global programs and organizations seeking liberation. In other words, we work with justice organizations to determine how the history of our 244 acres might be enriched by their work.

Dreaming is a luxury for many, including a boy like Joseph in his effeminate coat of many colors and Rev. Dr. Martin Luther King Jr. and his dreams for future generations of the Black diaspora. What happens to a dream undreamed? Those dreams are the ones often missing in our rural, poverty-laden community. FCAB empowers others to dream again by providing access. We till the land, plant the seeds, and invite the community to eat. I develop relationships with local community leaders who help ensure that food gets to the tables that need it. Why? Because if you eat, you can think. And if you can think, then you can learn. We welcome educators to our land, to learn the history of the community from those who lived it. We invite organizations that use our land for social justice trainings to build relationships with us, and we help our local schools to gain access to these organizational assets as they are developing curricula. Such assets feed the work of our local community, widening the doorways of justice and offering opportunities to dream again.

If my call is for a season such as this, for a season when dreaming is scarce, then it makes sense that I have been prepared for what is needed, both as an administrator who understands the business side of nonprofits and as an ordained minister in the United Church of Christ called to the work of justice. This, my vocation and ministry, helps me to create a table with more than enough for all. My role at Franklinton Center at Bricks creates the table for others to continue the work of justice, not from a place of scarcity but from a space of abundance. Understanding that while we continue to prepare and fight for equality in all her ways of being, we need also make room and space for the joy that comes with full liberation.

QUESTIONS FOR REFLECTION

1. For everything there is a season, including a season of dreaming. What dreams has God placed on your heart? How are you preparing to live into them?

2. Society tells us that we need to save toward retirement. God tells us that there is a season and a time for everything. Change comes when it is supposed to. Who/How are you preparing for the next iteration of your journey?

Becoming the Clay

Megan Shepherd

What was it like to be the clay?

This question opened my imagination up to a whole new way of praying, and ultimately led me on a path toward my vocation as a spiritual director.

It was just a few days into my experience of the thirty-day Spiritual Exercises of St. Ignatius of Loyola, and I had been struggling to pray well. I would slog through the five prayer periods each day, diligently reading the scripture passages as if they were assignments and then reporting back to my spiritual director what I thought about each one. Despite a well-developed prayer life, on this retreat my experiences of prayer felt dry and boring. I began to worry that I had made a mistake in committing to the retreat. Four days down, twenty-six more to go.

As I turned to the passage in Jeremiah 18 that morning, I read through it thinking about clay, the potter, and how God shapes us through our experiences. I felt that I had a good grasp of what I wanted to talk about so I started off our meeting by jumping into listing the ways that I am like clay when my director gently stopped me and said, "Yes, but what was it like to BE the clay?"

I sat there dumbfounded. Be the clay? What do you mean "be the clay"? I thought I had all sorts of deep insights to share and was annoyed at the interruption. But he had recognized how much I was stuck in my head and instead of letting me stay there, he invited me into the imaginative prayer at the heart of the Ignatian Spiritual Exercises.

Ignatius believed that if we open ourselves up in faithful humility, God will work in our imaginations to help us glimpse the wonders of God's grace. Reminding me of this, my director asked me to do a repetition of the passage and this time to imagine myself AS the clay. And then let God do the work.

After lunch I settled in to pray by clearing my mind of theological thoughts and then reading the passage anew. I sat in silence, and slowly began to imagine a cold and moist block of clay wrapped in a plastic bag, like I had seen in a ceramics studio back in college. But I realized that I was still thinking *about* the clay.

And so, trusting in the guidance of my spiritual director, I surrendered my imagination and BECAME the clay: cold and clammy inside a damp plastic bag, surrounded by darkness until the top of the bag opened. Light spilled over me as the bag was pulled down around me. Hands stretched a wire across my top, cutting off a chunk and releasing me from the larger block. I became this new lump of clay cradled in the hands of the potter—slowly warming from their touch as they molded me, working me into new shapes, building me up, smashing me down. I grew more pliant and flexible as I became something new, something beyond what I had imagined possible. Grace abounded.

That moment of prayer still strongly resonates many years later because of how it broke open my understanding of how to pray and introduced me to a whole new realm of spiritual growth. My spiritual director was key in that awakening; his simple question reoriented my approach to prayer and allowed me the opportunity to discover and explore the richness of scripture in dialogue with my imagination.

The next twenty-eight days were filled with grace, moments of beauty, deep sorrow, and abundant healing. Yet the retreat wasn't for me alone. Part of the reason I went on the retreat in the first place was to deepen my understanding of Ignatian Spirituality in order to more fully serve the community of the high school where I served as a campus minister.

Part of the faculty/staff formation at the school was making the Ignatian Spiritual Exercises in Everyday Life during the third year of employment. But when it was my turn, my year was disrupted by a variety of reasons (including medical leave). The following year when my supervisor approached me about trying again, he proposed something that transformed my ministerial trajectory. If I spent the summer making the thirty-day retreat and then participating in a year-long spiritual direction internship funded by the school, I could serve my colleagues when they made the retreat in everyday life.

Thus, a few months later I found myself sitting on retreat, returning to the passage from Jeremiah 18 for the second time, and becoming the clay. While it was God's grace at work in that moment, it was the insightful and provocative question from my spiritual director that opened me to a new way of embracing my imagination in prayer.

That moment—and particularly that question, "What was it like to be the clay?"—was pivotal in transforming my prayer life and guiding me toward a new dimension of my vocation. When I returned from the retreat, I dedicated myself to deepening my own skills to assist others in recognizing and responding to God's grace at work in their lives.

In my initial internship the following year I was challenged to learn how to really listen, how to focus on the religious experience of the directee, and how to humbly ask questions to help them recognize where God is acting in their lives.

Through my internship, ongoing training, peer supervision groups, and my own experiences of direction, I see my role as a spiritual director as holding up a mirror, reflecting to the person what I see, hear, and feel as they share their lives with me. I pose questions to help them recognize and articulate how they feel, understand their emotions, and grow in relationship with God. When appropriate I invite them to explore new ways of praying, just as my director did for me on retreat many years ago.

Over the past twenty years I have had the privilege to walk with many undergraduate students, young professionals, MDiv students, faculty, and staff through discerning relationships, making plans for after graduation, deepening their relationship with God, overcoming disappointment, managing grief, and delighting in joy.

It is a real gift to help them express their feelings to God. Especially powerful are those moments when they enter into a deeper authenticity as they finally feel free to be honest. I can't count how many times I've reassured someone that it is okay to be angry with God—God can take it! And God wants to hear how you are feeling! One of my greatest areas of growth has been learning how to get out of my own way, to pay attention to how God is working directly with a person and help direct their awareness toward that grace.

I often use the following to help focus a directee's attention on their relationship with God:

- Name a concrete time when you felt close to God.
- What people, places, events in your life have led you to desire a more intimate relationship with God?
- What helps you recognize the presence and action of God around you?
- What are your memories of being loved and cared for?
- What scriptures often evoke God's love for you?

My ministry as a spiritual director also helps cultivate my awareness of how God is at work in my life. In reflecting on my years of directing, I can see how God deepens my capacity to listen and receive another with compassion, to ask contemplative and evocative questions, and to attune myself to the promptings of the Spirit as I discern how to proceed with each directee.

QUESTIONS FOR REFLECTION

1. How would you describe your spiritual life and relationship with God right now? Who is God to you? Who are you to God?
2. What kind of listener am you? What skills come easy to you? What skills might you need to develop further?
3. How is a spiritual direction conversation—helping a directee reflect on their religious experience and relationship with God—different from the types of conversations you often have with people?

A Calling to Campus

Trygve D. Johnson

My senior year in seminary, I took a two-and-half week course in Israel. The goal was to encounter and experience the land and culture of the Bible and fill our imagination with a photo-album of the places where Jesus walked, talked, lived, suffered, died, and was resurrected. This excursion to the Holy Land changed the direction of my life; it gave me a vision for an ancient approach to ministry, and how I might be able to find correspondence with the way of Jesus in my own life on a college campus.

One of the places we visited was the "orthodox triangle," which consisted of three towns, Capernaum, Corazon, and Bethesda, that were each about three miles apart (and walkable) from each other. Some scholars argue that Jesus and his band of young disciples spent 70 percent of their ministry in this region—meaning this was a place where Jesus made a deliberate decision to do the deep formation and training of disciples for the work and witness he was preparing them to do. This training ground was made up of small towns, and was occupied by a large percentage of Pharisees, who lived apart from the power structures of Jerusalem and the ruling priestly class of Sadducees. This is an area where Jewish life was intentionally pursued and lived out with a rigorous discipline.

I remember visiting the triangle with our professor, who pointed out two interesting archeological observations. One is that many of the ruins were interconnected structures. This was called *insula*, a family household arrangement common in Jesus's day, where many room-residences for various family members were built around a central courtyard. When someone from a family got married, it was often the custom for the family of the groom to add on a room to their home. The second observation was that these towns had ruins of a synagogue. This was a context where God was worshipped daily. This struck me as significant. Jesus spent the majority of his time in a context where people would have been known by name (*insula*) and would have worshiped together as a community (synagogue).

When I reflected on the fact that this is where Jesus chose to invest in the lives of young adults, and that the context of this investment was in small towns where people would have been known and who embodied a life of worship, I felt a stirring in my soul. This resembled my college experience, where people lived and worshiped together in a concentrated location. College had been a period of critical growth in my faith, nurtured and shaped not by one experience, or class, or person. It was the weaving together of a totality of experiences, made up of a village of scholars and students, books and ideas, coaches, residential directors, and administrators that, over four years, shaped who I had become.

At the time I was preparing to enter a process of "calling." There were a variety of ministry options available before me: I could seek a calling as a pastor of a church, or pursue a life as a hospital chaplain or a director of non-profit or parachurch organizations, or even seek a teaching post at a Christian school. But I kept thinking about the context of Jesus's work—where he focused a bulk of his ministry in a context of relationship and worship.

As I thought about where I wanted to spend my life in ministry, I kept thinking about Jesus in the triangle. Prompted by Annie Dillard, who in *The Writing Life*, says, "How you spend your day, is of course how you spend your life,"[1] I discerned, there near the shores of Galilee, that I wanted to spend my day serving Christ on a college campus.

I love everything about college. A college is like a small town. It is a place where people live together in close proximity, living and learning, fighting and forgiving, praying and playing, and rooting for the home team, all in a shared space. It is a place where people fall in love, and discern a vocation, and imagine what it means to live a good and beautiful life. It is a place where futures are discerned, commitments are made, and life trajectories are set. A college is one of the last best places in our frantic culture where students are invited to ask and answer the foundational questions of the soul, such as "Who am I?," "Where do I belong?," and "What is my purpose?" For me, discerning a sense of calling to be a college chaplain, within this unique geography of learning, felt like a gift of revelation.

This is the calling I pursued, and by God's providence, I was called to serve as a chaplain at two different liberal arts colleges. Twenty years later I am still at this work, seeking to be a witness who seeks to articulate the gospel in a meaningful way to a suspicious generation.

SAY THE NAME

One of the primary responsibilities of a college chaplain is simply to say the name of God—clearly and with conviction, without shame, or embarrassment. The currency of a college chaplain is a relational presence that points to, and attempts to make plausible, the reality of God's presence, by naming God with intentionality. There is so much concentrated energy on a college campus that life becomes magnified. It is easy in this context for young adults to turn inward onto themselves and get locked inside their own experience. Similarly, within the culture of the secular age, the academy can relate to God, or religion in general, as an interesting relic, a curious historical phenomenon, which then often views campus ministries as one option on the menu of student activities. It is the task of a college chaplain to enter this intensified experience and open the door of a divine reality by speaking of God as present. In other words, the work of a college chaplain is to be available for a relationship that offers an alternative script for life, where the goal of education is more about communion, entering a fullness of being, than simply gathering competencies for a future job.

The tools that a college chaplain can use to speak God's name are prayer, preaching, the study of Scripture, the "ministry of books," trips, outreach, hospitality, conversation, and retreats. But by far one of the most important ways a college chaplain keeps the name of God before a college is by offering and inviting the community into a life of worship. More often, on a campus, this is called "chapel."

In chapel, the primary job of the chaplain is to gather students, faculty, and staff and to speak the name of God, who frees us to explore the wide-open country of salvation. This happens when worship ignites wonder, and wonder is the spark that lights the fire for learning the bigger and deeper things of life. In this way, the chapel works in a symbiotic relationship with the classroom. In the classroom we ask and answer the questions that encourage doxology, and in chapel, our doxology inspires us to go to the classroom to ask better and more honest questions. In this way, chapel can nurture an environment where students can experience an integrated life, where there is a congruence between our interior desires and our exterior realties, as we begin to weave together all the fabric of our lives into a tapestry of participation in the triune life of God. Here student experience comes together instead of being split apart, as it offers a life whole, without fragmentation.

Leading into and then out of worship a college chaplain can be an essential campus presence who can challenge the gnostic assumptions that divide the sacred and the secular, and in its place, offers a surprising but healing truth: the truth that there is in fact no such thing as a campus spiritual life—there is only life—and all of life is spiritual. In this way, in this place, where people live and worship together, we discover that "grace is everywhere."[2]

In sum, the primary work of a college chaplain is to help people enter and speak of the real world, as Gerard Manley Hopkins says, as one that "is charged with the grandeur of God."[3] In a context of the academy, where God is often neglected as a working assumption, there has never been a better time to be a college chaplain who can point us toward this truth.

QUESTIONS FOR REFLECTION

1. How was your college experience formative for your growth and maturity as a Christian?
2. How do you see the role of education as a place for God's work of discipleship and formation as a Christian?
3. If you are thinking about campus ministries, or a role as a college chaplain, how would you describe your understanding of your role on a campus for faculty, staff, and students?

Doing Campus Ministry Latinamente

Eddie De León

I have served in higher education for most of my ordained ministry. First, I directed Catholic campus ministry for twelve of my thirteen years at Missouri State University. Then, following a seven-year term in leadership as provincial of my religious order, I accepted an invitation to be a chaplain and director of intercultural outreach at the Catholic Chapel and Center at Yale University. Today, as a professor of preaching and pastoral ministry at a Roman Catholic graduate school of theology, I find myself preparing others for a diversity of ministries, including the accompaniment of communities on campuses.

So, this is my story. It was spring, and I was asked by the provincial of my religious community to consider going to campus ministry at the age of thirty-three. To be honest, I was not enthusiastic about the request; I had my own plans. I long imagined that I would be assigned to an urban Latinx parish community in Chicago. Now that dream was fast disappearing; the so-called opportunity did not, frankly, seem like one at all to me. I kept telling myself that the assignment would be for only two years, and then I could return for a new assignment that suited my dream. This provided momentary peace of mind. As a newly ordained missionary priest, I wanted to appear collegial; but I really didn't want to go. I wanted to stay in the Chicago area, not journey to an unfamiliar geographical location to serve in a ministry that I knew little about. I also was uncomfortable with the idea of doing campus ministry in the "Bible Belt" of southern Missouri; the thought was nerve-racking. What would I be doing there? God, help me!

Upon my arrival, I was perceived as a novelty simply because I was from Chicago. At this time, no one knew that I was Puerto Rican; nor was I willing to share this information as the number of people of color at the school were few. In my walks around campus, I saw firearms on dashboards of pick-up trucks and Confederate flags waving freely in greeting and heard a particular southern accent everywhere, reminding me that I was no longer in Chicago. I was a stranger, an outsider, a Yankee. Complicating matters further, I discovered that Catholics here were suspect. Often the target of prejudicial preaching, we were considered not to be "true Christians." Life limped along for this new cleric just trying to figure things out in this disquieting ministerial assignment.

In time, I met many in the campus community and was impressed and inspired by their intellectual pursuits and generosity of spirit. Because of them, I came to a new understanding of campus ministry as the official presence of the church on campus. I also learned that this ministry served more than students but also included faculty, staff, and even their families.

A year after my arrival, I was appointed both chaplain and director. I had to decide how I would approach campus ministry with responsibilities for two universities and a community college. I perceived that the role of campus ministry as church must be reflected in our presence, vision, and programming. As I considered what approach to take, I decided on privileging relationality. Looking back, I now realize that I began doing ministry *latinamente*. It wasn't a conscious decision at first. Rather, it was born out of my cultural influence and marked by the ways I negotiate space and relationships in the world. I focused on *lo cotidiano* and grew to comprehend my ministry as one of *acompañamiento* to be accomplished *en conjunto*.

Becoming attentive to *lo cotidiano*, daily lived experience, was necessary for me to better grasp what the campus community was going through on a regular basis. I could more effectively accompany those in my care through the daily rhythms of their lives—in their hopes, dreams, failures, successes, joys, and sadness. By embracing a ministerial approach rooted in concrete realities, my *acompañamiento* valued the other, began where they were (not where I thought they should be), and asserted, "You are not alone, and you matter."

Doing pastoral ministry *en conjunto* is both essential and effective, an affirmation that it is better when we work together rather than opt for a lone ranger approach. Collaborative styles of care encourage consultation, networking, and teamwork. They underscore the mutuality necessary for accompaniment. On the global stage, the synodality called for by Pope Francis is one example of doing ministry *en conjunto*. Such an approach centers encounters, deep listening, ongoing dialogue, and multiple and intersecting levels of consultation with diverse constituencies. The hope is that such engagement leads people to invest in community and achieve something for a greater good.

In the process of providing pastoral care authentically, I came to discover that I had to embrace my own complex *cotidiano* in order to be my genuine and authentic self. Being Latino was not a hindrance, as many had told me, but an asset in the landscape of the Ozarks. It was important for me to realize that I was good enough! When I was young in ministry, I tried to please everyone, especially those in leadership. I thought that their approval would validate me as exceptional. Why exceptional? Because societal cues were communicated to me as a child and young adult that we Latinos were not good enough. There were not many role models that I could call to mind except for those in entertainment and sports like Rita Moreno, José Feliciano, Chita Rivera, or Roberto Clemente. In time, I came to understand that who I was as a gifted Latino was a necessary component of how I cared for others. Claiming my own Puerto Rican identity, drawing on my cultural resources, and doing campus ministry *latinamente* proved to be not only creative but also generative, inspiring others to consider new possibilities for doing ministry and even for recognizing their own potential.

Ministry as *acompañamiento* takes *lo cotidiano* as context seriously and cultivates collaborative responses accomplished *en conjunto*. Instinctively, I was partial to such approaches because they felt familiar; this was how I was raised. In a certain sense, I developed this leadership style and honed my ministerial skills from a young age.

While I am grateful for my theological education, in too many spaces my Latinx-rooted approaches were not welcome even as an alternative to what had become, for too long, the preferred way of being and doing. Many times, I experienced so-called normative approaches as exclusive and even marginalizing. In my preaching, I encouraged those in the assembly to be their best versions of themselves. I, however, was not heeding my own counsel. The advice of Polonius to his son, Laertes, in Shakespeare's *Hamlet* continually came to mind:

> This above all: to thine own self be true,
> And it must follow, as the night the day,
> Thou canst not then be false to any man.[1]

I was not being true to my own self. I was afraid of the consequences, so I felt like a fake. It was not until years later, during my chaplaincy at Yale University, that I finally embraced more fully what it meant to be more myself. This comfort with my Latino self and its value for my ministries developed over time. In part, my membership in the Academy of Catholic Hispanic Theologians of the United States (ACHTUS) helped me to give expression to my familiar Latino self in ways that were pastorally and theologically relevant. The process of research and writing my doctor of ministry project allowed me to engage the richness of theologies arising from Latinx academics and pastoral agents. These insights challenged the stereotypes that I had succumbed to early in graduate studies and in my work in campus ministry.

Now, I bring all of these experiences, the wisdom learned from my journey, and my perspective as a Latino pastoral theologian to the graduate courses I teach in preaching and ministry at Catholic Theological Union. For example, taking *lo cotidiano* seriously, I invite my students to explore context through street art, regarding this art of our daily spaces as visual texts that tell the stories about the communities and barrios that they serve. Such art conveys local peoples' concerns, fears, sorrows, struggles, hopes, and dreams.

My attention to art emerges from Latinx theologies that consider the essence of life to be source, ground, and place for doing theology and ministry. To accompany students in ministry responsibly, I have found myself back in academia as a student studying art history at schools like the Courtauld Institute of Art, Sotheby's Institute of Art, and Oxford University. Never would I have dreamed of studying art in such prestigious institutions; but thanks to distance education, I am able to bridge multiple worlds.

I have discovered through my experiences in higher education, as a campus minister, and as one who teaches and prepares others for ministry that throughout the journey, I am continuously becoming my true self.

QUESTIONS FOR REFLECTION

1. What gifts, cultural identities, joys, and fears do you bring to campus ministry?
2. What must you consider when ministering in intercultural spaces on college and university campuses?

Unfolding

Kate Holbrook

It has always been about unfolding.
The unexpected way Spirit moves in my life
How one experience opens and unfolds into another
expands into another
into unknown possibility, unknown growth and becoming.
The invitation to embrace where space opens
To take time to discern and cultivate
Through the discipline of daily spiritual practices
Inner trust and faith
Grounds me
Helps flow with Spirit in the unfolding
Believing that if I seek to listen
Listen
to sense Spirit
Life's movement
I am open
each day
To the expansiveness that waits to be greeted
Within and all around
Form into formlessness
Formlessness into form
In this life
I call my own

My vocation unfolded into college chaplaincy. I did not expect to find myself in this specific vocation. I did not set out or intend to land in college chaplaincy. Working in academia never occurred to me in college or in the early years of graduate school. I couldn't see myself there. It was not a place I previously found belonging or felt valued, having desired an embodied integrative and heart-affirming education—and being queer and spiritual at a time when there wasn't space on campus for such intersecting identities.

Had you told me that I would one day work in academia, I would not have believed you.

Yet life unfolds, and after college I found myself working on farms and at a retreat center. Long hours of physical labor and lack of community erased any romantic vocational notions of farming and running a retreat center, yet that led to clarity about which seminary I wanted to attend. My seminary choice opened me to a field education experience at an urban Spanish-speaking congregation in San Francisco, which led to a curiosity about rural ministry and a summer internship with two small rural fishing village churches. For three of the four years of my joint MDiv/MA, I also worked as a student teacher poet (like a TA) for June Jordan's Poetry for the People Program at UC Berkeley, which empowered students politically and artistically to bring about social change. The combination of experiences in the parish and within the classroom helped me to realize that there was more space to give voice, to speak the truth of my life, in the poetry program than in the church. This moved me to be curious about educational chaplaincy at a high school level. When I was unable to find an internship in the Bay Area, I hand wrote to more than a dozen Presbyterian girls' schools in Aotearoa/New Zealand, where I had previously studied abroad. Miraculously, one wrote back, and the internship was arranged.

During the internship working with adolescent young women, something clicked as I engaged in creative spiritual care and teaching. I felt life's movement. This experience unfolded into a one-year chaplain's fellowship at a small college in the northwest, which led me into a vocation in college chaplaincy. During each of these vocational experiences, I would sit with these queries: "Am I open to this internship as a possible vocation? Do I approach new ideas and experiences with discernment? Am I open to spirit moving in this experience? Am I open to life's unfolding in this experience?"

Life unfolds, with awe and mystery, not to mention with irony. I find myself heading toward two decades in interfaith college chaplaincy at a small, competitive, driven, fast-moving private liberal arts college in Colorado, on the unceded territory of the Ute, Apache, Arapaho, Comanche, Cheyenne, and Kiowa peoples. In this community, part of my work includes cocreating space with students and the wider community where head, heart, and intersecting identities can come together in ways where spirit, philosophical thought, and ethical traditions can be valued.

I am a practitioner, deeply grounded in spiritual practices and working in academia. I have come to understand that the center of college chaplaincy is accompanying the community, especially students, as they seek and make meaning, and sometimes unmake and remake meaning, in the inner and external geographies of their lives. Coming alongside people through the unexpectedness of their lives—moments of expansiveness and joy, like aha moments and love, and through deep sorrow and contraction, like death, disappointment, anger, and grief of all types—is a daily practice. Context is everything, especially in our pluralistic, diverse campus—spiritually, religiously, and culturally. As a college chaplain, I hold space energetically, ritually, and with advocacy. I support our community in remembering the importance of the heart, the life of the spirit, the importance of space for contemplation, ethical questioning, and philosophical teachings in higher education. With others, I get to create space to ask questions of what it means to be compassionate and just and embody our values within our community and institution.

My experience of being a college chaplain unfolds in the everyday rhythms. Occasionally, I am in the public role giving ritual blessings. However, the majority of my work is not visible—which is a challenge at times. Much of the work is in confidential conversations; quiet advocacy for people, programs, and policy; unseen visits; connecting students/staff/faculty to supportive resources; building and maintaining relationships; maintenance and stewardship of our building; and endlessly moving chairs, meditation cushions, and tables. It is in the mundane, or what I think of as the spiritual practice of the mundane. It is in the programming, teaching of contemplative practices like qigong, and conversation groups. It is finding opportunities to collaborate with other offices and faculty where spirituality, interfaith, and religious literacy and engagement intersect with justice, art, and nature. It is in being attentive, flexible, and holding the work lightly and with humor. The heart of chaplaincy, though, is in the choice to be fully present, fully attentive in the moment with whoever may be present at that time—not just present in a thinking way, but present to the fullness of the person—embodied, energetically, and with intersecting identities—and in the space of pauses, silence, and fullness of words.

One of the challenges of this vocational space is practicing being fully present, as my work is to be interrupted. And I mean, I am interrupted. Constantly. College chaplaincy is about interruptions. It is amazing that I am able to complete anything. For me, there is a sacredness to the interruptions and the pause of remembering that whoever is at the door, on the phone, or in the text is the embodiment of the sacred. This is true at 2:00 a.m. when I'm on call for the college and at the hospital meeting with a student; sitting with a motion-sick student on retreat; dealing with an administrative issue; supporting a student in existential crisis or who is feeling anxious, lonely, unworthy, not good enough, wrestling with identity, family pressure, experiences of marginalization, and so on; assisting someone who desires to find a spiritual practice; or some other need. These interruptions are humbling. Being invited into people's lives is a gift, however and whenever those invitations may come. Each day, I ask myself, "Am I open to those I may encounter throughout the day? Am I willing to be changed by those I encounter? Am I willing to be open to interruptions?" And I say to myself, "May my heart and spirit be open to all I encounter."

It's not uncommon for me to be juggling twenty random unrelated tasks; keeping administrative, spiritual care, and programmatic pieces all afloat can feel like barely contained chaos. Most of my work challenges unfold at the intersections of institutional politics and administrative work, especially where space, budget, and specific student needs intersect—or when the institution makes decisions that do not seem people-or life-affirming. It is also challenging when there is a disconnect between words and actions, and specific communities on campus, especially marginalized communities, are hurt. Occupying this vocational position in an institution invites me to be creative about how I advocate for and support community members and nurture the community as a whole, discerning the politics so I can respond with what is most needed. The way academia can sow a sense of inadequacy is challenging; it can undermine the well-being of the community. Working with people in their strength and vulnerability is holy work. Accompanying community members through sudden deaths and navigating each one's unique complexity of timing, cause, location, community connections, not to mention shaping appropriate rituals of remembrance, highlights and reminds us of what really matters: questions of who and how we are to be together, and challenges like communal loneliness and deep desires for belonging. The joys and challenges in chaplaincy are of one piece, though, as everything belongs. As a chaplain, I hold the campus in the highest good, the highest compassion and healing. And my prayer has been—and always is—to be open to spirit's movement and life's unfolding.

QUESTIONS FOR REFLECTION

1. How may you find space to allow your life to speak?
2. Are you open to this internship or field education experience as a possible vocation?
3. Do you approach new ideas and experiences with discernment?
4. Are you open to spirit moving and life's unfolding in this new experience?

Called by Name for Engagement with the World

Mary Schaller Blaufuss

Mary stands in the place of the deepest hurt she knows. She is at the tomb of Jesus after his crucifixion when she hears her name, "Mary." She turns to see the one who is calling her by name, thinking it was the gardener. Upon challenge, she realizes that she is in the presence of the risen Jesus, who is sending her into the world to work with others for the reality of new life for all God's creation.

This post-resurrection text of John 20 is the framing story for the paper I wrote in preparation for my ordination almost thirty years ago. It continues to motivate and provide vision for the way I perceive my identity, meaning, and purpose—my vocation. The story emphasizes presence and solidarity in uncomfortable places of brokenness and exclusion. It enables a recognition of the living God already active there. And it empowers a purpose with which God sends us to accompany others in making real a wholeness and well-being for all.

I sensed my call to ministry from before the time I can remember. Although as a child I knew no women clergy, my family and home congregations always encouraged me in the calling to church leadership. For that I am grateful. But the shape of that calling continued to emerge as it tugged at a church that was bigger than the group of people who gathered on a Sunday morning for worship, education, and fellowship. The form of that calling began to take shape through my young adult leadership in church camp, college campus ministries, and seminary contextual education. These experiences expanded my communities of trust, gave me space to test my role in different forms of church, and presented new opportunities for activism.

As a child, I attended church camp every year. Normally, as an introvert, interaction with lots of new people made me uncomfortable. But I experienced camp as a safe space to make friends who openly explored faith and questioned the expectations of the world. During the summers of my college years, I returned to camp as program director and found those same experiences, only accelerated; I also was helping shape those experiences for other staff and campers.

If camp experiences highlighted community for formation, college campus ministries that enveloped those summers presented opportunities to explore new questions and test new leadership identities. A trusted college chaplain enabled me to break open possibilities of an adult identity that transformed expectations shaped in childhood. I also tried on a preacher's identity with a small congregation in town that took seriously their own vocation to nurture future church leaders by opening their pulpit to college students. And I took the opportunity to be among the college's first study-abroad students at a time when this educational movement in US schools was just beginning. The college organized arrangements for my cross-registration with a school in London, England. I had neither been on a plane before nor traveled by myself. As I turned from my family in the airport to board the plane on my own, I realized in that moment of formational clarity that I was free to test out new ways of interacting with the world. I read newspapers and textbooks and engaged in dialogue with people from the United States and other parts of the world. I opened myself to embrace the world from the perspective of my questions and to use critical analysis skills as normative. In the process, I began to recognize that I had a role in the global community.

Trusted communities of reflection and critical analysis, places to test new leadership identities, and activism for social transformation came together in the formational experiences of my master of divinity education that followed college. The contextual education program at Eden Theological Seminary immersed students in both community organizations and congregational placements to practice ministry, to integrate classroom learnings, and to discern vocation. In my first year, I chose placement with Unleashing Potential (then named Neighborhood Houses) because it enabled me to work in north St. Louis. I have been part of their ministry in some way ever since. I had grown up in the metropolitan St. Louis area and had been taught to fear and avoid that part of the city. I knew that I needed different perspectives and relationships. The journey of authentic relationships and leadership as a white person alongside Black communities and leaders was and is intense and life-giving, providing continuing moments of formational clarity.

That continually deepening engagement with the world then took me from my doorstep to the literal other side of the world. Part of my MDiv studies was at the United Theological College in Bangalore, India. I fell in love with the interfaith pluralism, diverse Christianity, and bright cultures of the people of India. In continuing moments of formational clarity, I committed myself as a feminist ally in advocacy with Dalit and tribal peoples against exclusion. I identified my own social location as a North American amid economic systems that produce extremes of poverty and wealth. I worked with others in movements for equity. After receiving my PhD in mission theology and history, I returned to teach on the faculty of the United Theological College for three years, to cross boundaries and to share life.

I treasure these formational experiences and give thanks to God for the ways they have shaped my identity and meaning and purpose in life. In my previous position as executive for volunteer ministries for the national setting of the United Church of Christ, I inherited a program for young adult leadership development and its predecessor denominations that was in transition. I learned that through the years, leaders formed through these programs had been instrumental in shaping the identity of my denomination as ecumenical and committed to God's just world for all. I listened to the hopes and goals of young adults currently involved in experiential service and advocacy. And I reflected on my own formation as a young adult. The result was the creation of national networks of Young Adult Service Communities (YASC) and Summer Communities of Service (SCOS).

The YASC/SCOS model has multiple layers and intended outcomes. Hosted by a local congregation, a small group of young adults form intentional community with each other. An assigned role in the congregation's life and leadership connects each participant with the local church. Young adult participants are immersed in the work of community organizations engaged in justice advocacy or direct service in the wider community. Boundaries between congregations and community service and activism become more permeable. A spiritual sojourner (mentor) sparks deliberate reflection with the group on these experiences and their interdependence. The young adults explore the meaning of their experiences for their own vocations, much like I had done in my own young adult years in similar experiences. In many ways, my journey of discernment as a young adult prepared me to help prepare the journeying of other young adults.

While I no longer serve in that setting, my vocational calling continues in my current ministry setting with Eden Theological Seminary, where I interact with many younger (and older) adults along the path of discernment. The contextual education program of Eden that influenced my own MDiv vocational discernment as a young adult continues. That formational experience accelerates for me; I now am involved in supporting and shaping its influence for new generations and new settings. In my current and in other ministry settings, including my role in the YASC/SCOS networks, the post-resurrection story in John 20 continues to guide and frame my vocation. I continue to hear my name called as I am sent to accompany and engage with others in the world for the purpose of God's well-being for all.

QUESTIONS FOR REFLECTION

1. Where are places of discomfort in which you have placed yourself to experience God's presence in new ways?
2. What skills do you need to practice that will enable you to accompany others in the new work God is doing?
3. How have you experienced your vocation accelerated while forming opportunities for others to experience it for themselves?

So, You're the Bishop

James Hazelwood

Several years ago, following Sunday morning worship, I sat on the deck of one of our church's parsonages with the pastor and an intern seminarian. We enjoyed lunch and a conversation about the ministry of the congregation. At one point, the intern turned to me and said, "So, you're the bishop; I think that's something I'd like to do someday." I smiled and said, "Well, let's first get you through seminary." I wanted to share with him the realities of the work involved in serving as a bishop, but I refrained.

In the following week, I faced several difficult crucial conversations. One involved an investigation into a case of misconduct by a minister. Another task ahead of me included a meeting with a staff person whose performance was subpar. Then, the following weekend, I attended a church council meeting in a highly conflicted congregation over divisive political matters. It was not the kind of work I thought I would be doing when elected at a synod assembly in 2012.

In most mainline protestant traditions, bishops arrive in their leadership position through several pathways. The typical pattern includes an election or selection process by one's peers and lay leaders. In Lutheran, Episcopal, and Methodist traditions, we serve with the title of bishop. But in the United Church of Christ, one would be called a conference minister. Some denominations have a polity (church governance) that rejects the idea of a single leader and operates under an assembly of gathered elders, such as Presbyterian and Reformed traditions.

In recent years, I've observed many of my bishop colleagues to have demonstrated their leadership skills in congregational settings. This brought them recognition in their ecclesial bodies when it came time to elect a new bishop. Another common route to the episcopacy is through experience serving on a denominational staff as a specialist working for a regional judicatory.

When I was elected, a colleague who had recently become an Episcopal bishop of a diocese said to me, "I was told when I began in this office that I'd probably use about 30 percent of what I knew as a parish priest. That other 70 percent has been on-the-job learning." I think my new colleague was reasonably accurate in his estimates.

The work of a bishop is not what I thought it was while serving as a parish pastor. I had bold visions around expanding congregational vitality, stretching people's theological and spiritual capacity, and developing social justice initiatives. While some of that has been addressed, it reflects a small portion of the workload.

When asked "What does a bishop do?" I respond with three words: Thank, Truth, and Trouble. Yes, I've oversimplified the work, but this response either shuts down the conversation or, more likely, prompts the inquirer to ask a follow-up: "What do you mean?"

Max De Pree, author of *Leadership Is an Art*, once said that a leader has two jobs: saying thank you and telling the truth.[1] I've taken liberty with that statement and added "causes good trouble" with credit to the late Congressman John Lewis. I maintain that a bishop does three things: offers gratitude, defines reality, and causes trouble.

Offering gratitude is more than simply saying thank you. Increasingly, I find people in the pews and pastors in the pulpit beaten up, weary, and living with shame. Nearly two years of the COVID-19 pandemic has exacerbated tensions in many of our congregations. A common theme of my conversations with people in ministry, both lay and ordained, is exhaustion. In this context, it's not productive to offer false hope or challenges to embrace the latest innovation tools. Instead, I find my role is to be an agent of appreciation. My sermons, letters, and video communications need to embody gratitude for who they are and what they have done.

Ministers and congregants tend to be relatively poor at celebrating who they are and what they have done. Too often, the focus is on the shortcomings and who is not present. My view is one of abundance and celebrating the gathered. All too often, the church is filled with stories of decline and angst about the many challenges. I won't deny those, but there are still people feeding and clothing the dislocated in society. Yet, our congregations embody a Gospel-centered hope through word and deed. People are still going to ministers for guidance, support, and spiritual companionship. Thanks be to God. I believe a bishop is called to affirm and appreciate the engagement.

Defining reality or telling the truth might seem on the other end of the spectrum from my encouragement to offer thanksgiving. While needing words of appreciation, there is also a need to be realistic. Since many of our congregations believe their best days are behind them, they tend to compare that imaginary glorified past with what they think should be the current situation in their congregation. As bishop, I am called to remind them what year it is now. It's 2022, not 1972. In my interaction with church leaders who describe the good old days, I ask them to describe those days. They often begin with descriptions of a church with filled pews, the coffers overflowing, and the lawns nicely trimmed. I then remind them of some of the realities of that era. It was great if you were white, male, straight, abled, and Protestant. I continue to remind them that in a previous period of Christendom, the church had a home-field advantage since stores were not open and sports were not an option on Sunday morning.

The conversation can lead to inquiries of easy solutions. For example, on a Sunday morning during an adult forum with members of one congregation early in my tenure as bishop, a thirty-something mother of two asked me, "What's one easy thing we can do to attract new people to our church?" My instinct was to laugh but then realized she articulated the secret desire of everyone in the room. So, after offering thanks for what they are already doing, I shifted into defining reality. "I have to be honest with you. There is no one easy thing. That's like asking what's an easy way to raise a teenager." The room chuckled, and I then continued to describe our current societal context and offer a perspective of building a culture centered on collaboration and building relationships with people, organizations, and businesses.

A bishop or denominational leader needs to stand amid the people, define reality, tell the truth, and articulate with clarity and conviction. But here's the real challenge. You must do it in such a way that the people can hear it. One can't simply spout off, chastise, and denigrate. That produces nothing. Instead, you must find a way to speak so that others can hear what you are saying. I have often found the best approach to be responding with a series of questions rather than making a speech. This is something Jesus practiced in his ministry, and I aspire to ask questions with his poignancy.

The third aspect of my work as a bishop involves causing trouble by challenging people and structures. If bishops do not embrace the prophetic role, they can easily succumb to a church bureaucrat. I'm not suggesting that every bishop must go out and be a celebrity for a particular cause, whether for a culture war issue or social justice matter. Instead, I'm suggesting that part of a bishop or judicatory leader's role is a challenger. Stirring the pot, agitating, and provoking are all legitimate aspects of this role. That can include a challenge to the bureaucratic strictures within one's denomination or a challenge to inequities one observes within society.

These three roles shape my work as a bishop. Other regional judicatory leaders will define their guiding principles. Each bishop finds a compass that directs them in their ministry, and these are mine. There are many other practical matters to this office, such as dealing with conflict, attending to legal and church governance matters, and clergy discipline. One critical task involves the supervision of staff. I chose to hire people who possess two qualities: a desire to learn and eagerness to work hard.

My staff has more significant opportunities to work closely with congregations. I wonder if they have more impact than I do. If the bishop is responsible for the big picture, the associates are charged with the implementation. They are often tasked with working directly with congregational leaders and pastors or deacons in such matters as the call process for new clergy leadership, conflict resolution over disputed issues, and helping plan new initiatives in these challenging times of post-Christendom.

Sara, who serves on my staff as an associate with responsibilities for about sixty congregations, recently summarized her work well. "I think of our job as being coaches, ones who point others to (and work to create) possibility and opportunity for the gospel—in practical, spiritual, and intentional ways. A central aspect of our work is reminding people that we are resurrection people. That means death and resurrection, grief, and joy, and they dance together."

That's a helpful frame for the work of judicatory leaders.

QUESTIONS FOR REFLECTION

1. Do you know a judicatory leader or denominational staff person? Have you considered contacting them with your own questions about their values/principles for their work?
2. As you read the above chapter, what surprises you most about Bishop Hazelwood's description of the work of a denominational leader?

To Say Yes, Again and Again and Again

Karen Oliveto

"Have you ever thought about being a pastor?"
The question was posed in a church kitchen. I was eleven years old. The questioner was the music minister of my church. When he said those words, my heart burst open with a giant "yes!"

I did not come from a particularly religious household. My dad was an atheist. My mother, while raised in the United Church of Canada, was not a churchgoer. She did, however, take seriously the vows she took at my baptism and dutifully dropped me off at Sunday School at the Babylon (New York) United Methodist Church every Sunday.

I remember the first time I stepped down into the damp and musty church basement. It felt like a homecoming. Taking my seat on the floor each week, I eagerly listened to the new Bible lesson, sung with gusto each hymn, and dutifully dropped my coin in the collection basket. That church wrapped me not only in the lessons of faith, but also—through the pastors, teachers, and friends' parents—helped me experience God's unconditional love and acceptance of me. I thrived there.

Even at that early age, I became more and more involved in the church, singing in one of the children's choirs. Rev. Ken White, the music minister, had a joy that was infectious. If this was what a life of faith looked like, I wanted to know more!

So, when Ken asked me the question, it was as if all that I loved the most had found expression. Even though I had never seen a woman pastor, I suddenly realized that, of course, where else would I want to serve? How great would it be to spend my life sharing this love of God that I had experienced?

From that point on, I prepared for a vocation in ordained ministry. My call was affirmed by my local church and my seminary professors. I breezed through the many years of ordination interviews. I gladly went where the bishop appointed me and loved the unique settings I was blessed to serve.

Yet over the years, a pall began to fall upon me. In 1984, the General Conference of the United Methodist Church (UMC) approved language that restricted LGBTQ people from serving in ordained ministry. I had already been ordained a deacon in 1982 and was looking forward to elder's orders in 1985. Even though it was clear to myself and others that I was called to ordained ministry in the UMC, could I continue to fulfill my call here?

Still, God kept calling and I kept saying "yes." Saying "yes" was costly. But isn't following Jesus always costly? For me, it meant willingly entering into a closet where my love would be hidden from view. In the 1980s, this was what most LGBTQ people expected, whether in ministry or not. But as AIDS pushed more and more gay men out of the closet, LGBTQ people began to live more openly. In spite of greater visibility, I knew that I was choosing to remain in the closet in order to fulfill my call. I never denied who I was, but there was a huge part of my life that I never discussed.

There were times when the call became too costly, and I tried to leave it. I went to school for a PhD in religion and society, hoping to serve the church in a less public way. But even from the safety of the academy, the bishop kept calling me: "Would you be a consultant for a local church?" "Would you step in and be the director of one of our church camps for the summer?" I kept saying "yes."

Saying "yes" meant going to places I never dreamed of going. From rural ministry, I entered campus ministry, serving first in New York and then in San Francisco. I was three thousand miles away from my home conference, serving as campus minister in a self-proclaimed gay capital. I stepped out of the closet and felt a deeper sense of power and agency than I had ever felt before.

But then, the bishop of the Cal-Nevada Conference asked me to serve a local church. This was unexpected! I was a guest in the conference serving in campus ministry. Did I feel called to return to the local church? Did I want to do this, since what I knew most intimately of local church ministry was that it meant being closeted?

I literally ran into the wilderness to discern my response to this request. I camped for a week at Lassen National Park in northern California, taking one day to do a solo hike to the top of Mt. Lassen. It was a slow and laborious climb. The atmosphere grew thin and the air chilly as I made my way to the peak. Standing at the top, looking out at God's vast creation, a "yes" leaped from my lips and I came down the mountain ready to accept the call.

I quickly learned that there would be no closet to return to. The congregation already knew I was a lesbian. In fact, they had given my name to the bishop as someone they would like as pastor. When I arrived there and began to reenter the closet, the leadership of the church sat me down and said, "We want you to be your full authentic self. We know that entails a risk, but we have your back."

We shared a powerful ministry for twelve years. Together, pastor and parishioners, we challenged each other to greater discipleship. This meant being a visible witness to the denomination of the richness found in a church where everyone was welcomed fully into the family of faith, challenging injustice through civil disobedience, and being a resource for other churches on ministry with LGBTQ persons.

Then, in 2004, we were called to a very public stage as Mayor Gavin Newsom opened up marriage for same-sex couples. I officiated at nine weddings for church members. This resulted in a complaint against my ministry. Instead of being charged for being a lesbian (a fear that I had woken up with every morning), I was charged for performing a pastoral act. I had no idea if this would result in the loss of my credentials, which meant the loss of income, housing, and even identity. Once the initial fear and shock wore off, a peace descended upon me. I had exercised my pastoral leadership in a way that was pleasing to God. This peace helped me hear God's affirming "yes!"

The complaint was later dropped, but not before it led to Pacific School of Religion inviting me to the position of associate dean of academic affairs and adjunct professor of United Methodist Studies. Four years later, this led to an invitation to be the first lead pastor of one of the largest United Methodist Churches, Glide Memorial. Did I ever dream these doors would open for me? No. It took a heart willing to say "yes."

In 2016, I began to sense that the work I was called to do at Glide was being completed, and I began to wonder what God had in mind for me next. I prayed fiercely for clarity, but none came. What did this mean? Was my professional life coming to a close?

At this same time, the United Methodist Church came close to imploding at its quadrennial meeting. Tensions around homosexuality had reached a tipping point. In a last-ditch effort to preserve the unity of the church, a commission was created to bring a proposal to the body at a special called session in 2019. I wondered if *this* was what God wanted of me. Perhaps my voice, as an open lesbian serving one of our denomination's largest churches, would be a place I could serve well.

But I wasn't asked to serve on the commission.

Colleagues began to ask me if I would consider allowing my name to be brought forward for the episcopacy. Throughout my ministry, people would comment that I would make a good bishop, but I never gave it much thought. Now, however, it was time to take the comments seriously. Call is given by God and confirmed by community. While my community was affirming the gifts I had for this role, what did God want?

My spouse and I talked and prayed long and hard about this. I knew I loved her, and I loved the church. I worried what impact being a lesbian bishop in a denomination that disallowed LGBTQ persons from serving openly and considered homosexuality as "incompatible with Christ's teaching" would have on my relationship and on the church. I was afraid and didn't want to harm either one. One night, as we were discussing it, I named the fear I was carrying. Robin looked me in the eye and said, "Perfect love casts out fear." That Bible verse removed the fear and allowed a "yes" to emerge. And with that "yes," the Holy Spirit took over. One month after saying "yes" yet again to God, I was elected to the episcopacy unanimously on the seventeenth ballot of the Western Jurisdiction of the United Methodist Church.

QUESTIONS FOR REFLECTION

1. How has God worked through those around you to help you identify your call?
2. What is the cost of this call for you?
3. What role does fear play in how you respond (or not) to God's call?

Ministry in the Public Square

Traci Blackmon

I've answered the call to ministry many times. I worked as a registered nurse for fifteen years, work I call healing ministry, before answering God's call to authorized ministry and serving bivocationally as both pastor and nurse for eighteen years. Currently, I am the Associate General Minister of Justice & Local Church Ministries for the United Church of Christ. I am also what many would call a public theologian, meaning that I am one who also theologizes social matters for the public's consideration.

Neither of these callings was my idea. I was not raised in an environment with a theological framing that was affirming of women in authorized ministry, yet they were very affirming of my personhood and my place in the community of faith. This is why our public exegetical work is so critical to the health of the church. The church of my youth loved God and God's people, and the limitations of their welcome were framed by their limited understanding of scripture. Expanding that understanding is a huge part of what we are called to shepherd.

During my final year of seminary, I registered for a cultural immersion trip to Ghana, West Africa. I use the phrase *cultural immersion*, as opposed to *mission trip*, because the latter is widely understood in religious circles as trips to other cities, states, or countries for the purpose of providing humanitarian aid and/or religious exposure to the God of our colonized understanding. However, I attended a United Church of Christ seminary, and our denominational understanding of missions is not one that presumes the need to take God anywhere. We serve with others in diverse places, paying attention to what God is already up to and how God is understood by the people there. I learned from this experience to always enter space and place with the wonderment of asking: *What is God up to in this place?*

In the book of 1 Kings, the prophet Elijah finds himself in a harrowing situation after answering his call to serve God. His "yes" to God meant confronting the idolatrous worship of the prophets of Baal at Mount Carmel.

Elijah answered the call and defeated the prophets of Baal by God's might, but the consequences were severe. Elijah ran to Mount Horeb to hide himself in a cave, hoping to escape what he imagined as imminent death. The situation was dire, and Elijah felt all alone. Yet the same God who was with Elijah when he faced the false prophets was with him in the cave. He was not alone, and there in the cave God asked Elijah a question (1 Kings 19:9): *What are you doing here?*

These are the anchoring questions of my ministry: *What is God up to in this place, and what am I doing here?*

Every ministry path I've taken has been illuminated by these two questions. Sometimes our ministry paths are clear, and we are filled with confidence; sometimes we are not as clear where this "yes" is leading, but we are trusting the process in uncertain waters. At other times, we may find ourselves hiding in caves. What I know for sure at this stage of my ministry journey is that God is always with us, in both the "yes" and the questions, and while at times the call to ministry can be lonely, we are never alone.

My current journey only became clear to me in hindsight. I now know every experience of my life prepared me for the next. Prior to my election to this position, I served as pastor of a small local congregation. It was not the position, location, or even denomination I imagined; but I remember asking myself the question: *Where is God in this, and what am I doing here?*

I knew that God was in the mix, so much so that the church reopened a closed process to interview me; but I didn't know why I was there. The church had twenty-five remaining members, of which only twelve were completely engaged, in a sanctuary built for five hundred.

Prior to seminary, I'd also served as pastor to a small rural congregation with similar membership numbers in a different denomination. I knew well what it meant to serve a congregation that was not prepared to financially sustain a pastorate, and I wanted to end my bivocational path and focus solely on the church. Accepting this assignment would not allow me to do that, and yet I was clear that this is where God wanted me to be.

Faith is much easier to preach about than it is to live. I was clear that my dreams and God's direction were not fully aligned, but I understand ministry in any capacity as an unqualified "yes" to the urging of the Holy Spirit. So, I said "yes" in spite of my fears. For me, faith has come to be defined as the confident expectation that all God intends for my life is possible, and I believe God intends well so I trusted the path set before me.

It is because of that "yes" that I was able to serve with a small group of lavishly loving people who believed God as well. The ministry we began to shape there did not expand our membership exponentially, but it did expand our ministries significantly. And I am certain that if I had not said "yes" to God there, I would not have been in place to eulogize a young woman killed by gun violence in August of 2013. And if I had not been in place to eulogize that young woman, her best friend—who had rejected church because of being hurt in a faith community—would not have heard me preach the eulogy of her best friend. And had she not heard that sermon, she would not have been compelled to ask the usher for my contact information. And although she never returned to the church that year or contacted me, because she kept the information she was able to call me on August 9, 2014, when Michael Brown Jr. was killed in her community.

And had she not called and asked me to come as her pastor, I may not have been present in Ferguson in all the ways the Holy Spirit led. And had I not been present, the word of my public witness might not have ever been known outside of my community, my denomination may have never called me to serve the wider church, and I most likely would not be included in this book or living out a ministry I now know I am called to live.

God really does move in mysterious ways and the question will always be: *Are we willing to go where God leads?*

The older I get, the less confined my understanding of the Call to ministry becomes. I now understand my "call" as descriptive of the principles and teachings of faith that compel my journey, wherever it takes me, as opposed to the particular function I hold at any given time. Such reorientation does not excuse me from the responsibilities of my office, yet it does anchor my ministry in something greater than current or even past functions, and this matters to me. Ministry means a "yes" to God, wherever that may lead.

There have been many challenges along the way, and those will always be a part of the journey. I served bivocationally throughout my entire pastorate. My nursing career informed my pastorate, and my pastorate changed my approach to nursing. It wasn't until I settled into my call as associate general minister that I resigned from congregational ministry to focus solely on where God has placed me in this season. I miss being the pastor of people. My heart is still with the local church. But I also love the ministry to which God has called me in this time and place.

A challenge of my current role is to offer a pastoral presence to people I do not serve personally, to apply the principles of discernment and discipleship at the intersection of personal piety and public praxis, and to never lose the hope of the faith. I don't know what God has in store next, and it really doesn't matter to me. The answer, for me, remains an unqualified "yes," and the questions will always be: *What is God up to in this place, and what am I doing here?*

QUESTIONS FOR REFLECTION

1. What practices of spiritual discernment have you cultivated to guide your ministry path?
2. How do your past experiences inform your current ministry practices?
3. What shifts, if any, in ministry might you make if you were not afraid to go wherever God leads?

The Inward and Outward Journey of Ministry

Wesley Granberg-Michaelson

H. LeRoy "Pat" Patterson, a star football player at Wheaton College, served as pastor of South Park Church in Park Ridge, Illinois, the independent, evangelical congregation faithfully attended by my family. Early in high school, I went to a Youth for Christ rally in Washington, DC. Upon my return, I shared about my experience at the Sunday evening service. A few days later Pastor Patterson wanted to talk to me. "I rarely suggest this to any young person, because it's serious," he began. "But I hope you will consider going into the ministry." It's a conversation I didn't forget.

But I wasn't so sure. My abiding interest was politics. At that time, I was a conservative Goldwater Republican, like my parents and most others I knew, including Hillary Rodham, who attended the same high school. At fifteen, I attended the Republican National Convention in Chicago, part of a group of young Republicans carrying American flags down the aisle. I was the "good kid" who got elected president of the church youth group, president of the Young Life club, and to the student council. I always seemed comfortable speaking and leading groups.

That pathway continued at Hope College, affiliated with the Reformed Church in America, where I became student body president and a leader in the newly emerging Student Church. My preoccupation to integrate my faith with politics persisted and was deepened by reading books like Reinhold Niebuhr's *Moral Man and Immoral Society*.[1] I was uncertain about my future after graduating college with a philosophy degree. A Rockefeller Fellowship for a "trial year" in a seminary of my choosing suited my indecision perfectly, and I selected Princeton Seminary.

By then the civil rights movement was emerging, the Vietnam War was raging, and my previous political worldview was completely upended. I knew of only one prominent political figure who described himself as an evangelical Christian and who was courageously opposed to the Vietnam War—Senator

Mark O. Hatfield. I met him at a conference and became an intern in his office after my year at Princeton. As things happen in Washington, before long I was his legislative assistant, responsible for his anti-war efforts, writing his speeches, and acting as his liaison to a variety of Christian groups and institutions. Now I was living faith and politics.

But my soul was still restless. Church of the Saviour, an ecumenical, innovative congregation begun by Gordon Cosby, became my spiritual home. Gordon became my mentor and spiritual director. Elizabeth O'Conner, whose books shared the stories and dynamics of the church's "inward and outward journey," became a good friend. And I embarked on my own inward spiritual and psychological journey.

As a high-commitment congregation structured around "mission groups," Church of the Saviour believed that every member needed to discover and follow their calling. This was a particular calling to the outward journey of mission and service in the world that God was beckoning them to follow. However, hearing that call was only possible through an inward journey to clear out the clutter of one's soul, becoming more deeply attentive to God's presence. Prayer, journaling, silence, and retreat were the tools.

I left my desk in Senator Hatfield's office one rainy December day for a retreat at a Trappist monastery in Berryville, Virginia. It changed the trajectory of my life. Father Stephen, the guest master, helped guide me then and in visits that followed, including a month-long stay, as I tried to open myself to the presence of God's love, and to hear God's deeper calling. It led me to my marriage with Kaarin, and later to step away from nearly a decade of intense political service with Mark Hatfield.

We joined Sojourners, which was establishing itself as an alternative Christian community (sometimes we'd attach the adjective "radical") in a neighborhood just off the Fourteenth Street corridor in inner city DC. I assisted Jim Wallis in starting and growing the new *Sojourners* magazine. But eventually my inward journey, and Kaarin's, beckoned us away from the frantic activism and frequent superficiality of political life in the nation's capital. By then I had been reading Stringfellow, Yoder, Ellul, Bonhoeffer, and similar voices.

Community Covenant Church in Missoula, Montana, a congregation on an engaging journey to become a deeper community, attracted us with their hospitality. We left DC behind, but more crucially, I was trying to leave behind a life where my identity was rooted in all the external impressive things I was doing as that "good kid," and instead find my deepest worth and identity in "being," rooted hopefully in Christ's love. Only then did the question of my call to ordained ministry re-emerge.

Life was good and felt full of grace in Missoula. I wondered whether I should go into local politics. My persistent desire was to participate in God's ongoing redemptive and transformative mission in the world. But how? On retreat the direction became clear. I was called to do so through the life and ministry of the church. And I recalled that conversation with my pastor twenty years earlier.

Completing my MDiv was the next step, and I did so at Western Theological Seminary in Holland, Michigan. The Reformed tradition claimed me. I felt it understood grace more deeply than my evangelical heritage, and it reinforced my desire to forge an integrated worldview of faith and politics, as well as culture and creation. My ordination, however, was lived out in "specialized ministry," not as a pastor of a local congregation. I was drawn to institutional expressions of Christianity, and to ecumenical work.

I had no preplanned pathway. Once my inner calling was clear and rooted deep within, outward opportunities were discovered. Most remarkable and unexpected was the invitation to join the staff of the World Council of Churches (WCC) in Geneva, initially as Director of Church and Society. My first responsibility was leading the WCC's work on "integrity of creation," beginning its efforts to address climate change in 1989. Ecumenical politics intrigued me, and I worked with staff colleagues on organizational restructuring, on a long-term effort to clarify the WCC's "common understanding and vision," on building more reciprocal relationships with the council's Orthodox churches, and similar initiatives. Being part of a large organization that assisted churches from differing traditions to seek unity and join in common witness became central to my ministerial calling.

Then one day I had lunch with the general secretary of the Reformed Church in America, Ed Mulder. He startled me with an unexpected question. Had I thought of applying for his position, since he planned to conclude his work? Not at all, came my quick response. And I listed the reasons. I'm not Dutch, I wasn't raised in the RCA, my formative congregational experiences have been with faith communities like Church of the Saviour, and I've been out of the loop, working with the World Council of Churches. Ed smiled thoughtfully and then said, "Well, those are all the reasons why you should apply."

A whirlwind journey ensued, ending when the search committee flew Kaarin and me to Chicago for a long interview, and then came to our hotel room announcing that I had been selected. For the next seventeen years that's how I lived out my ministerial calling. My time with the WCC was providential preparation. I led a process to clarify the RCA's central mission and vision, tried to focus on tools to nurture congregational revitalization, and facilitated a process leading to our adoption of the first new confession since the seventeenth century, the Belhar Confession.

Denominational politics intrigued me. My colleagues and I kept experimenting with innovative ways to build trust between the wide diversity and divisions within the denomination. Unity within the denomination seemed just as challenging as ecumenical work in the WCC. Always, we kept asking how belonging to the RCA could help empower congregations to place their focus outward, on participating in God's ongoing mission in the world, beginning in their local context.

Mistakes and failures punctuated those years, frequently. But I became convinced that the biggest challenge of such a ministry is trying to transform organizational culture. That requires careful discernment, theological reflection, and the meaningful integration of spiritual resources within the fabric of institutional life.

In the present, my journey with institutional ministry continues. Serving on the boards of Sojourners and Church Innovations is a spiritual calling requiring ministerial gifts to facilitate their vital work. Navigating the politics of these and any religious organization is a continual part of that service. Ecumenical ministry, needed more than ever today, continues through service on the governing board of the Global Christian Forum.

Finally, ordained ministry includes what we say or preach, and for some, what we write. I've come to regard my writing, during this chapter of life, as a highly significant way to fulfill the ordination vows I made in 1984.

My advice? Do the inner work so vitally necessary to clearly hear God's calling on your life. Root your identity there, and then expect the unexpected.

QUESTIONS FOR REFLECTION

1. At what points in your life have you sensed that you heard God's call? How did this happen?
2. How would you describe the roots of your identity? Does it mainly come externally or internally? Have you ever explored this, and if so, how?
3. Who have served as mentors and guides for you up to this point in your journey? How have they done so? Do you expect or hope to have persons in that role in the future?

The Communion Table as Vocational Pathway in Nonprofit Leadership

David Harrison and John Senior

REFLECTIONS FROM DAVID HARRISON

I am currently the Executive Director of New Communion of the Triad and pastor of First Christian Church in Winston-Salem, North Carolina. New Communion is a faith-based nonprofit organization. Its goal is twofold: to enhance community relationships while also diminishing the impacts of hunger and food insecurity, a primary marker of poverty in our region. New Communion provides nourishing food via our mobile food pantry, which serves Winston-Salem, North Carolina, in neighborhoods that are at high risk of poverty. The work of distributing food to hungry people is necessary, but we aspire to much more. New Communion is fundamentally about creating and strengthening relationships with persons and communities who experience food insecurity.

New Communion began as a seminary course assignment. In a course on public health and food security, a seminary colleague, Rev. Monica Banks, wrote a proposal for a United Way grant as a final course project. This particular grant program funded projects that sought to address pressing needs in several census tracts in our city. The grant proposal was submitted, and incredibly, it was accepted!

We saw an opportunity to create a mobile food pantry to address hunger in our community. Our commitment to the Communion Table helped us to see that the way that we would go about this work mattered as much to us as the work itself. Drawing on an asset-based community development framework, we wanted New Communion to ground the cultivation of relationships in the neighborhoods we serve. Our work begins when our neighbors and community partners invite us to distribute food in their neighborhoods. Neighborhood partners serve in leadership positions and on the board of New Communion. All are welcome to the resources of the food pantry; we do not check our guests' poverty status, and we do not limit access to the pantry. In these ways, we hope that New Communion convenes the Beloved Community even as it provides food to hungry neighbors.

The metaphor of the Communion Table has come to occupy a central place in my theology and has profoundly shaped my journey in ministry. Many of the iconic moments in the Christian tradition center on meals and table fellowship. The table signifies the human need to build and enjoy community through engaging a wide variety of identities and experiences. Table experiences of laughter, fellowship, and tough conversations, among others, are universal; everyone can relate to them. In the face of food insecurity, the metaphor of the Communion Table raises a number of challenging questions: How can we deny a seat at the table to anyone? Why have we denied access to food to those who are marginalized? And why have we weaponized food in our society? These burning questions began to change my views of life and frankly the views that were within me from my embedded theology.

Through my work with New Communion, I have come to understand Holy Communion as more than just a Sunday morning practice. Communion *is* and *should be* more than a Sunday morning practice. Christ's work was always done in communion with people whom he often gathered around meals. Indeed, the work of Christ is the work of communion. With this realization, I was convicted that my ministry and my vocational desires to fight food insecurity did not have to be two separate pathways. In fact, they could be one. For me, Communion is at the heart of the Gospel and the very definition of the Great Commission that Jesus gave in Matthew 25 to *"Therefore go."* My commitment to the Gospels and the work of Christ began to fuel my desire to respond to the very tangible need for food security in our regions. And my work with New Communion meets my spiritual need to live into ministry "outside the walls" of the church.

At New Communion, the Communion Table welcomes holy chaos. Just as the story of the Last Supper is a beautiful moment amid a chaotic time, and the feeding of the five thousand takes place in the face of overwhelming need in a community, this work is at times chaotic. The need for food is overwhelming. However, in the midst of the messiness and complexity of community work, the miracle of shared abundance is revealed. The table principle of shared abundance that fed the five thousand—the gathering of shared resources for the betterment of all—gives shape to each food distribution. The shared resources of many come together in this symbiotic dance, moving to the rhythm of life. Each life, though not the same, is united through the open table. The praxis of Holy Communion is on full display; all are truly welcome at this table. In welcoming each person, each story, the mobile Communion Table honors the image of God in each person, bearing witness to the Gospel in action.

The spirit of Christ that guides me to the Communion Table each Sunday is the same spirit that guides me into the community every week. We break bread and drink from the cup at the Table every Sunday in church as a community of faith. Through my work with the mobile food pantry, we partake in the holy moment of Communion with each passing of peanut butter and jelly jars in the community. In community spaces, the blessed Table is not in fact a table; it is a sliding pantry shelf in the back of a mobile van. The sacred appears not in the form of liturgy or the words of institution, but in simple fist bumps, hugs, and laughter, and in each of the wide-ranging conversations we enjoy with our neighbors. The sacred emerges in experiences around the intersections of life, community, and food. I have found my vocation in these very intersections.

REFLECTIONS FROM JOHN SENIOR

New Communion provides a creative answer to a challenging question for religious leaders: what difference, if any, does it make for nonprofit leaders to be theologically trained? What do the resources of religious traditions—in this case, the Christian tradition—provide to support the work of nonprofit leadership in ways that may not be found in other forms of professional education, or at least not in the same way? Shouldn't nonprofit leaders be trained in schools of business, social work, or elsewhere? On some levels, the particular skills and practices of nonprofit leadership are what they are and can be learned in many different contexts. That is, there is wisdom about organizational management, budgeting, finance, fundraising, program development and assessment, grant writing, leadership development, etc., that, in the day-to-day, may not shift much in a theological frame.

But framing matters a lot in nonprofit leadership. Framing is articulated in an organization's vision and mission statements—its sense of what the world ought to look like and how the organization is going to work to bring that world about. Mission and vision in turn give shape not only to *what* an organization does but also *how* and *why* it does it. The theological frame of Communion, for example, challenges the logic of transactional provision that so often mires nonprofit work in "toxic charity"—forms of provision that reinforce rather than challenge the very conditions that make provision necessary in the first place. In the theological frame of Communion, leaders must not only ask questions about effective provision. More fundamentally, the frame of Communion invites the question: what kind of community are we building through the work of food provision?

Another way of saying this is that the theological frame of Communion raises important questions about equity, understood as the provision of what is necessary to each to enhance the flourishing of all. Neighbors who are minoritized and marginalized may need food to address hunger. They also need to be included as full participants in their own flourishing. The theological metaphor of the Communion Table occasions the sharing of food, but it does so in the context of community building that invites the participation of all stakeholders.

It's easy to miss the power of a mobile food pantry in a city like Winston-Salem, North Carolina. Winston-Salem, like many cities in the American South, is deeply divided by the legacies of racism, racial violence, and the intersecting forms of structural injustice that come with them. Highway 52 is a physical marker in the built environment of the city that represents the partial destruction of predominantly African American neighborhoods on the east side of town, and their physical division from predominantly white neighborhoods on the west side of town, all in the name of "progress." New Deal–era maps of redlined neighborhoods correspond neatly with contemporary maps of the city that show disparities in household income and employment, food and health-care deserts, access to public transportation, and the like.[1] In short, there is a lot about Winston-Salem that has not changed. A mobile food pantry that moves from the west side of the city to the east to do its work is therefore a transgressive project. But that's true only if the work of food provision is done in ways that promote equity and challenge, rather than reinforce, the structural conditions that make the experience of poverty in the city what it is.

QUESTIONS FOR REFLECTION

1. How would you identify your deepest sense of value? Where does that come from in your experience? And how do your values and commitments orient your leadership in nonprofit spaces?
2. What difference does it make to be a religious leader in your area of nonprofit work? How might theological resources give shape to the work of justice and equity in that area?

Discovering God's Call in Prayer and Community

greg little

It's 7:13 a.m. on a chilly morning in November as a few neighbors meander into our home through the living room into our little chapel in the back corner of the house. I light the candle on the altar and lay out some prayer books. A moment of quiet unites the dozen of us who showed up, intersected by the rustling of the couple of children who settle in with their berries and coloring pages to participate in the morning's worship. We gather like this, morning and evening, every weekday, to open ourselves to the reality of God's love giving shape to the rest of our daily lives. In preparation for reading the gospel passage of the day, we commonly recite Psalm 95 in unison: "Come, let us sing to the Lord. . . . Today, listen to the voice of the Lord." This is a daily prayer of vocational yearning.

All vocation rests on the voice of God, and my vocational journey is one of learning how to listen. In my thirty-five years of life, the two primary schools for this sort of receptive listening have been prayer and community. At the heart of both is encounter. Indeed, my vocation is oriented around this realization that God is unceasingly and lovingly encountering me. I am called to cultivate this awareness and to grow in my readiness to say "yes" to the transformation that follows. I am committed to living my vocation as a way of life proclaiming Jesus as Lord in all the small, mundane dailiness. I am discovering that it is precisely in those little, ordinary gestures and rhythms—like gathering to pray each morning and evening with a few neighbors—that I encounter a God who is already encountering me.

I am thankful that my daily life positions me right at the intersection of these two schools: prayer and community life. The current concrete expression of God's call on my life has led me to creative, shared homemaking at the Corner House here in Durham, North Carolina. Six years ago, several of us opened ourselves to the possibility of creating a home of care, hospitality, and prayer. It began with a simple desire to deepen some of the relationships that were forming at Reality Ministries, a place that proclaims that the deepest reality of all of our lives is the loving-kindness of the God we find in Jesus by making space for friendships to grow among people with and without developmental disabilities.

Over time, we were tasting and seeing the beauty of the gospel in these friendships, and a few of us began to ask some questions: *What if we lived together? What if we created a home—some of us who are very different in age, gifting, race, challenge, ability, etc.? What if this was a home of gentleness and peace amid a world so saturated with efficiency, competition, fear, and violence?* All of us crave home—a place to belong—to know and to forgive, to be known and to be forgiven. So, seven of us moved in together five years ago and are giving it a shot, inside the grace of Jesus.

With the addition of two young children, we are now a peculiar sort of family of nine. We've got a little chapel for prayer, a Christ room for hospitality, and a big table for all the eating we do together. Our ages range from two to seventy. Some of us live with developmental disabilities, and some of us do not. Some of us are Black and some are white. All of us are bearers of Jesus to one another and gift-givers in our little shared life, which is centered on people often pressed to the periphery of society. And yet we seek to be a home of mutual tenderness and belonging for all. We want to help one another discover our free, full selves in Jesus through the little things, like cooking and eating and cleaning and praying together.

I have volunteered and worked at Reality Ministries for ten years now. Over the years, Reality has come to own and support three homes, one of which is the Corner House. My work as the director of residential life involves nurturing the shared life within these homes, which are filled with people of all abilities yearning to grow in friendship in an atmosphere of mutuality and welcome. My daily work involves paying attention and offering accompaniment to residents who have chosen the dynamic littleness of living a creative shared life amid difference. Learning to live peaceably for one another is a daily way of confrontation (with oneself and others) and beauty, and I receive joy in this work of care.

What has led me to this way of life? Perhaps changing the "what" in that question to a "who" is a good start. I've been changed and shaped by encounters with living, breathing signposts of God's kingdom here and now. The thread of encounter has been woven through my journey of vocational discovery and remains central even now. *How can I engage with the world around me with a sort of hesitation, pausing in reverent awe at the reality of God's presence always here, always now? How can I slow down to listen and see the heart of the matter in a world intent on convincing me that I need to move faster? How can I posture myself to notice and participate in the stirring vitality of holiness residing in the depths of small, ordinary existence?* I have received vocational direction in exploring these questions through attention to my own encounters in creative communal life and in prayer.

I grew up in a family committed to hospitality, with compassionate parents relentlessly offering themselves to the wider community. My three siblings and I were established in a vision of life open to the wondrous reality that we could discover Christ's presence everywhere. In the first five years of my twenties, God met me in a handful of schools of justice and peace, including two years as a Methodist missionary in Baltimore and a few months each in four international communities: teaching in a Muslim village in northern Ghana, joining a home of care for people with disabilities in Haiti, apprenticing with a pastor's family and their orphanage in a Ugandan village, and working at a farm, home, and school to more than sixty children in northwest Kenya. I learned to meet God. More truthfully, perhaps, I learned to notice God's persistent encounters with me and received the grace to begin cultivating a daily way of being in the world that attempted to proclaim Jesus as loving Lord in all the little patterns and gestures of my life.

During this time, I was introduced to companions in the faith who kindled in me a sense of adventurous hope for a life radiant with the beauty of the gospel. Saints like Francis, Therese of Lisieux, John of the Cross, and Basil spurred me on in love of God. Howard Thurman, Dorothy Day, and Mother Teresa offered me an alternative vision for how to live justly with creativity and passion. I read, I talked about what I read, and I lived some aspect of what I had read. My encounter with these (and so many other) friends in the faith were alive in the Spirit and activated my imagination for how to enflesh God's life in my own particular way.

I entered Duke Divinity School with all of these shaping encounters, which helped me to see the season of study not as an end or achievement in itself, but rather a contributor to a full-orbed way of life sourced and aimed in God's love. My home life anchored me during this time, including a Catholic Worker hospitality house committed to the works of mercy, and an intentional community of divinity students living with young adults with disabilities. These homes illuminated the insights of the classroom and cultivated a lived wisdom that hit the ground every day.

"You think about God a lot. But God is not primarily an object of your thoughts. God is a 'Who' lovingly present to you, inviting you to simply be." This was the wisdom of Father Guerric, a friend and monk at Mepkin Abbey, a Trappist monastery in South Carolina. Seven years ago, I went in to share with Father Guerric my struggle with silence. I could sit still for hours with a book or in conversation, but to sit still for more than nine minutes in silence, that was just too hard. He challenged me to engage with God as a Being and not an object, opening for me a way of understanding prayer in terms of presence and loving encounter. Mepkin has become a place of regular refreshment for me over the years, even hosting our community for annual retreat over New Year's. I have been discovering the integration of prayer and community life through encouragement to show up every day to silence. In silent practice I am learning to listen, discovering God's presence in my own depths. I am learning to remain watchful and alert, open to the next step in the little way of love in which Jesus is calling me.

It's 8:27 p.m. at the conclusion of another brisk day in November as a few neighbors take that same pathway through the living room into our little chapel. I light some candles and lay out prayer books. The dim, flickering light cuts through a quiet darkness, and the seven of us present this evening welcome the restful stillness after days of varied activity. "We belong to You, O Lord. You are always with us." This call-and-response echoes in our morning and evening prayer liturgy as a community and proclaims simply the heart of my calling. May I always remain receptive to the transformation of your faithful presence, Lord, and in my daily life of discipleship may I be a herald that all creation belongs to you.

QUESTIONS FOR REFLECTION

1. What are a few vocationally illuminative encounters in your own story? Receive some time to sit with the encounter(s) in your memory, perhaps write it down, and ask God how that encounter is impacting the way you live out your call today.
2. In your own vocational discovery, how connected is your calling for ministerial work and the dailiness of your way of life in discipleship? If you haven't considered this, receive some time exploring that connection and forms of integration going forward.
3. How can you posture yourself to be receptive to God's self-communication in your big and small encounters with other people, with the world around you, and in the solitude of prayer?

Ministry Connecting Faith and Health

Kathie Bender Schwich

I serve as chief spiritual officer of Advocate Aurora Health, one of the ten largest health systems in the United States, covering parts of Wisconsin and Illinois. The Advocate (Illinois) part of the organization is faith based and affiliated with the Evangelical Lutheran Church in America (ELCA) and the United Church of Christ. The health system values its relationship with our faith communities; my executive leadership role is evidence of that commitment. How I got here is an interesting story.

I came to this call having served calls in all three expressions (congregation, synod, and churchwide organization) of the ELCA and an affiliated organization. In looking back over my ministry experiences, I realize that each of these calls, though varied in scope, focused on what gives me meaning and purpose: connecting faith to health and well-being.

I entered seminary as a second career student, having spent my undergrad years discerning a vocation in medicine or dentistry, and graduating with a degree in dental hygiene. I first experienced the inner call to ministry as a confirmation student several years prior, but my denomination wasn't yet ordaining women. So, I pushed the call aside and explored other vocations through which I could find meaning and purpose through serving others. I worked as a dental hygienist for a dentist with whom I frequently talked about the faith and well-being connection. Years later, and still feeling the call to ministry, I enrolled in seminary.

There I was inspired and energized by the variety of pastoral care course offerings and did all I could to learn as much as possible about pastoral care ministry. I was eager to know more about how pastors can nurture in others the connections between faith and emotional and physical well-being. The three months I spent in an acute care hospital setting fulfilling my denomination's requirement for clinical pastoral education really shed light on those connections for me as I walked alongside people during times of illness, tragedy, and grief. I also was intrigued by the sense of purpose and meaning that colleagues found in their work in health care and had conversations with everyone from neurosurgeons to environmental service and cafeteria workers about their sense of calling in doing what they did to serve others.

Upon graduation, I was ordained to serve a large congregation as assistant pastor with a focus on pastoral care and family ministry. The congregation was a member of Stephen Ministries, an organization whose mission is to equip lay members of congregations in providing care and support to others during challenging times in their lives. I led the Stephen Ministry program there and was inspired by the stories of those who received Stephen Ministers' care. I also had the opportunity to write some training materials for Stephen Ministries. A few years later I was offered, and accepted, the call to be on the executive staff of the organization and to serve on the teaching faculty. While in that role, I found great meaning in equipping and empowering others to make the connection between faith and well-being that I valued so highly.

My growth as a leader there helped equip me for my next call as an assistant to a synodical bishop in the ELCA. I loved the work I was doing and the title I was given of Bishop's Associate for Developing a Healthy Ministerium. The bishop with whom I served encouraged me to view myself as a guide for candidates pursuing rostered ministry in the church, and as a pastor to the pastors of the synod. As part of the bishop's staff, I had the sacred privilege of journeying with servants of the Gospel during the highs and lows of their lives and ministries. I helped them find new ways to connect their faith to their own sense of health and well-being, working with them to ensure they were taking care of themselves so that they could effectively minister to others. My "flock" went from being the members of one congregation to the rostered leaders of many congregations.

Not long after my term on the synod staff concluded, I answered the call to serve as an assistant to the presiding bishop of the national church with a focus on serving the denomination's Conference of Bishops. In addition to other duties of this call, I was honored to be in a sense a pastor to our denomination's sixty-five synod bishops. My call as a parish pastor and my call to serve on synod staff affirmed for me that pastors are people, too. They experience grief and loss, frustration and burnout, and need spiritual support for their own well-being just as their flocks do. My call to the churchwide organization taught me that those called to the office of bishop are pastoral leaders who also welcome the pastoral, caring presence of another to support them as they face the many highly confidential, stress-filled challenges of their vocational calling. In addition, the various leadership roles I was asked to assume in staffing the Conference of Bishops, doing strategic planning with synod councils, and supervising local and deployed staff provided me with valuable leadership experience and increased confidence in sharing my ideas within groups of other leaders.

It was during this call that I was invited to serve on the board of a local faith-based, ELCA-affiliated hospital. I hope that I was able to provide helpful insights to hospital leadership as to how the hospital's mission reflected the mission of the church. I know for sure that I gained insight and enthusiasm for pastoral leadership in health care through my service on that board. I readily volunteered for various board committees and attended all optional events, not out of obligation, but out of my desire to explore and learn as much as I could about the ministry of health care. I also invited other members of the board to lunch or coffee to learn from them and to hear their thoughts about how I could best serve in this leadership role. During my board tenure, the hospital's vice president of mission and spiritual care announced his retirement. I was elated and humbled when the hospital president suggested that I apply for the position. I did and was offered the position and found myself preparing to leave a call I thought I'd be in until I retired.

Talk about a steep learning curve! By this point in my ministry career, I knew something about pastoral ministry, but the language of health-care leadership was very unfamiliar. I looked for opportunities to talk with other leaders and hear their vision for the role that I was in. I listened to their stories and asked about their biggest challenges and the areas that brought them joy. I also was eager to find ways to help my executive colleagues and the clinicians with whom I regularly interacted embrace spiritual care and well-being, not as an add-on, but as part of the DNA of the health care we provided. The hospital president gave me some great advice in my leadership development by encouraging me to become credentialed as a fellow in the America College of Healthcare Executives. The education required for the credential helped me to better understand the broad context in which we worked and the challenges faced by those with whom I served each day. It also gave me even more credibility in their eyes. Since then, I have continued to explore opportunities for further education as the health-care landscape changes. And I continue to have those one-to-one conversations.

I also looked for opportunities to be more involved in leadership in our larger health system. I met with leaders across the system to learn more about what they do and explore ways that we might work together. And when the senior vice president of mission and spiritual care for the system retired, I applied for that position. I was offered the call, accepted it, and served in the role until 2018, when the health system merged with another, doubled in size, and I was named chief spiritual officer for the entire organization. I now oversee spiritual care, clinical pastoral education, ethics, faith outreach, environmental sustainability, our trauma recovery program, and our physician and team member well-being work. Yes, this is a wide variety of functions! They all are led by amazing people who feel called to the mission of our health system and the areas in which they are striving to make a difference. The scope of my leadership responsibilities is large, but I find my greatest sense of fulfillment in hearing stories of individual lives being changed because of what we do in connecting their personal faith to their sense of health and well-being.

QUESTIONS FOR REFLECTION

1. As you explore the many opportunities for ministry that exist, what are those that most excite you and ignite your sense of purpose?
2. What do you need to do to prepare yourself (education or experience) for the call in which you envision yourself?
3. What people do you need to connect with? Learn from?

Called by Community

Marilyn Pagán-Banks

I have been serving as executive director of A Just Harvest in Chicago since October 2002. If someone had told me then that I would be serving in one place for so long, I would not have been able to imagine it. My journey has often been one of feeling unrooted—too often with one foot planted in one place and the other not quite planted anywhere.

I first engaged with the organization as associate pastor and founding board member as we transitioned from a soup kitchen ministry of Good News Community Church to a self-standing 501(c)(3) organization. Having served in the nonprofit industry in various roles for more than ten years, I was asked by the senior pastor to represent the church in this new move, especially since many of the longtime volunteers, donors, and partners in this collaborative work were not from the communities we serve, were predominantly white, and were from much more affluent communities.

As we completed the community assessments and began the strategic planning, those of us on the new board with a deep commitment to community organizing became agitated by the fact that the soup kitchen had been feeding the community since 1983 and many who came to us were regular patrons. Grateful that we were known as a reliable source of free food and nutrition—no proof of need required, and no questions asked—we knew in our gut something was not right when one of the wealthiest cities in the richest nation of the world had community members experiencing chronic hunger and poverty.

When we had a plan in place to incorporate community organizing and advocacy into our mission and work, I was asked to apply for the position of executive director. My immediate response was, "Thank you, but no thank you." I did not feel called to this type of ministry. I had seen and experienced how "free stuff" can go from heartfelt to ugly really fast, on the side of the giver as well as the receiver. I wanted nothing to do with that dynamic.

A year later, while still serving on the board of directors, the person who had been called to fill the role changed their mind; and once again, I was asked to apply. This time, witnessing a real shift in the mission of the organization toward social justice and with a bit of cajoling by church and board members who insisted that I was "going to miss my blessing," I interviewed and got the job.

I have been blessed in leading the "soup kitchen" to become an interfaith-led, trauma-informed, asset-based, power organization that intentionally centers community and whose mission is *to fight poverty and hunger in the Rogers Park and greater Chicago community by providing nutritious meals daily while cultivating community and economic development and organizing across racial, cultural, and socioeconomic lines in order to create a more just society.*

The vision embodied by our work at A Just Harvest is "cultivating a world of shared abundance and radical belonging." From the moment I arrived, I have talked about putting ourselves out of business—meaning we believe that one day all will have plenty and no one will go without. We strive toward this goal while remaining an accountable partner and space in the collective work of centering the well-being and thriving of the community and addressing systemic oppression.

I came into this work ready to fight!

I have not always been clear where this *fight* comes from. My parents, part of the Puerto Rican diaspora, were not particularly political or civically engaged. They were hard working folx whose union factory job and bilingual client skills at the local clinic allowed us to be a part of the lower middle class.

This fight has always been there.

I remember it growing up in Catholic school as I defied authority while loving Jesus and dreaming of following him—believing in my young heart that I was only allowed to do this in limited ways. I remember it at my first "real job": when I defended a coworker being bullied by the company owner's daughter, as she backed off she asked me, "Why do you care?" I remember it when I demanded quality education for my child struggling with learning differences. I remember it when I was arrested at our US senator's office for refusing to leave until he committed to protecting and increasing vital services for the most vulnerable.

I entered seminary unclear as to what my ministry setting would be. While I loved church, I did not see myself in full-time parish ministry because I did not fit into the boxes I had perceived as needing to be checked off. I didn't think I could be a pastor and truly be myself. I wasn't male. I was a single mom. I didn't buy into performing respectability. I wasn't holy enough. My edges were too sharp. I cuss! I spoke my heart and mind. I was bold and not apologetic about my passionate energy. I am queer, claim my Blackness, and love my Puerto Rican culture! *¡Pa'que lo sepa!*

I did, however, clearly believe that I was called to ordained ministry. To care for people—not as a social worker as one member of my discernment committee suggested, but as an intentional leader within the faith community to share in the sacraments and to learn and teach in community. After all, I had experienced my call *in* community. My call came from the community. They saw what I could not see.

And so it was in seminary, too. Community kept calling; and I served as the first assistant helping to further expand the language and resource lab provided by the seminary, working with mostly international students and all those seeking support with seminary studies.

Community kept calling, and I served as support staff to the seminary's Hispanic Ministries program. I spent time building and deepening relationships with Latinx students, as well as those from the other racial/ethnic programs, and making connections and building collaborations with the communities represented by these students, faculty, and leaders.

Community kept calling, and I served a small urban mission church as a licensed lay minister during my last year of seminary. While there, I engaged with an ecumenical coalition of Latinx churches and began to really experience the powerful reach of the church in the public square. Prior to seminary, my understanding of church was small and limited. I had not known a church that fought against the powers and principalities. I had not experienced a church that engaged its members in the work of social justice, that made space for rage and lament, as well as praise and worship, or that knew the power it had to transform the community—and not simply help folx get to heaven.

I hadn't understood the church as *us*—the people.

Community kept calling, and I served as an outreach minister and community organizer. This work affirmed my understanding of the importance of community and authentic relationships, of being present, of listening and making space for folx to share stories in their own voice, of politicizing and organizing our experiences so that we can build collective power, dismantle white supremacy, and fight for liberation and love.

Not knowing it, I was being prepared for the work that I would lead and grow at A Just Harvest. After denying the call for more than a year, I arrived excited and ready to fight! I wanted to turn the world upside down, build power with people, and call the church out of its four walls. I love the church but did not feel called to full-time parish ministry. The folx on the street, many who have never stepped into any church I have led, call me *Pastor*. They are my congregation, my people.

I do serve as the part-time senior pastor of a local church with the same embodied values and compassion in action as A Just Harvest. I have *always* served in both roles during my time in authorized ministry, sometimes feeling set apart from those in full-time parishes and struggling with the label "bivocational."

It wasn't until I was attending a training with WomanPreach in 2017 that I publicly declared that I am not bivocational. WomanPreach founder and CEO, the Rev. Dr. Valerie Bridgeman, led us in an exercise where we each introduced ourselves in our own voice, based on how we *know* ourselves and not on how others label us. Since then, when asked about my vocation, I start off by letting folx know that I am not bivocational. I have one vocation: to accompany God's people on their journey. I learned this in relationship with the neighborhood community in Chicago that I initially thought I was called to save, to "mother." I was taught this by the call to love those whose blood was spilled by violence before their gifts were given life. This is the call to love God's people as they are—just as God has loved us.

I simply choose to live out my one vocation in various settings—the nonprofit organization, the church, the seminary setting, and in most of my daily life—not because I haven't found the "one" perfect place, but because this is how I embody my call as I continue to discern and live into my purpose.

Coming to know this in my bones is how I have been able to embrace my *renaissance ashé* unapologetically, *con buya*, and curiosity. While I did briefly mourn the years of feeling *less than* because I was so *nontraditional*, I refuse to give this any more energy. I now find a life-giving joy in the freedom I experience throughout all of my ministry, my personal life, and the strength and deep beauty of relationships and collective building.

When I need to remember or begin to feel lost or alone, I go back to community—where it all began—where my faith tells me it all matters and my roots find connection.

QUESTIONS FOR REFLECTION

1. If you could create a way of "doing" ministry that would be a dream come true, what would that look like?
2. What do you view as the necessary boundaries between life and ministry?
3. What is your call story?

Spiritual Entrepreneurship

Patrick G. Duggan

An entrepreneur is "a person who organizes and operates a business or businesses, taking on greater than normal financial risks in order to do so."[1] A *spiritual* entrepreneur is one who launches or operates a business out of a faith-driven or religious mission. My own story is illustrative of this definition.

Since 2012, I have served as executive director of the United Church of Christ Church Building and Loan Fund (CB&LF), a financial ministry that for nearly 170 years has financed more than four thousand churches with mission-driven building projects. In addition, the organization has helped dozens of churches interested in launching community development projects and affordable housing on church-owned properties. Most recently, we created a program to help spiritual entrepreneurs launch or expand for-profit and nonprofit ventures called the Adese (pronounced Ah-DEH-seh) Fellows program.

Often, I am asked how I moved from traditional ministry to running a loan fund for churches and working with spiritual entrepreneurs. Here is my typical response to that question:

> I said "yes" to a series of opportunities. I said "yes" to Christian ministry, to serving as a capital campaign consultant for the United Negro College Fund, to running a $170 million economic development agency, and to founding a church-related community development nonprofit. Without knowing why, I collected knowledge and experience to do this work all along the way.

And then I learned that my "yes" to these opportunities had little to do with me and everything to do with my grandfather, Sam Jones.

After nearly twenty-five years of searching, I met my mother's family in January 2018 at the funeral of my Aunt Beatrice, who died at the age of ninety. Realizing that I knew almost nothing about my family, another aunt sat next to me after the funeral and said, "I'd like to talk to you about your grandfather. He and his brothers built this church."

It filled me with pride to know that I was sitting in a church that my grandfather helped to build. But then my aunt said, "When Daddy Jones would go to a town, he would find a plot of land. He'd stay in that town for a while; and by the time he left, there would be a church building on the land and it would be full of people." About a hundred years ago, Rev. Sam Jones worked for the Fire Baptized Holiness Church, establishing congregations, raising funds, and erecting church buildings around the country. Then my aunt said, "The last place Daddy Jones built churches was in Cleveland, Ohio." CB&LF is headquartered at the United Church of Christ National Offices in Cleveland. I get chills every time I think about that.

God said to Jeremiah, "Before I formed you in the womb I knew you, and before you were born I consecrated you; I appointed you a prophet to the nations" (Jer. 1:5). I make no claims to be a prophet, but I am certain that I "do" church buildings because of Sam Jones's DNA.

The motivation to launch a venture out of faith and an idea that perhaps only you believe in comes from something deep within you that is uniquely yours. Most spiritual entrepreneurs are tortured souls because we fail often and are too stubborn to quit. We feel that if we do not do it, nobody will. It takes that kind of commitment—continuing to do something so difficult that it causes you pain—for you to achieve your outsized dream.

Today there is a rising tide of both for-profit and nonprofit organizations that generate revenue and solve social problems—ventures that "do well" and "do good." Organizations and businesses globally are concerned with aligning social impact to the advancement of the United Nations Sustainable Development Goals.[2] Centuries ago, religions created the world's first banks, hospitals, schools, and other commercial ventures and were at the leading edge of the socially responsible investment movement of the 1970s and 1980s.[3] However, religious communities are only recently engaging in the new wave of social impact ventures led by spiritual entrepreneurs.[4] Most church leaders do not completely understand what spiritual entrepreneurship is, but they feel a certain newness and energy about it. The idea seems to encourage longtime churchgoers who worry about the future church.

I have been surprised by the successes. One of the individuals in our spiritual entrepreneurship program went from being homeless to running a successful credit repair and personal finance organization. There's a bakery that employs recent immigrants, a woman-owned construction company that trains the hard-to-employ for construction jobs, a distributor for African American hair products, and an ordained minister and Wall Street professional who now runs the family natural juice business. One individual left a job as a senior executive for a very large nonprofit and started her own nonprofit organization. One year later (during the pandemic), she had raised more than a million dollars and was operating a thriving human service agency.

The range of entrepreneurial ventures, as well as the series of opportunities I've experienced in my own professional life, begs the question, "Exactly what does a spiritual entrepreneur do?"[5] Just as a traditional entrepreneur engages in business activity with the primary aim of generating a profit, a spiritual entrepreneur engages in business activity for the primary purpose of advancing a religious mission and/or bringing about societal transformation. The spiritual entrepreneur might even be somewhat agnostic when it comes to the business structure (sole proprietor, corporation, for-profit, nonprofit, and/or church-affiliated) or type of business (e.g., a monastery that makes and sells beer, a multinational used clothing business, or a church that offers a professional counseling service or runs a home health-care agency), as long as the venture is fulfilling the mission or transforming community.

Prospective seminarians who embrace liberation theology or the Catholic social teaching of the "preferential option of the poor" will find ample resources within the theological academy that speak to the efficacy of spiritual entrepreneurship as a means to individual and social transformation.[6] The same cannot be said about courses or other resources on entrepreneurship at most seminaries, however. Those who sense a call to spiritual entrepreneurship as ministry may need to explore the growing number of theological institutions that offer dual MDiv/MBA programs, or seek out fellowship programs like Adese that equip, train, and coach aspiring spiritual entrepreneurs. Those who intend to lead impactful ventures must be well trained in both business *and* biblical hermeneutics, as well as adept at theology and ministry praxis *and* social marketing and reading financial statements. The call to spiritual entrepreneurship comes to those who are inclined to blaze trails, who understand that God has called you to something that has no roadmap.

And yet, the world is hungry for more spiritual entrepreneurs and mission-driven ventures. We need people—church leaders—who may not think of themselves as entrepreneurs but who love the Lord and want to do a new thing. We need people who do not fit within traditional religious roles and are proud that they do not fit. We need to look for spiritual entrepreneurs the way nineteenth-century preachers in the United States recruited converts. We need to move with a sense of urgency because the world is changing at light speed.

We need people like you who are excited to do a new thing. Perhaps you are the next new spiritual entrepreneur.

QUESTIONS FOR REFLECTION

1. Which is more convincing to you: that the church will soon decline to irrelevance or that the church can still be an instrument of transformation through the work of committed Christ followers?
2. In what new ways can religion use its considerable wealth to be the change we claim to seek through our theological rhetoric?

A Way Out of No Way

Tawana Davis

As a Black woman who grew up in the African Methodist Episcopal (AME) church, I often saw leaders who did not look like me, and these leaders were men who were in pastoral/ordained roles in the church. As I discerned my call, I was mentored and guided by men who solely focused on traditional pastoral ministry. Nevertheless, there is so much more than pastoral ministry as one is discerning the call.

Spiritual and social entrepreneurship broadens the scope of the call to ministry to one that responds to the needs of the community in a robust, eclectic, and nonlinear way. When I received the call to ministry, I did not know a call outside of traditional pastoral ministry. A call to ordained ministry can be unique, but the church leaders imposed the trajectory of the traditional church pastor. I consider myself to be a life-learner, so I watched and listened with a desire to learn more about this call. I listened to my Spirit, body, and environment. Acquiescing to the linear trajectory placed upon me and my call, I went through the ranks of being ordained. I was an assistant minister, a youth and young adult minister, and an executive minister. (I used the term *minister* because in the AME church there was only one *pastor*.) To move through my call, I was required to attend seminary to receive my ordination as an itinerant deacon and then an itinerant elder.

I attended the Interdenominational Theological Center in Atlanta, Georgia. I served in a couple of churches, worked as an intern and then a resident chaplain, and later relocated to Denver. Although I discovered my womanist voice in seminary, I found my activist voice in Denver. Unfortunately, for what I deem political reasons, I knew that I would not be allowed to pastor a church that matched my experience and educational acumen. During my reflection over the years, I realized that patriarchy and misogyny would hinder my call to pastoral leadership in the traditional sense. My voice, spiritual awareness, business skills, and leadership prowess were needed; unfortunately, it was at the behest of an oppressive, toxic leadership environment.

As an activist and advocate, I found my voice outside of the four walls of the church and in the larger community. My G-d[1]-given gifts created space for me to lead in a way Spirit would have me lead. My theological training and hands-on experience allowed me to lead in ways that connected me back to my call at age thirty-six. Even though I did not know my call's specifics in 2006, I knew that I had to explore and find where G-d would have me be and not contend with the challenge of the triple consciousness of being Black, American, and Woman in the traditional church. As unorthodox as it was, I had to own my voice and call and move into the public sphere of pastoring in the community.

Spiritual and social entrepreneurship appeared in the form of activism through nonprofit communal work. As clergy, I sat on various boards as the active voice of diversity, inclusion, justice, equity, revolutionary love, and leadership. My call evolved and morphed into pastoring community in my sphere of influence and care. I discovered my influence of care in domestic violence awareness and advocacy as a domestic violence survivor. I am an activist and advocate for breast cancer awareness as I am surviving metastatic breast cancer. I imbue a womanist epistemology where Black women and Black women's experiences are centered for the liberation of all while centering, redefining, and refining my call to ministry.

Theologian Monica A. Coleman, in her book *Making a Way out of No Way: A Womanist Theology*, states that the call is an invitation into power and participation in relationship to G-d and the community of faith.[2] In the novel *Parable of the Sower*, author Octavia Butler writes, "We are called to a new and renewed awareness of our humanness and our infinite possibilities. . . . G-d makes demands on us to live into our faith in a radical way."[3] So after attending an HBCU for my master of divinity degree, as mentioned earlier, I moved to Denver to be a youth and young adult minister and then was promoted to the role of executive minister at an AME church. Nonetheless, I felt the call to something else. Unbeknownst to the community, my ties and relationship with community helped me to home in on my call to racial justice work. I resigned from my position in the church in 2015, retired in 2016, and began a womanist-centered, faith-based, racial justice nonprofit called Soul 2 Soul Sisters. The nonprofit is still flourishing today. It went from earning $7,000 for the year with no employees to hiring five staff members and eight contractors with a million-dollar budget to do the unique, first of its kind, communal Black-centered justice work.

Being the cofounder and curator of a nonprofit focused on social and racial justice is no easy feat. Proverbs 18:16 articulates that your gifts will make room for you. It takes trust and faith in G-d to be the provider, way maker, and sustainer through budding social entrepreneurships. Two Black women with families making $7,000 each for 2015 required a leap of faith. Honoring the call outside of the norms of pastoral ministry required a passion for the work and an unwavering faith that resulted in six years of growth and a national presence through patience and perseverance. After curating, implementing, consulting, and facilitating Soul 2 Soul Sisters programming, including its signature Facing Racism training, I had the opportunity to partner with nonprofit organization Odyssey Impact and Transform Films to cocurate and moderate important conversations on domestic violence and youth mental health.[4] Truly, G-d made a way through my call and beloved community.

I liken the community to my tribe. Leaders emerge from tribes/communities, particularly in leaderful, transformational, liberating spaces. According to *Tribes: We Need You to Lead Us* by Seth Godin, leaders are the ones who challenge the status quo, who get out in front of their tribes, and who create movements.[5] Tribes are about faith—about belief in an idea and in a community.[6] Practical skills, courageous attitude, dreams, hope, faith, love, encouragement, and teamwork are essential in thinking outside of norms that historically oppress, marginalize, dehumanize, and silence. There is an opportunity to lead in the discomfort of change, challenge the status quo, and foster a liberating imagination in discerning the call. Some calls to ministry are to an existing structure, and others are to create structures that fill a gap or meet a need.

I saw a need, had a tribe, possessed leaderful skills, and recognized the G-d in me to cocreate a movement to liberate the historically oppressed and the oppressor. I realized my call was not a traditional call to ministry after eight years of service in a traditional role in traditional churches. My call was leaderful, leading together with others at the same time. There are so many ways to serve, needs to be met, and much work to do. If not us, then who? If not now, then when? "There's going to be all kinds of roads to take in life. . . . Let's not be afraid to take them. . . . Let's live our lives without living in the fold of old wounds."[7]

QUESTIONS FOR REFLECTION

1. Take a moment, sit in silence, close your eyes, and silently ask yourself, "What does my call feel, look, sound, taste, and smell like?"
2. Describe and name (if possible) the feeling that welled up in your soul as you thought of your call.
3. Reflect for a moment and think about what aspects of your call bring you joy, hope, and courage and why?

A (Non) Sacramental (Non) Ministry of Food

Mariah Hayden

As an elder in the United Methodist Church, I understand my pastoral role as inherently sacramental. It is a unique privilege to pull together the profane, ordinary, even heretical moments of life nearer to a place where God's people can encounter the sacred. It's how the Church can take ordinary elements of wheat, fruit, and water and remember centuries' worth of Christians following Jesus and manifesting God's reign in the world. It is a profound responsibility to be called on for the work of cultivating the sacred in the midst of the ordinary, and one I never take for granted.

It was startling to me that I could hang up my stole and take a leave of absence from ministry after a particularly tumultuous appointment. I moved across the country with my family to a place where my spouse had taken a ministry position. At the time, my spirit could not remember my deep call to these sacred moments and sacramental events within the life of the church. I started over in a different conference, halfway across the country, in a place where I had no ministry connections. I became the primary at-home parent, worked part-time as a church administrative assistant, and set my focus toward entrepreneurial efforts. It was truly starting over; for many years, I did not miss the institution. I traded the ministry of tending souls for tending chickens and took a course in beekeeping.

As I encountered a new neighborhood, I witnessed a high rate of food insecurity among seniors, families, and children. There were free lunch and dinner programs for school-age children. Produce giveaways at local churches and nearby libraries could not make up for the lack of a local grocery store. The evidence of significant class and racial disparity inspired me to address food security issues alongside neighborhood blight and vacant lots. I had the time and an abundance of creative freedom in which to develop an idea that became a business and social enterprise. UpCycle Farm, LLC was founded on the principles of putting abandoned urban land back into productive use, utilizing sustainable agricultural practices, and prioritizing community engagement. My small urban farm grew from a tiny seed of inspiration into a focus point of the neighborhood flourishing with dozens of varieties of vegetables, an eclectic group of colorful chickens, a couple of beehives, and a 3,200-square-foot greenhouse.

I loved living and working in Cleveland because of its grit and the seemingly dissonant nature of urban living. It's the place where flowers grow and drugs are sold, where neighbors buy tomatoes and then get on the bus to go to work, where kids walk freely but not after dark, and where God's smattering of all different people coexist in the same area, though not necessarily in relationship. Beyond the obvious goals of growing good food and running a small business, I wanted to offer a place that surprised people into delight. My goal was to create a space where the beauty and taste of a garden, the sounds of happy hens, and the drips of newly extracted honey met the grit of a Cleveland neighborhood. Sacred in the midst of the ordinary. Many of the people I met would exclaim "I didn't know this garden/chicken coop/farm stand was here!"

I called myself the farmer, not the pastor; and my goal was to feed people, not their souls (as if those things are completely unrelated!). I networked with government and community development organizations instead of direct service nonprofits. I submitted grants to develop an urban farm instead of grants to restore sanctuary windows. I developed a system of shares for the food I grew (called community supported agriculture or CSA) instead of stretching myself thin in too many areas. When I went home, my body was tired, but my soul was fed. UpCycle Farm was not a church; but for me, and many of my neighbors, it was a sanctuary.

Jesus knew grit. He knew what it meant to be transient, homeless, and hungry. He surrounded himself with the nobodies and rubbed elbows with both lepers and temple officials. He brought the upside-down Gospel of radical love and incarnate God to women, outsiders, small towns, and cities. Rooted in the dirt, his stories embodied imagery of sowing, growing, harvesting. Jesus ate with people, and this radical act was so backward and odd that it frames our stories of faith because of who he ate with, what he ate, and how he talked about it.

After years of urban farming, I have experienced how much one can learn and grow by connecting our lives and our faith formation to the very stories Jesus told. Getting our hands in the healing power of the soil can deepen faith in transformational ways. In addition to the healing work of the soil on my soul, Jesus and I spent a lot of time talking while I worked. Interrupting the sounds of car alarms, traffic noise, the daycare center playground, and pedestrians, Jesus spoke words and stories that I had come to know well. As I learned to carefully prune tomatoes to a single string, hoping for a more abundant harvest, I heard the story of pruning branches (John 15) in my head, touching my heart in a new way. When I learned to save the seeds of my most prolific peppers, I remembered Jesus's metaphor about abundance. Each and every seed I placed in the ground was an act of faith. Sometimes I cast carrot seeds indiscriminately across the ground, hoping enough of them would stick to grow the sweetest rainbow carrots. Sometimes, I carefully planted bean seeds in neat rows of poor soil, hoping to replenish needed nutrients used up by the previous year's crop of peppers and tomatoes. Sometimes I planted one tiny broccoli seed in rich soil to be carefully transplanted into the greenhouse at the first signs of spring.

Over the years, I reconnected my call to the work of my hands and named what already was: A ministry of food and presence. My experience running UpCycle Farm inspired me to think about ministry differently. I learned to listen deeply to the needs of my neighbors and customers. Curiosity drove my leadership as I sought to connect people to the land, more just food systems, education, and beauty. The entrepreneurial spirit taught me to stay flexible and change directions based on the feedback of my neighborhood. Market Gardening 101 says to sell your product before you plant the seed. In other words, know someone wants what you're peddling before you even start planting. The first step is listening.

After pastoring churches who "have always done it this way," it was a relief to respond to what people in the neighborhood *really* needed and separate what is feeding people and what isn't. Diseased plants were immediately pulled and burned or trashed. Overabundant vegetables fed the chickens and the compost. I only grew slightly more kale than people wanted to buy, planting three times as many collards, beans, and tomatoes—things of which people could not get enough. Deep listening allowed me to discern the difference between "that's too expensive" (I'm not willing to spend the amount of money that matches the value of the produce) and "that's too expensive" (I see the value and my circumstances prohibit purchase). People in the latter group were always amazed by how far their money stretched, and the former were never satisfied. I've met a few churches like this, too.

There were disappointments along the way. The new church development people asked why I needed an appointment as an elder "because the work isn't sacramental." A few thefts set my goals back weeks or months. There was a difficult neighbor. The surprises, however, were exuberant and frequent. Youth groups spent days doing manual labor to help move the mission along. Numerous children who spent time at the farm knew (and learned they love!) the taste of peas and that not all green beans start out that way. Curious kids shyly asked to taste the difference between white cucumbers and "regular" green ones. Kind neighbors watched the farm in the evening and morning times. Most of all, the greatest gift of this space was the abundance of food, color, and delight that grew on a vacant lot in the middle of the city. It fed people. It showed them God's variety and beauty. It surprised them into noticing. Seeing chickens digging near the fence never got old. Even in early spring when the land was fallow, the garlic was proclaiming its abundance, proudly sprouting green shoots as soon as the snow disappeared.

Wearing a stole or wearing overalls, sacramental ministry is everywhere; it is everything that seeks to connect what is right in front of us with that which is beyond us. Here on an ordinary corner, in an ordinary city, grew a (non) ministry that connected the people to sustenance and beauty. I never decided whether the work was growing ordinary food for God's extraordinary people or growing extraordinary food for God's ordinary people. Either way, I cannot think of anything more sacramental than the meeting of grit, beauty, and the nourishment of body and soul.

QUESTIONS FOR REFLECTION

1. Where do you see Jesus show up in extraordinarily ordinary places or occasions?
2. What are the hyper-local needs that call ministers and churches to engage in their neighborhood?
3. What makes a church? Would you consider UpCycle Farm a church?

A Thread You Follow

Nathan E. Kirkpatrick

When I was in seminary, a story circulated through the hallways. It was clearly apocryphal; the details changed regularly depending not only on who was telling it but who was hearing it. Most often, it involved a United Methodist bishop in the southern United States who, whenever he was about to ordain a person into professional ministry, would whisper into their ear, "If you can imagine yourself doing anything else and being happy, then you should do it. But if you cannot, you are where you are meant to be." My classmates and I would tell each other that story on exam days, in paper-writing seasons, or whenever we were just frustrated with our life and work as seminarians. Within my friend group, sometimes we would just shorthand it for each other—"If you can imagine yourself"—and that was enough to get us back to the books, the keyboard, the classroom, or the internship.

Two decades later, I can see that we repeated the story because of what we heard in it—something about the irresistibility of God's calling in our lives. We were where we were meant to be, and that place was special, set apart, sacred even. In the movie *Keeping the Faith*, the Catholic priest says it this way: "[we] went off to seminary the way other [people] go off to the army or the Peace Corps."[1] We were caught up in something bigger than any one of us, greater than all of us together.

The problem, of course, is that the point of the story simply was not true. My classmates were wildly talented, and any of us could have excelled in any number of fields. There wasn't just one thing we could do that would be vocationally fulfilling—nor did any of us really want to believe that the ranks of the professional ministry were filled with people who could only be priests or pastors, as if no other vocation would have them. No, of the options before us, we had chosen to go to seminary. We had a sense that this was right work to be sure, but we chose this work, this life, this future.

This reality was underscored in just the few years after we graduated from seminary as classmates began leaving professional ministry for other vocations. My best friend found the church unwelcoming to his understanding of vocation and headed to law school. He was met there with excitement and support for his passions. A colleague left full-time parish ministry to direct a nonprofit in DC, spending her days with the homeless and the hungry. Another became a teacher and found his joy working with second graders. I left parish ministry after two years to become a seminary administrator and teacher, working with the next generation of people who were telling each other "If you can imagine." What I learned in that season was that vocation was capacious, that calling was an invitation to explore an open meadow rather than drudge down a narrow and one-way corridor.

In those days, I was introduced to the poetry of William Stafford. In his poem "The Way It Is," he writes:

> There's a thread you follow. It goes among
> things that change. But it doesn't change.
> People wonder about what you are pursuing.
> You have to explain about the thread.[2]

Those words taught me more about vocation than any book, article, or sermon ever had. Rather than vocation being about a single or static role, there's a thread that runs through—through my life and yours—connecting gifts and skills with experiences and opportunities. This thread makes divergent elements of our stories cohere. It sustains us on our hardest and longest days. When we feel lost, it can help us find our way. This thread can find its way through a wide array of jobs or roles, institutions, or organizations. Our work is to recognize, articulate, and appreciate what that thread might be.

With the aid of two spiritual directors and three executive coaches over the years, I have named that the thread that runs through my life centers on the reconciliation that God longs for among the peoples of the world. It should have been obvious. In college, I spent considerable time researching religious-based violence, particularly genocide, studying how people leveraged religious and political power toward heinous ends and how other people used those same levers toward peace and justice. In seminary, I explored how religious leaders stopped violent spirals with the weight of their witness and the power of alternative visions. Working in a congregation, I did some of my most meaningful work with people who found themselves in significant conflict with others, often their own families, about their core values and commitments. While working at the seminary, I made trips to Côte d'Ivoire shortly before their 2011 civil war and immediately after to meet with denominational leaders on the front lines of peacemaking and peacebuilding. Now, working as a consultant with my own firm, I find my deepest fulfillment helping the leaders of organizations and congregations navigate meaningful tensions within their communities. There's a thread I follow; it's about the reconciliation and restoration of relationship that is at the heart of God's vision for the healing of the world.

"If you can imagine yourself doing anything else," the bishop allegedly chastened years ago. What I like to believe is that today somewhere there is a bishop or a pastor or a counselor or a friend who says instead, "There's a thread you follow. Let me help you find it because it will bring you—and the world—unspeakable joy."

Speaking from experience, that's a life-giving, life-shaping message.

QUESTIONS FOR REFLECTION

1. What stories have shaped your understanding of vocation both generally and personally?
2. When you hear people talk about vocation, what assumptions do you hear in what they say?
3. Looking back on your life to this point, what threads of vocation or passion could you name?

Holy Friendships: Ecumenical and Interfaith Connections

Katie Crowe

In a 1976 interview with Landrum Bolling, theologian and mystic Howard Thurman describes what he calls the paradox at the center of conscious life: on the one hand, the drive to experience one's own uniqueness of being and identity and, on the other, the absolute necessity of relating to everything and everyone else, of which one is a part.[1]

"Deep within the experience of my own self in its profoundest sense is the key to experiencing every other living thing and person." He then goes on to describe how religion takes one down into oneself and universalizes what one discovers there, so that when a person looks into the face of another, they see their own face. Given this, Thurman says, "I'm always on the lookout. . . . I'm on my own scent, all over the world. And my assumption is that if I can't pick it up in you, my sniffer is off. So that I have to work on my sniffer, because it is there."

I was taught in seminary that the essence of the Reformed tradition (within Christianity), of which I am a part, is freedom and form: the freedom to approach those who are different from us in love while maintaining the integrity of our own tradition. This sentiment is reflected in the Presbyterian Church (USA) Confession of 1967, which reads,

> Christians find parallels between other religions and their own and must approach all religions with openness and respect. Repeatedly God has used the insight of non-Christians to challenge the church to renewal. But the reconciling word of the gospel is God's judgment upon all forms of religion, including the Christian. The gift of God in Christ is for all. The church, therefore, is commissioned to carry the gospel to all whatever their religion may be and even when they profess none.[2]

Those words have been essential guides through my years of pastoral ministry. They pressed me to delight in the joys of ecumenism when I would have otherwise been inclined to circle the wagons with like theological minds in the name of ease. They served as insistent mentors who challenged me to lean into relationship with colleagues whose hermeneutics and ideals were far different from my own when every impulse within me was to push away.

Standing squarely in the unique form of my theological identity helped me to avoid perceiving difference in others as a threat and encouraged me instead to welcome it as a friend.

When working with colleagues or congregations across Christian denominational lines, this framework enabled me to wonder over the nuances that get parsed over centuries of church history and praxis and varied cultural locations. But no matter how diverse my Christian conversation partners may be, we always had the Trinity as the foundational element among us that could be returned to when distinctiveness began to transgress into division. Within the context of inter-religious relationships, however, and one in particular, this was not the case. Absent such a foundational premise, my seminary learning would take on new meaning.

Rabbi Daniel Greybur of Beth El Synagogue and I met in 2012 at a new clergy luncheon hosted annually by a local congregational collaborative. We had arrived in Durham, North Carolina, within a year of one another, but our paths didn't cross regularly until I took up running laps around Duke University's East Campus—a mile-and-a-half-gravel loop that serves as the staging area for any number of health and wellness routines for locals. There I'd quite literally run into Rabbi Daniel, whose synagogue was a mere five blocks from the church where I pastor. We would smile and wave as we passed one another, and I'd wonder how he kept his kippa in place. Soon we started to walk together and chat.

One day I reached out to ask if we might hold a retreat for our Session, the governing body of a Presbyterian church, in their facility as a change of scenery for us and a chance to become better acquainted organizationally as neighbors. Their hospitality was easy and warm and the learning curve for what it meant for Protestants to gather in a kosher Jewish space was humorous and steep. Shared commiseration over the woes of aging facilities united us further.

Months later, our Session enthusiastically affirmed the synagogue's request to host occasional services during the holidays over the year that they were to be displaced from their facility as it was undergoing renovation. But when the location for their weekly Shabbat services fell through, our church facility became their new home.

After months of planning, on a freezing January Sunday morning in 2018, the assembly of Beth El Synagogue gathered for a special service to bid farewell to their building and processed through the neighborhood to Trinity Avenue Presbyterian Church, carrying their Torah scrolls shaded by the canopy of a chuppah, singing.

Members of Trinity Avenue lined the sidewalk along the final block to the church, waving and cheering them on until all gathered in the fellowship hall and swayed together as they sang the refrain of Psalm 133:1, *Hineh ma tov uma na'im, shevet achim gam yachad*. "How good and pleasant it is for kindred to dwell in unity." A mezuzah was presented by the church to the synagogue and affixed on the doorway to the fellowship hall by the rabbi, christening their new home in the first known liturgy of its kind.

My heart grew many times its size that day. And with it my clarity on what pastoral leadership is about.

What unfolded over the course of the next sixteen months of their residence with us was a commixture of mutual practical and theological learning, deep institutional friendship, a steady stream of comic relief as we aimed to take the gospel seriously but not ourselves, and a redefinition, for our members, of what made church home.

Christmas decorations were put up in the sanctuary, taken down for a bat mitzvah, and put up again. Our alcohol-free campus rule was suspended so that wine and whiskey could be enjoyed at Shabbat meals ("You don't allow whiskey? But Presbyterians are from Scotland!" the Rabbi marveled). We enjoyed snacks in the sukka on the church grounds during Sukkot.

In advance of Passover, I became the proud temporary owner of all the synagogue's leaven for the low price of $1. Church and synagogue members enjoyed meals in one another's homes. Rabbi Emeritus Steve Sager introduced the primal call of the shofar in Sunday school and unfurled the Torah scroll for our members, inviting us to approach Scripture not as a problem to be solved but a mystery to be enjoyed. I made my "What's Not to Like?" Yiddish Song Festival choral debut.

But for all the levity and learning that took place, there were points of pain and poignancy too. With centuries of experiences between Christianity and Judaism behind us, trust was not initially a given. Our denominational stance on the conflict in the Middle East surfaced difficult and honest discourse on matters layered with complexity and schooled me on holding tensions that would have to be redeemed where they resisted resolve. The October 18, 2018, mass shooting at Tree of Life Synagogue in Pittsburgh yielded a churchwide offering of letters of solidarity, grief, and love to members of the synagogue. But we knew that such a heinous act compounded the communal trauma of ongoing hate crimes and anti-Semitism in the world, reverberating existentially in ways we could never comprehend.

The day that Beth El members processed their Torah scroll back through the streets of our neighborhood to their newly refurbished synagogue was laced with tears and smiles and a journey that shaped us all indelibly. A love offering to our church of $18,000 was presented by Beth El and applied to the sanctuary entrance to the church that was badly in need of renovation and repair. Accompanying the gift was their prayer that it would help our church extend the same hospitality to others that enabled a season of dislocation to be one of consolation and joy. A piece of artwork created by one of their members was commissioned and presented to Trinity Avenue Presbyterian Church. It now hangs in the beautifully renovated sanctuary entrance, commemorating the friendship that taught us that the church building is just a structure, but it is love that makes it a home.

"I think that, whether I'm black, white, Presbyterian, Baptist, Buddhist, Hindu, Muslim, that in the presence of God all these categories by which we relate to each other fade away and have no significance whatsoever," Howard Thurman continues in his interview.

> Because in His presence I am a part of Him being revealed to Him. And anything that I do that blocks that, from my point of view, is sin because it is against God. Because it is against life. And whenever, in my experiences with my fellow, this can be awakened, then a door between us is opened that no man can shut. Because, you see, I feel that the only and ultimate refuge that any man has in this world is in another man's heart. So my feeling is my heart must be a swinging door.[3]

The essence of the Reformed (Christian) tradition may well indeed be the freedom to approach those who are different from us in love while maintaining the integrity of our own tradition. But my holy friendships across denominations and religions have refigured my understanding of the phrase. The Reformed tradition not only affords me such freedom; it gifts me with a deeper comprehension of the integrity of divine love that sets free a multiplicity of expressions in creation and the human family. It sharpens my sniffer, leading me to the side of new friends, and opening wide the swinging door of my heart in which I welcome my God, my neighbor, and myself home.

QUESTIONS FOR REFLECTION

1. What practices can you take up to sharpen your "sniffer" and better acknowledge and celebrate the image of God in others?
2. To what extent does your own tradition identify with or depart from the paradigm of "freedom and form"?
3. When has the swinging door of your heart invited someone unexpected in and how did that experience draw you deeper into yourself, the human family, or God?

An Unexpected Way

Liddy Barlow

In fall 2013, a colleague of mine sat down with a friend. "Did you see the news about Christian Associates?" he asked. "The director is retiring next spring. I wonder who'll serve there next."

"Do you think they would ever call a woman for that job?" my colleague mused.

His friend laughed. "That would be a cold, cold day," he said.

His skepticism made sense. Christian Associates of Southwest Pennsylvania was an old-fashioned, legacy institution: a regional ecumenical agency bringing together twenty-eight Protestant, Catholic, and Orthodox judicatories in the ten counties of greater Pittsburgh. Its director, formally titled the "executive minister," had a sprawling job description: fostering collegiality and collaboration among diverse Christians, representing the church in civic and interfaith spaces, and keeping the small nonprofit afloat. No woman had held the post in the organization's forty-three-year history. Many of its member church bodies don't ordain women at all; even among those that do, few had ever placed women in key roles of leadership. At the time, Christian Associates' governing board, composed of each church's bishop or executive, included only one woman—and she was an intentional interim.

And yet, the following winter, those same church leaders came downtown to install a thirty-four-year-old woman—me—as Christian Associates' executive minister. In a bitter wind, they hurried into the church and removed their hats, scarves, and gloves. The temperature outside was three degrees Fahrenheit. It was, indeed, a cold, cold day.

I'd moved to Pittsburgh to join my husband seven years earlier, with some trepidation about how my professional life would turn out. I wanted to be a pastor, but there are only a small handful of United Church of Christ congregations within commuting range of the city. I was convinced that I was called to ministry and equally certain that I was called to marry Greg. If both those calls were true, I figured, then surely, as the Quakers say, "Way will open." God would find some way for me to heed both callings.

Knowing that I might need to look beyond the local church for employment, I made a list of dozens of possible vocational paths. "Lead an ecumenical agency" was notably absent from my brainstormed options. In retrospect, however, I can see the sneaky ways the Holy Spirit was preparing me for this calling, long before I knew roles like this even existed.

For instance, I grew up in an ecumenical family: my grandparents represented the scandalous coupling of a Methodist and a Lutheran, with my parents the first-in-their-families pairing of a Protestant and a Catholic. I'd attended a women's college, Mount Holyoke, noted for preparing trailblazing women in historically male professions. While there, I'd held leadership roles in a robustly ecumenical campus ministry, planning chapel services and Bible studies alongside women who were Methodist, Presbyterian, Episcopal, Ethiopian Orthodox, and evangelical. My seminary shared a campus with a rabbinical school; our interfaith student group had shaped my spirituality. I served as a pastor in two local churches, honing skills in organizing events and public speaking. Through it all, I'd developed a tolerance for meetings and administrivia: the tasks that many clergy can't stand seemed bearable or even fun to me. Leading Christian Associates was an unexpected way forward, and yet exactly the right fit.

On the surface, Christian Associates seemed like a stodgy institution, but I soon discovered its legacy of innovation and risk. It traced its history back to the earliest organized ecumenism in Pittsburgh in the 1830s; in the decades that followed, these groups became the Council of Churches of the Pittsburgh Area, a well-resourced, established part of the region's religious landscape. In the wake of Vatican II, however, the council dared to make a fresh start: working closely with the Roman Catholic Diocese of Pittsburgh, the all-Protestant Council voted to close its doors and reopen with a new name and new focus. The new agency, Christian Associates of Southwest Pennsylvania, would be the first regional ecumenical group in the United States to welcome Catholics as full members. With a story like that in its living memory, taking a chance on a young woman's leadership came naturally.

The ecumenical fervor of the mid-twentieth century had cooled by the early 2000s. Many similar organizations in other cities closed or reorganized. Christian Associates faced budget pressures, decreased engagement, and missional uncertainty. Psychologists Michelle K. Ryan and Alexander Haslam first described a phenomenon called the "glass cliff," in which organizations facing crisis tend to call their first woman leader.[1] When I applied for the executive minister role, the search team told me they could guarantee my salary only for two years; beyond that point, it seemed possible that Christian Associates would cease operations altogether. From this perspective, my call was a Hail Mary pass, a desperate attempt to do something dramatically different in hopes of institutional survival.

We caught the pass. Eight years later, I'm still here, and so is Christian Associates. Some credit surely goes to my own creativity, strenuous effort, and sheer audacity; but I'd offer much more acknowledgment to all the others who have come alongside this good work: the church leaders energized by the ideal of our unity and the very real friendships they developed with one another; our interfaith partners who eagerly include us in their projects and ideas; the foundations and other donors who invested in this ministry. Ultimately, of course, credit goes to the Holy Spirit. After all, Jesus prayed that the church would be one, and surely his prayers will be answered.

I frequently claim to have the best job in the world, and I really do think that's true. This role has brought me to fascinating places to meet the most interesting people. I've received a blessing from His All Holiness the Ecumenical Patriarch, and I've wept with an inmate at the county jail. I've done 2:00 a.m. shots of vodka with an Orthodox archbishop after Paschal liturgies, and I've interviewed a Buddhist monk in Myanmar for an online dialogue series. I've been the only woman in an auditorium full of Catholic priests, the only white person in a sanctuary full of Black worshipers, the only progressive in a meeting full of conservative believers. In 2018, when a gunman killed eleven worshipers at a local synagogue and the attention of the world's media turned to Pittsburgh, it fell to me to speak on behalf of the church, repudiating anti-Semitism and standing with our Jewish siblings. So often those who speak for Christianity are those with the brashest and most exclusive voices. Doing loving, inclusive public theology at such a tender time, while visibly representing as a young(ish) ordained woman, was the greatest honor of my life.

This work is never boring. There are always new projects to take on, new people to meet, and more to learn, whether about the breadth of Christian traditions or the nuances of nonprofit management. There are always new ways to discover that the Spirit is alive and at work. Some of my deepest spiritual experiences have come in unexpected settings. Once, I grudgingly sat through a bleak sermon presenting theology that was the precise opposite of my own, only to find myself moments later weeping at the altar rail, certain that Christ was really present in the Eucharist before me. In such moments, the unity of the church is no mere slogan, no abstract ideal: it is a tangible reality for me to experience, to name, and—most importantly—to share.

The call to share, to "go and tell what you hear and see," as Jesus instructed the disciples (Matt. 11:4), is central to this calling. The experiences I'm privileged to have are not for my own personal enjoyment, but for the benefit of the whole church of Southwest Pennsylvania. My role is to tell these stories, to reflect a varied church back to itself, to make connections among diverse traditions so that all of us, together, might better understand and live out our true unity in Christ. I never imagined this role as a seminary graduate newly arrived in Pittsburgh; I did not see the shape it would take on that cold day when I promised to serve. But the Spirit opened a way for me to do this work, and for that I will always be grateful.

QUESTIONS FOR REFLECTION

1. How does your call to ministry intersect with the personal callings in your life (to family, relationships, other responsibilities)? How has "way opened" for you to pursue these callings simultaneously?
2. How have encounters with the diversity of Christian traditions, or with our interfaith neighbors, shaped your vocation?

The Unexpected within a Call

Michael Bos

My journey into ministry has been filled with surprises. I grew up in western Michigan in a traditional church amid a rather homogeneous population. I say this because the community was almost exclusively white, and as far as I knew, I had not met a person from another religious tradition. This was the only world I knew. I imagined I would go to seminary and then pastor a church much like the one in which I was raised that was in a community like that of my birth. It's hard to believe I now pastor a church in Manhattan and teach a course on Islam to high school students at a prep school. The journey from where I was to where I am has been a confusing yet exciting adventure in finding and following my call to ministry.

THAT GNAWING FEELING

It all began in seminary when I arrived ready to learn how to be a pastor. I admit I was naive and had little idea about what to expect. My conception of being a pastor was formed in my home church. I knew I would preach, teach, and visit parishioners in need. My vision centered on caring for a congregation, and I had given little thought to how to engage the community in which a congregation found itself.

In my classes I found myself in conversations about post-Christian society and the waning influence of Christianity in North American society. With this, I realized I would need to learn to navigate a world with other cultural and religious influences. I am not sure how I can explain it, but this sparked my curiosity about other religions. I had never thought about the content and practices of other religions. I had never thought about the meaning of my faith in relation to other faiths. I had never thought about how I would engage a family whose members represented different religions. These questions began gnawing at me and would not let me go.

For the first time I noticed how our story of faith contained encounters with other religions, especially in Hebrew scripture. There were influences to which Israel said "yes" and influences to which it said "no." I wondered why we weren't talking about this more, and what was being communicated to us about our faith in relation to other faiths. I discovered verses like Jeremiah 29:7, which spoke to a people in exile surrounded by foreign influence: "But seek the welfare of the city where I have sent you into exile, and pray to the Lord on its behalf, for in its welfare you will find your welfare." I wondered to myself: how does one even go about doing this?

Over time, I discovered these questions required an answer for me to follow my call to ministry. I ended up with so many unanswered questions that rather than move from seminary to ministry, we moved to the Netherlands so I could do additional study in Hebrew scripture and the theology of religions. Beneath it all, what began as a wonderful curiosity began to feel like a crisis of faith. I think it was because I kept adding to my list of questions but could supply little in the way of answers. I know there are those who say, "It's all about the questions," but as one who only had questions, I can tell you that it's not a good place to be. I needed some answers, something to hold onto, to be able to move forward in ministry.

After two years, we moved back to the States, where I started my first position as a pastor. The room to explore and question proved to be a pivotal time of preparation for my ministry. I can now see that, without realizing it, I was wrestling with a call within a call. Yes, I was called to be a pastor; but there was a part of it emerging that I hadn't anticipated: interfaith work. The curiosity and crisis would redefine what my ministry would be.

TURNING POINTS ALONG THE WAY

There are so many things that happened along the way that it is hard to capture the confusing and complicated journey I was on, but two turning points stand out for me.

The first turning point was around whether I should spend time studying other religions. There was so much I didn't know about my faith and areas within Christianity about which I was also curious. With a demanding seminary schedule and a young family, shouldn't I make the study of Christianity my priority? As I struggled with this, I had a conversation with a professor who, knowing my struggle, quoted Max Müller's often-used aphorism, "The person who knows one religion knows none." This really stuck with me; while I think it is overstated, there is a truth to it that invited me, even encouraged me, to study other religions. I no longer saw this pursuit as a confusion of priorities but as one that was needed for me to better understand my own faith.

It wasn't easy. When questions arose and my faith was challenged, when doubt crept in and I wondered what I really believed, I couldn't force myself to ignore these things. However, I could remind myself of this aphorism as a way to reassure myself that in the end, I would have a deeper faith. But getting there would involve some struggle.

I was fortunate I had someone with whom to share this struggle. It was this same professor who told me you can only have depth perception from two points of reference and studying other religions will give me another point of reference to see deeper into my own faith. For me this was God-sent encouragement to continue my journey, and in the end my appreciation of my faith grew.

The second turning point was around what to do with what I was learning about other religions. Do I incorporate it into what I believe? Do I pick and use parts I find useful? As I was asking these questions, I listened to an interview with Huston Smith, author of the best-selling book *The World's Religions*. A caller asked him the question, "Since you've learned so much about the world's religions, do you pick and choose the best from them to use for your faith?" Huston, who was also a Methodist pastor, said without missing a beat, "No, ma'am." Then he used the analogy of drilling for oil. He said that when you drill for oil, you have a much better chance of striking oil if you dig one deep well rather than many shallow ones.[1] This made so much sense to me, and it help me clarify that whatever I was learning, the well I was digging was Christianity.

These turning points helped me find a place for the study and engagement of other religions in my life of faith. In fact, interfaith work would become the call within a call I needed to live fully into the ministry to which God was directing me.

A CALL WITHIN A CALL

I don't think I am alone in having a call within a call, and I am so thankful I didn't ignore that gnawing feeling that was drawing me to explore other religions. I learned that through my general call to ministry, there were other calls awaiting me. I can't imagine my ministry without this. Interfaith work has brought a breadth to my ministry. It helps me seek the welfare of the city where I have been sent by God, and it is something so desperately needed in this world. As Hans Küng once said, "There will be no peace among the nations without peace among the religions."[2] For me, this involves teaching Islam. Certainly, a part of this is that I lived nearly a decade in the Middle

East and did my DMin thesis on the origins of Islam, but it is something more. It is here I do my utmost best to engender a fair understanding of this global faith. After all, how can we expect the same about Christianity unless we do this for our neighbors and friends from other religions?

QUESTIONS FOR REFLECTION

1. Is there anything creating a gnawing feeling in you that is calling you to learn and explore more? And who do you have to help you process what this means for you and your ministry?
2. What points of reference do you have for how you understand Christianity? Have you explored other religious traditions in ways that not only inform your understanding of them but also enlarge your understanding of Christianity?
3. As you prepare for ministry, do you have any sense of an emerging call within a call for your future?

Just Keep Walking

Amanda Henderson

The path has been winding and unexpected.

What I now call my "calling" began to take shape during Lent in 2007. I was walking on a masking-tape labyrinth marked out on the maroon commercial carpet in the open sanctuary at Heart of the Rockies Christian Church in Fort Collins, Colorado. I was a tired mom to two young children and awaiting a third child through adoption. I knew I loved being a mom, and I knew I was ready to serve in new contexts, but I had no idea what that might look like. I remember looking down at my bare feet and feeling the anxiety of not knowing what the next phase of my life would bring.

With each step forward through the path to the inner circle, I felt a deep peace wash over me. The peace said, "Just keep walking; you are on your path."

In all honesty, I am skeptical of messages from God. I see God as simultaneously unspeakably Holy other, and intimately close in the earthy spaces of life. Even as I feel the presence in my bones, I resist any naming of that presence. Most often, I call this feeling peace, assurance, or in the words of theologian Paul Tillich, the "ground of being."[1] At that moment in the labyrinth, I knew that I did not know, and I knew that I was okay in the not knowing. So, I kept walking.

This process of putting one bare foot in front of the other and listening for that assuring presence would sustain me through the year after adopting my third child (one of the most challenging years of my life) and continue to push me to pursue an education in theology and ministry. The process of listening and following led me to choose seminary to pursue a master of divinity degree at Brite Divinity School in Fort Worth, Texas. Our family—me, my husband, and three kids ages three, five, and seven years old—sold our house and many of our belongings and moved from Colorado to Texas. Throughout this path, the well-being of my children and deepest relationships would be a reliable prognostic of the integrity of my path. When I look back, I see that in this move we were wildly brave and perhaps I. At the time, we were up for an adventure. We traveled to seminary without a clear plan for where this would lead, but simply as another step in the labyrinth of life.

As we traveled, I would come to see clearly that the path I was led to was one of community, creativity, continuous learning, embracing radical differences, and speaking and acting for justice. These pieces of clarity did not come all at once, but as steps on a rocky trail where I slowly found my footing.

An early moment of clarity in my path came on a trip to Israel and Palestine, where I traveled with my home church pastor and a group of leaders from across the United States to experience "holy stones and living stones." We toured the sights I had learned about over the years, visited refugees and advocates navigating political turmoil and frequent war conditions, and stayed with local Palestinian families who extended generous hospitality. In this experience of meeting Muslim, Jewish, and Christian people navigating war, peace, and daily life, I was struck by the power of relationships and the impact of multiple religious traditions and divergent understandings of God, religion, and care for one another. These learnings empowered me to keep walking and pursuing deeper questions and authentic relationships.

The next step on my path was in taking an opportunity to work with a multicultural education organization in Fort Worth. Through developing and leading interfaith dialogues, I was able to see the ways religion shapes people's lives and relationships firsthand. I witnessed people challenging fear and assumptions to build real connections. This opportunity was an affirmation that my calling meant moving out into the community, being around tables and talking about things that matter. It felt simple yet profound and would be a pivotal step in my path.

After I completed my master of divinity degree in Texas, my family decided to move back home to Colorado. In this move, I had the opportunity to serve as a congregational pastor in Denver. While serving in this urban, creative, and historic community, I experienced both an affirmation of my path forward and a deep awareness of what my path *was not*. While I loved the work of pastoral ministry, it felt clear to me that the places I felt most alive were found outside the walls of the church. Through engaging with the local neighborhood and building a community night market with food trucks, vegetable stands, and live music, I saw the community come alive. I learned that while I love the work of the church, my gifts and energy were most generative when connecting with people who may never pass through the doors of the sanctuary. Through this time, I questioned the path I was on and struggled to discern how to navigate complicated leadership questions.

My body responded to the stress with sleepless nights and grinding teeth that eventually led to two emergency root canals. My physical health has been another marker of the integrity of my path. When I am making time to follow my love of running and moving my body and eating healthy, I know that I am aligned with the rhythms of my path. When my physical and mental health are suffering, I know that I am not. With time, I listened. Feeling a sense of clarity, I knew that while I was still on my path, I needed to change directions. This was a challenging moment as I learned to listen to that still, small voice and just keep walking.

The next step on my journey would be an opportunity to grow, serve, and thrive in ways I never could have predicted. Amid the deep questioning of my path in congregational ministry, I learned about the opportunity to serve as the executive director of the Interfaith Alliance of Colorado, an organization that worked in the community to bring people together across differences for a common vision of rights and equality for all. It was as if the job description had been written for me. However, the organization was in a stage of rebuilding and had very few resources to enact the potential of the mission. The work would be fruitful but would require intensive learning about public policy and legislative systems, fundraising, grant writing, and managing a growing staff. I decided to take the challenge.

Through continuing this path, I discovered the power of sitting around the table with advocates, activists, policy makers, and faith leaders to envision and catalyze new paths forward together. I was able to call upon my curiosity and belief in the power of relationships across differences to build strong coalitions. I was able to grow and utilize my administrative gifts to lead a staff, board, and growing organization. This work was an emotional roller coaster of community vigils, legislative hearings, street protests, and political strategy sessions. I found myself in these spaces, and I felt the deep presence of *knowing* that my gifts were meeting the needs of the community in which I live.

And yet, after seven years, I found that the time had come to take another turn in the path. Through my experiences at the intersection of religion and politics, I felt a continual frustration with the lack of deep understanding of the ways religion shapes the way people see and move in their lives and in the community. I have a strong pull to be able to better understand this and to communicate it to those serving in public leadership as we work to build transformational political structures. Leaving work that I knew in my bones was my path was harder than I thought. And yet, I continue to discern and listen to the spaces where I feel most alive and generative. When I feel the energy of connection, curiosity, and authenticity, I take another step and *just keep walking.*

QUESTIONS FOR REFLECTION

1. What are the signals that assure you of alignment with your path?
2. Have there been times when you questioned your path? What did those feel like, and how did you respond?
3. What work makes you feel most alive and energized? How does it feel when you lean into this?

Starting New Faith Communities: What's the Point?

Chris S. Davies

Starting a new faith community or ministry is not an easy task. It will likely be one of the hardest things that you've ever done, and I'd encourage you to think carefully about whether this is really, *really* what you're called to do. In fact, if you can think of *anything* else, maybe do that instead.

You may be wondering why I'm introducing this section at such a place when we are in the context of a world that seems so desperate for the language of meaning making and liberative faith intervention, and hungry institutions seemingly ready to leap up and support the kind of "innovative" and "creative" ministries we've been saying we have wanted for decades.

I will tell you: It's because I have not met a new church start pastor or leader who hasn't also been walking through the valley of Institutional Nonsense and unnecessary barriers to funding and support and unrealistic expectations placed upon them from within and without. It is not a reasonable expectation that this will be a career that can financially sustain you, at least immediately; it takes a lot of perseverance, privilege, and access to resources to make it work. I say this with deep awareness that these circumstances are not just, but you must come into this with informed consent about how difficult starting a new thing can and will be.

It can be a difficult and isolating journey to hold vision for what is possible without a clear pathway before you for actualization in the post-institutional era of proclamation. It takes an enormous amount of faith, clarity of call, and—dare I say—obstinacy to continue when things get really hard. So, if you are still reading this through and thinking, "God, that's still for me," then I pray the following advice and stories and testimonies to both the sacredness and the shittiness of this work carry you with a measure of discernment and care toward the call, however it evolves. Do know that it is offered in service to your discernment and connection to the Divine and the world we seek to build, together.

With every faith community I've started, I've done so with a particular carelessness of structure and a boldness of vision. And many of them have failed spectacularly when held to modern metrics and are no longer actively ongoing! From Guerilla Queer Bars and epiphany parties of "Beers, Queers, and Baby Jesus" to house churches and Queer Clergy Trading Cards, the creation of networks of innovators and spiritual rabble rousers has been an integral part of my work in the faith. When my vocation moved from the experimentation in creation of such communities to directly supporting them, I set about building the structures I wish I had in trying to start something from the ground up. The following are a few things I've learned or observed from both the outside, and the inside, of making ministry happen in creative and chaotic ways.

Know the *problem* and consider many *solutions.* In teaching and learning alongside Rabbi Elan Babchuck of the Glean Network, I recall that he often starts with this question for spiritual innovators: Are you more in love with the problem you are seeking to solve or your solution for that problem? Consider your own call through this lens. When you imagine your new faith community, how do you perceive its formation and success?

For example, here is a *problem*: Souls need healing after collective grief and trauma through COVID-19 and continued racialized assault and macro/microaggressions from personal to systemic. People need meaning making for this world as it is, and community to experience it alongside. A common *solution* that churches often point toward is this: gather people for an hour and a leader will talk at them for fifteen minutes, with a few songs and some speaking back and forth in the mix. Does this solution address these problems? Which one of these are you more in love with, and why?

Know your people. Define clearly *who* you are called to serve in community. It isn't "everyone." That kind of vagueness simply doesn't fly anymore, and the more specific you get in seeking those whom God is calling you to transform, the clearer you can build a matching structure to support it. Do twenty non-leading (consensual) interviews of who you think you are called to serve and test your theories and ideas with them before starting anything concrete.

Know your team. Beloved, as much as you may want to, you simply cannot do this alone. Pull in the trusted people who offer you wisdom outside of your own circle and listen to them. Connect to people who will support you, challenge you, work beside you, and be a part of your successes and failures. This is a team effort. Be aware that early groups reflect their leader, so align your own identities with the people you seek to serve, and/or get really clear in supporting other leadership who more closely align with those whom you are called to be beside in the Gospel work.

Know your support system. Reach out to the people who are your support team. This includes coaches, mentors, leaders, folks who have been here before you and can speak to some of the pitfalls and successes, those who will be completely separated from your work and hold you accountable to the joys and passions that you had *beyond* starting something new for the sake of the Divine—you'll need all those people! Also, make connections with the institutional bodies with whom you hope to be in relationship, whether through associations, conferences, districts, synods, regional ministry missional developers, or more. For better or for worse, early relationship goes a long way toward a smoother institutional process if you are looking to affiliate with a particular tradition.

Know your limits. You cannot know everything, and your idea is not 100 percent correct. One of the things that funding sources will look for is whether you are "coachable." In other words, when presented with a need to pivot, are you able to shift? Or are you so committed to *your* solution that you are unable to adjust to the consistent change of the world in which we live, in service to those whom you are called to lead and serve?

In my own early work of starting something new, I wish I had more of a sense of how to set about sustainable structures from the beginning. I went all in—hard and fast—and burned out quickly in leadership. I wish that I had been more careful in setting up teams of people through intentional leadership development and learning more carefully of the systems and structures that I needed through things like a business plan and clear budget. However, I do not regret the learning or growing into different aspects of ministry. The problem that I was seeking to solve then is the same that I continue to work toward now: people need to be connected to each other in the work to help build a world where all people are loved in abundance, liberated from that which oppresses them, and connected to each other for the sake of all our great-great-great-granddaughters. Whether this is practiced in the micro or the macro, in the home, the church, or the nation, it is still the problem and opportunity that drives my own vocational (and life!) discernment. Regardless of what you choose to do in relationship with God, I pray that you find that which calls you into action, for the sake of the Gospel!

QUESTIONS FOR REFLECTION

1. What is the problem you are seeking to solve through your ministry?
2. Who are your support people along the way?
3. What connections and experiments and interviews do you want to be doing *now* in preparation for the actualizing of your call in starting a new ministry?

On Starting New Things While the World Is Burning

Tyler Sit

When social justice–minded church people talk about privilege, we usually ask questions like:

Who is welcome at the table?
Who is at the head of the table?
Who gets to be heard at the table?

What these questions miss, however, is exactly what church leaders need to be asking ourselves if the church is to have a future at all: *Who gets to build the table?*

In other words, if we think of ministry only in terms of reconfiguring existing pieces within existing structures in existing communities, we will not get to where we want to go. The justice of the church should include not only passing inclusivity statements within the congregation but also starting new communities that are inclusive from the jump, not only mobilizing existing congregation members to show up to a protest but also starting new movements entirely.

This realization, in combination with some empathy and bold mentorship, is how I discerned a call to become a church planter. I looked around at the congregations in my area and thought, *I'm not sure any of my friends would want to go to these churches*. Which, mind you, doesn't mean that *I* wouldn't want to go to these churches. I love the mainline! I love United Methodism! There is a roped-off pew in my heart reserved just for hymns, church aunties, and the liturgy I grew up with. But my friends outside of the church? Not so much. They are, like so many Millennials and Gen Xers, running off to make a difference in the world, whether it be through activism, mutual aid, education, social work, business, or the ubiquitous "all responsibilities as assigned" job in a nonprofit.

All of these friends flock to difference-making jobs because the perils and injustices of our communities are in front of our faces—all the time. And, as much affection as I have for the mainline congregation, I found most congregations' responses to be entirely insufficient to the challenges our planet is facing.

I have participated in some climate change activism, and one time a speaker at a rally said something that convicted me to my core. He said, "Climate change is the greatest moral challenge that humanity has ever faced."

Ever faced? Yes. Climate change will make life worse for everyone in general and definitely worse for Black people, for Indigenous people, for women, for queer people, and for children. All of the cracks existing in our society will widen more and more in a hot planet.

And the response that I saw most churches taking—the anemic "recycling committees," the tragically unproductive "creation care" team—felt so dramatically apathetic that it bordered on gaslighting. How can these churches look at the same burning world that I am seeing and do so little?

Fortunately for me, I had some good mentorship in my life. Mentorship, truly, is one of the greatest gifts that the local church can offer. A few months before I heard that "ever faced" line about climate change, I was sitting across the table from my district superintendent (that is, the United Methodist supervisor of pastors) talking about my ordination process. She told me, "Tyler, you think like an entrepreneur, and you pray like a mystic. That is all you need to be a church planter. Would you pray about whether God is calling you to start a new community?"

The offer completely gripped my imagination. For months, it was the last thing I thought about before I went to sleep. It was the first thing I thought of when I woke up. I started reaching out to other church planters, signing up for trainings, and devouring church planting books. Could a church plant be a chance to confront the deep pain of our world with the highest potential of the local church? Could the Gospel transform us so deeply that it actually changed the injustices our world is facing? *That*, I thought to myself, *would be the kind of church that my friends would go to.*

Before the conversation with my mentor, church planting was not even a concept to me. I assumed that my call to ministry meant that I would pastor an established church that had a bell choir and a radiator, and if I were lucky my church would one day start a recycling committee. Once my mentor spoke planting into my life, things changed almost instantly. Following that day, when I was asked what Christians should do about the greatest moral challenge that humanity has ever faced, I could respond, "I don't know, but do you want to start something with me to find out?"

Of course, mentorship is in itself a dimension of privilege. As I laid out in the leadership development chapter of my book, *Staying Awake*: "One of the injustices in our society is that some people have victory and opportunity spoken into their lives every day, while others wake up in the morning to blame and fall asleep at night to shame."[1] When I wrote that, I was thinking specifically about what a blessing it was to have church planting spoken into my life. I am both Asian and gay, and Asian gay people don't have an overabundance of church planter role models to look up to. I haven't met too many starters, entrepreneurs, or organizers who have a voice like mine or who face the intersection of challenges that I do. And yet, when my mentor said what she did, it freed me to my calling.

I want to pass on the blessing. You, my reader, might not have had church planting spoken into your life, either. If you are a person of color, or female, or queer, or poor, you might not have heard that starting a new thing was even an option. Sometimes people receiving scraps at the table don't realize, as I didn't, that it is even an option to build a new table. But if, as you're reading this, you become fixated on the idea; if you immediately start journaling about what a new thing could look like—church planting may be for you.

To conclude, let's fast-forward through what happened over the subsequent few years. Through deep community listening, I realized that "a church that focuses on climate change" did not resonate with the Black, Latinx, white mixed neighborhood in south Minneapolis where I was planting. So, we became New City Church, because the Revelation 21 image of an inclusive community where there was no violence and the whole earth was renewed appealed to folks more than the phrase "climate change." As a multiracial community, we started looking at issues like trauma healing, and how spiritual practices and Creation all are part of God's salvation plan to make us whole.

Then, the racist murder of George Floyd happened, just minutes away from where New City Church worshipped.

The ensuing uprisings took place on Lake Street, just one block from our building. It was indeed traumatic. Fortunately, though, God had given us a few years of a head start to understand how the Gospel, trauma healing, and the very soil beneath our feet all require attention in moments of crisis. With ministries like the Incarnation Fund, a mental health reparations program, New City was able to (in harmony with extremely talented and generous churches) respond uniquely to one of the most significant racial justice moments in the United States—in the world—in the past century.

This is why we need to start building new tables: because God needs all hands on deck for the healing of the world, and our existing tables are good but insufficient. If God has put it on your heart to start a community, please start now. You never know what God might be sending your way.

QUESTIONS FOR REFLECTION

1. If you had infinite time, money, and talent, what new thing would you start to join God in healing the world?
2. How do you think the church could respond powerfully to the injustice and trauma in our world?
3. Sit's mentor said he "thinks like an entrepreneur and prays like a mystic." Complete this sentence to apply to yourself: *I _____ like a _____ and _____ like a _____.*

Mi Camino

Rhina Ramos

Becoming a pastor was not a straight path for me. I took many detours, and that has shaped me and my ministry.

I first started my professional life as a labor rights attorney. As a child with big dreams, I was eight when I decided to be an attorney. I wanted to be the first female president of El Salvador. So, I did my research about what world leaders do to become presidents; when I learned that Indira Gandhi and Fidel Castro were both lawyers, I decided that I was going to be one too.

When we left El Salvador to come to the United States, we crossed the border and endured the perils that many other immigrants had to go through in attempting to get to US soil. I was undocumented for the first three years in this country. My dream changed then; I was going to become an immigration attorney to help immigrants like myself.

In 1992, I started law school at Hofstra University in Long Island, New York. Law school was the most difficult academic challenge of my entire life. I only had basic English writing skills. I couldn't complete all the required readings, and I struggled for every C that I earned in my courses. My determination and my friends who tutored me helped me to move forward.

In the middle of my second year at law school, I started volunteering at the Workplace Project, an immigrant workers' center. I learned how to advocate for the rights of immigrant workers who had been cheated out of their wages. I also learned how to be a community organizer at this organization. Its founder, Jennifer Gordon, mentored me and taught me how to write for law school. Thanks to her, I improved in my law school performance. One of my law professors even accused me of cheating because my written English had improved so drastically. She said, "A person who speaks like you cannot write a paper like this." I suffered great discrimination during law school because I was an immigrant with a big dream.

I graduated from law school in 1995. At the Workplace Project, I helped recover thousands of dollars in unpaid wages and taught hundreds of workers about their labor rights. However, at the end of five years, I was burned out.

I began thinking of going back to school. My mentor Jennifer—an atheist Jewish lesbian—suggested that I check out seminary. We still laugh about the irony of my atheist mentor encouraging me to apply to seminary, but Jennifer knew that faith was an important part of my life. She had met me when I was still in the closet and a member of a very fundamentalist conservative and homophobic Baptist Church. Jennifer was also instrumental in my coming out. She humanized for me something I feared in myself.

My coming out was traumatic, to say the least. I was married to a Salvadoran man whom I met in our church's youth group. I was nineteen years old and running away from all my fears of being a lesbian. I thought that getting married, praying hard, and trying to be a good Christian wife were going to make my attraction for women go away. I used to pray to God, "Kill me or change me."

Then one day, I told my then husband that when I hugged him what I really wanted was to hug a woman. I was at the end of my rope. We started going to couples counseling with Pastor Raymond Santos, a Methodist pastor and a clinical psychologist. He helped me come to terms with the fact that I was a lesbian. With his compassionate care, I learned that I was not possessed by demons and that I was not destined for hell. After a year of going to counseling, I decided to separate from my husband. I was rejected by the church in which I had grown up because they decided that I was to blame for my divorce.

Like many others, religion wounded me; but being a Christian was something I couldn't leave behind. In 2000, I moved to California to take a job connecting with El Salvador. It was at that time that I applied to Pacific School of Religion, and they offered me a full-tuition scholarship. It was in seminary that I reconciled my faith and my sexual orientation. I could be a follower of Jesus and a lesbian too.

After graduating with a master of divinity degree in 2003, I continued working in the nonprofit sector. I couldn't imagine myself being a pastor, so I did not pursue ordination in seminary. In my eyes, pastors were infallible; and I was too human and too flawed.

Around 2006, I started visiting Plymouth United Church of Christ (UCC) in Oakland, California. All of my church formation—the singing, the praying, and the preaching—had been in Spanish; worshiping in English felt strange. But Plymouth was diverse and multicultural, and I felt welcomed.

After a year of attending Plymouth, the senior pastor encouraged me to enter the ordination process with the UCC. This process took five years to complete all of the pending requirements for ordination. On May 26, 2012,

I was finally ordained as a minister by the UCC. It was one of the happiest days of my life, and presiding at the Communion table for the first time felt so affirming.

My call (the last requirement to be ordained) was to establish the first Spanish-speaking, open and affirming congregation in Northern California. My dear friend and coconspirator, Karla Perez, a Nicaraguan immigrant woman searching for her own spiritual path, helped me to begin this work. We held the first service of Ministerio Latino in a Guatemalan family's living room in December 2011, just a few months before my ordination. Starting my own congregation centering the LGBTQI community has been life giving and healing for me and many others.

In 2016, I had the unique experience of going to Orlando after the Pulse shooting. Forty-nine people—mostly from the LGBTQI and Latinx communities—had been killed because of a hate crime. I remember waking up that morning to the news and feeling consumed by the pain. I told my wife, "I know what pulpits at conservative Latinx churches are saying right now. They are blaming their deaths on them being LGBTQI. They are telling their congregations that these people deserved to die." My wife, who is not a believer, told me, "Last I checked, you are a lesbian, you are a pastor, you speak Spanish, and you have to go there." So, I did. With the help of the national office of the UCC, I arrived in Florida a week later to provide pastoral care to the families of the deceased. Praying with the families, holding space for them to grieve, felt like my real calling. This experience after Pulse was defining and led me into further living out this sense of call.

As a result, in March 2018, I quit my nonprofit job to become a full-time pastor. I had been working with a life coach, Carmen Iniguez, a Latina Chicana queer woman, who was challenging me to live out my life purpose. The other reason for my leap of faith into full-time ministry was a growing sense of urgency to respond to the Trump administration's attacks on immigrants and members of the LGBTQI community.

My wife backed me up; and with her support, I began fundraising for my salary and all the expenses of growing and operating Ministerio Latino. When COVID-19 hit and we all went into lockdown, Ministerio Latino raised more than $25,000 to help eighty-five individuals and families, most of them immigrant trans women, seeking asylum in the United States. The fact that I could dedicate myself full-time to pastoring a community so deeply affected by the pandemic affirmed my decision to quit my secular job. I was born for this. My path to ministry has had many colors and shapes, just like my queer self. The lawyering, organizing, fundraising, and nonprofit management—all of it—has prepared me to be Pastor Rhina.

QUESTIONS FOR REFLECTION

1. How do you know you are living your life's purpose?
2. What experiences/people are shaping your vision?
3. What are the sources of your vocational inspiration?

Farm Church

Allen C. Brimer

On July 16, 2014, at 3:17 a.m. Central Daylight Time, the Rev. Ben Johnston-Krase awoke from a dream. He had dreamed that he received a call to serve a new church. On the first Sunday, he arrived at the church to discover there was no building. It was a farm—then he woke up.

That was the whole dream—embarrassingly short for all that has happened. Mercifully, Ben waited until morning to call the only farmer/pastor he knew: me. I had left a career in farming to enter seminary some fifteen years prior. Both of us had since spent our post-seminary careers as pastors in tall-steeple, downtown Presbyterian churches, but we and our families were ready for a change. This dream set into motion the beginnings of what became Farm Church: a congregation that meets on a farm and leverages the resources of the farm to address food insecurity in Durham, North Carolina.

We agreed early on that Ben would serve as the pastor, and I would serve as the farmer/administrator. Ben's charism is attractive, creative, improvisational. I am a manager, process-oriented, and connectional. We hit the ground running like two husbands and fathers who did not know where their next paycheck was going to come from, because we didn't. We had to hustle in a way that being the salaried pastor of a comfortable church never challenges you to do. We met with anyone who would listen to us and drank endless cups of coffee regaling the dream: the move of two families halfway across the country to a town where they did not know anyone, and the imagination of a congregation that would meet on a farm. We wrote letters to everyone we had ever met asking for financial support. Money began to show up. We told countless people in Durham about the church. People would say, "I've got ten acres." or "I've got thirty acres—do this at my place!" Land was raining out of the sky like manna.

From the beginning Ben worked full-time, and I worked quarter-time because that was what we could afford. We also understood that building up the congregation's "membership" required the bulk of the attention at the beginning. So, I started looking for a full-time job and would work at Farm Church "on the side." (P.S.: there is no "on the side" in a church start-up. You're either all in—paid or not—or your church is not starting up.) Nothing about serving the church in a well-established denomination—like the PC(USA) or UMC, etc.—prepares a pastor to search for a job outside of the church. I was a fish out of water and really struggled to find employment. Those first months were very difficult. Eventually (long, long story aside), I partnered with a local home inspector who was about to retire and wanted to pass his business on to someone. He would train me up, and then the business would be mine in a year. So, I went to school for three months, took a grueling state licensure exam, and started belly crawling through crawlspaces and attics. Simultaneously, I was approached by a community college to be an adjunct faculty member and teach a World Religions course online. Providentially, three jobs converged to make a modest income. The things you do to follow your calling—the things God does to get you to follow your calling!

We moved to Durham in August 2015, and Farm Church opened its doors on May 1, 2016, with great support and curiosity. Every week, a few more people would wander in. We struck up a partnership with an inner-city gardening program in a gritty, complicated neighborhood. It had a great building with a roof in case of rain and plenty of places for us to put our hands in the soil. A little bluegrass band spontaneously combusted right there in our midst and led music every week. We secured a one-quarter-acre garden in an adjacent downtown neighborhood on an empty lot through a partnership with a family that had always wanted to see it become a garden. We were growing compost and vegetables and delivering those vegetables to local pantries. People were showing up and learning new skills and finding the Holy Spirit of Christ in the surprising smorgasbord of metaphors embedded in the garden. These folks were spiritually hungry. They were also institutionally suspicious, but a church like this—in a garden, with no building or cross or stained glass or dogmatic Apostles' Creed—was not threatening. It did what it said it would do. It met in a garden and leveraged the resources of the garden to address food insecurity. It bore fruit worthy of its calling. It was the right amount of simple, active, institutionally unincumbered, educational, change-making and spiritually nourishing all in one with dirt under your fingernails.

Things were going well. We were making partnerships. Parishioners were committing and investing. Funding was secure. We were telling the Farm Church story to wider audiences across the country. People were paying attention. God was moving!

Then, in November 2017, Ben was diagnosed with stage-four lung cancer. Everything went sideways. Ben was now faced with a new calling: cancer patient. Forty-seven years old. Never a smoker. The father of three daughters under age fourteen. After a year of prayer and a herculean fundraising campaign to support him and his family, Ben followed his calling by going on medical disability in November 2018 and left Farm Church.[1]

All eyes then turned to me. I honestly cannot even remember if I prayed for guidance about what to do. We had sacrificed so much, had taken so many risks, people had given so much—time, money, effort, prayer, encouragement. I was working and grinding so hard to keep this thing going that I don't even think I paused to wonder what my calling was now. I felt enormous responsibility to keep the "dream" alive, to ensure that all of this was not for nothing. So, by grace or force of will or lack of better options, the church's fledgling leadership team hired me to be both the pastor and the farmer of Farm Church.

I immediately got to work on training others to share in the leadership of Farm Church. We wrote a constitution—because institutionally suspicious believers do not adopt denominational standards! We solidified our bylaws and nonprofit status and incorporation status. We put financial policies in place and hired an accountant. We elected a council of stewards to serve as the board. We got to work on getting everything out of my cofounder's brain onto paper and into the hearts and minds of the congregation so that we could all carry the ministry together.

Just as we were really beginning to build momentum, the COVID-19 pandemic hit. Farm Church, like the wide world, came to a halt. However, we quickly realized that Farm Church was perfectly positioned to thrive. We met outside already. We were not dependent on a building. We were delivering fresh, local produce to people in need who were now *really* in need. When everyone else stopped, we sped up. In 2020, Farm Church grew and delivered more produce and had more volunteer hours than it ever had previously. The pandemic paralyzed many churches, but it created the perfect opportunity for Farm Church to thrive and be its best!

By May 2021, I was tired. It was becoming clear that my calling to Farm Church was coming to a close. Perhaps I had fulfilled everything that God had called me to do. For much of my time at Farm Church, I was not sure what my calling was. I just followed my instincts and my prayers. I did managerial things because—I'm a manager, a high and necessary calling. I managed the farm. I managed to train the congregation. I managed the funding. I also preached and served sacraments and provided pastoral care, but what stands out is the management. It is only in retrospect and having stepped clear of all that good and grinding work that I can now begin to understand what God was doing through me. I was called to build a foundation: guidelines, stability, shared vision, know-how, spiritual depth, partnerships, and service—that would allow God to build the next phase of Farm Church.

I have always seen far-reaching possibilities for Farm Church: food-resilience education, mobile farmer's markets in low-income neighborhoods, farm-to-table programs in prisons, pick-your-own gardens at public bus stops, Sunday School in a chicken house—the list is very long. But none of these things—as invigorating as they are—was my calling. Like Moses, neither Ben nor I got to lead Farm Church to the "promised land," that is, to all that we imagined. I am resistant to the understanding that Moses was being punished when he was not "allowed" to enter the Promised Land. Perhaps it felt like a punishment. I lean instead to the possibility that Moses had simply fulfilled his calling as a foundation builder, and it was now time for others to lead the next phase of all that God is building.

QUESTIONS FOR REFLECTION

1. How can you know what your calling really is?
2. What are you willing to do sacrificially to follow your calling?
3. What do you recognize as God's help so far in following your call?

Introducing Bivocational Ministry

Darryl W. Stephens

"Pick up your nets!"

This is the heartfelt advice I would like to offer all who feel called to ministry—bivocational or otherwise. Use the gifts and skills you already have.

Too often, pastors and those they serve perpetuate the mistaken idea that being in ministry requires abandoning our practical skills and careers. Jesus's call to the first disciples at the Sea of Galilee has caused no end of confusion for the church. "'Follow me,'" he commanded. "Immediately they left their nets and followed him" (Matt. 4:19–20). Centuries of interpretation have spiritualized this simple passage to our detriment, as if it would have been sinful for Peter and Andrew to fish in the sea anytime thereafter. (If only the church and its leaders took Matthew 19:21 as seriously!) Yet, the resurrected Jesus also commanded Peter—three times no less!—to feed and tend his sheep (John 21:15–17). This conversation occurred shortly after Jesus instructed Peter to cast his net to the other side of the boat to haul in his catch. His skill with a net was needed for post-resurrection ministry. The same is true of the skills and gifts each of us has been blessed with.

Fish and nets. These images serve to remind us of both task and tools, feeding and fishing. Fish meet our basic, bodily need for sustenance. During the miraculous feeding of thousands, Jesus multiplied the fish that the people provided (Matt. 14:17; 15:34). The people did not come empty handed. They offered themselves and what little they had. Nets are the means for bringing what we have to the feast. Giving thanks and blessing what they offered, Jesus returned the fish and loaves to the crowd, and it was more than enough to feed them.

Intentional bivocational ministry reflects the abundance of Jesus's miracle of provision. In bivocational ministry, we bring what skills and resources we have in order to feed Christ's sheep. We pick up our nets, bringing our whole lives to ministry. But, you might ask, what exactly is bivocational ministry?

Generally, the term "bivocational" describes the work life of a pastor who also holds another job, although the form of ministry is limited to neither pastoral ministry nor a congregation.[1] Bivocational ministers, whatever their context and calling, are representative ministers. They are called by God and affirmed by the church. They may be lay or clergy, paid or volunteer. They are usually licensed, consecrated, ordained, or authorized in some way to represent the church and to provide leadership in a variety of settings, including congregations.

For many people accustomed to fully funded pastors, bivocationality is saddled with stigma. Questions arise and assumptions abound, spoken or unspoken. There is collective shame: "Our congregation can only afford a part-time pastor—we must be a dying church." There is blame: "If that preacher were better educated, he could find a full-time pastorate." There are assumptions: "She must not be a very effective pastor, or she would not need another job." There is judgment: "If they were fully committed to the ministry, they would not continue their secular career." These misperceptions need not be the case.

Multivocational ministry, as the term implies, is a recognition that many ministerial leaders piece together more than two employments as a response to God's call on their lives. In fact, each of us embodies a rich "multiplicity" of gifts and functions, recognition of which "helps us understand how we are able to occupy many roles simultaneously."[2] The idea of vocation gives divine purpose to this multiplicity. Frederick Buechner offered a poetic understanding of vocation, connecting the minister's passion with the needs of others: "The place God calls you to is the place where your deep gladness and the world's deep hunger meet."[3] Where your skills and passions can be used to tend and feed Christ's sheep—that is your place of ministry, and there may be more than one place.

The practice of holding multiple jobs, paid or unpaid, is actually quite common, although it does have its challenges. In some traditions, such as the Black church, or in immigrant communities, partially funded or unpaid ministry is the norm. Across all traditions, women and others who have historically been restricted to positions of servitude may become bivocational by default, finding fewer opportunities for fully funded ministry available to them.[4] Systemic barriers, such as patriarchy, classism, and racism, compound the difficulties inherent to bivocationality. Balance, integration, and time management are requisite to the success of bivocational ministers.

Various expressions of bivocational or multivocational ministry go by many different names. Tentmaking, marketplace, and covocational ministry are strategic ways to engage in pastoral ministry in adverse contexts such as non-Christian cultures, extreme secularization, political repression, or antagonism to Christianity or other forms of organized religion.

Tentmaking is a missional strategy for postmodern church planters. Following the footsteps of Paul, some pastors work a day job while organizing evening prayers groups and Bible studies. Once these groups coalesce into a worshipping congregation, they can become the sponsors of another church plant, and the process repeats itself. In this model, the tentmaking pastor may work themselves into a full-time ministry position, move on to plant another church, or establish a collaborative ministry with lay leaders, allowing the pastor to remain bivocational.

Marketplace ministry is a form of tentmaking emphasizing the evangelistic potential of working side by side with potential congregants. When the pastor joins the labor pool, sets up shop, or engages in the world of commerce, they find connection and build relationships with people of all walks of life in the community. Through marketplace ministry, the pastor shares the everyday experiences and material concerns of their flock.

Covocational ministry is similar to marketplace ministry, with one major difference: the secular job is itself the intended site of pastoral ministry. The factory worker, coffee shop barista, and firefighter engage in ministry in these work settings without the intention of establishing a congregation. The job is no longer a means to an end but the end itself. The workplace becomes a site of a nontraditional pastorate.

The diaconate, sometimes expressed bivocationally, expands ministry beyond the pastoral role by exemplifying the ministry of all Christians. Diakonia is the ministry of service to which all the baptized are called; the ordained form of diakonia is the diaconate, or deacon in some traditions.[5] Deacons lead the laity in service to the world through calls to specialized forms of ministry, often through the helping professions, such as social work, teaching, and health care. A deacon claims their "secular" profession as a ministry with its own integrity; it is neither a means of founding a congregation nor a covert form of pastoral ministry. Many deacons combine a primary ministry calling outside the church with a call to lead the laity into the world in ministry.

Part-time ministry is perhaps the most common and least accurate description of bivocationality. The concept of "part-time" is derived from federal or state laws governing worker rights and employer responsibilities. In the United States, thirty hours per week is considered "full-time" and more than forty hours per week is considered "overtime." However, a difference of ten hours a week is hardly the most important factor in describing one's exercise of divine calling!

The truth is, all ministry is full-time, even though some jobs in ministry are only partially compensated or even volunteer. Ministry is a public vocation, an identity, and seen through the lens of baptism, there is never a time when one is "off the clock" as a Christian.

Bivocationality is expressed through many different configurations of remuneration and time commitment, going by labels such as dual career, nonstipendiary, worker-priest, voluntary, and self-sustaining ministry. Is the calling to be a parent or guardian or to be a caregiver for another person any less valued because one also holds a paid job? Is one's role as a community volunteer any less impactful because one is not paid in that capacity? We must shed the mentality of capitalism if we are to see the wondrous diversity of ministry opportunities in our midst.

Rooted in the priesthood of all believers, bivocationality overturns systems of hierarchy, prestige, and entitlement. Corporately, "the members of the body that seem to be weaker are indispensable" (1 Cor. 12:22). The fully funded pastor cannot say to the nonstipendiary clergy that "the church has no need of you" any more than the eye can say to the hand, "I have no need of you" (1 Cor. 12:21). Living into bivocationality means honoring the ministry of laypersons just as much as the ministry of the ordained clergy. This is not to say that there should be no distinction between lay and clergy, "For if the whole body were an eye, where would the hearing be?" (1 Cor. 12:17). However, distinctions should not manifest in relative value judgments. A bivocational mindset respects the partially funded pastor as much or even more than the fully compensated pastor.

Intentional bivocationality is a theological mindset with material implications for how we live and work together during these post-resurrection, in-between times. Jesus implored Peter to feed and tend his flock until his return. If we are to respond with Peter, we must use all our gifts and resources as we minister to and with each other. Whatever your net, whatever your skill, offer it in ministry! With Jesus's blessing, it will prove an abundance in the task of tending and feeding his sheep. We must pick up our nets, make tents, and wait tables—and do so with an assurance of vocation, divine calling. It will be more than enough for the task.

QUESTIONS FOR REFLECTION

1. Pick up your nets. What skills, experiences, and life-wisdom do you bring to the practice of ministry to enhance the formation and education expected in seminary? Imagine ways in which these skills could contribute to ministry within and beyond congregational settings, perhaps through multiple employments.
2. Feed Christ's sheep. Who are you called to serve? Which neighborhoods, communities, and brokenness are you uniquely suited to tend as a ministerial leader? Consider, from a missional perspective, a variety

of jobs in the community that would allow you to build relationships with those persons you are called to serve.
3. Remember your baptism. We are each called into ministry through baptism and discover our vocation(s) though passionate engagement in the world. What part of God's work renews your soul and draws you in? Tap into your passions to rediscover (again and again) the joy you experience loving God and neighbor.

RECOMMENDED READINGS

Bickers, Dennis. *The Art and Practice of Bivocational Ministry: A Pastor's Guide*. Kansas City, MO: Beacon Hill, 2013.

Edington, Mark D. W. *Bivocational: Returning to the Roots of Ministry*. New York: Church Publishing, 2018. http://www.bivocational.church.

Lindner, Cynthia G. *Varieties of Gifts: Multiplicity and the Well-Lived Pastoral Life*. Lanham, MD: Rowman & Littlefield, 2016.

MacDonald, G. Jeffrey. *Part-Time is Plenty: Thriving without Full-Time Clergy*. Louisville: Westminster John Knox, 2020.

Stephens, Darryl W., ed. *Bivocational and Beyond: Educating for Thriving Multivocational Ministry*. Books @Atla Open Press, Scholarly Editions, Teaching Religion and Theology series, 2022.

Thank God for Friends

Scott Cameron

In 2005, I finally finished my formal medical training. At the time, I was thirty-five years old, married, and had three young children. I was hired as a NICU physician in my hometown. In the months that followed, I purchased a new truck, a new home, and even a vacation home. I was a nominal Christian who inconsistently attended Sunday worship out of guilt (I was baptized and confirmed in the United Methodist Church). If pressed, I would've told you that I was really only interested in maintaining a church affiliation because of daycare needs.

In 2006, my life and my family's life began to change. The changes were undetectable at first, but they ultimately became swift and dramatic. Today, in 2022, I am still married with three children. I still work in the NICU in my hometown. But I am also a Presbyterian chaplain living with my family in an intentional community of young adults with intellectual and developmental disabilities (I/DD) and health-care professional students. I am paid by the hospital as a physician, and I volunteer as a chaplain. The truck, as well as the primary and secondary homes, have all been sold. They have been replaced by weekly community meals, evening prayer, and randomly themed celebrations. If someone had approached me in 2005 and predicted this life trajectory for my family and me, I would have responded with a VERY hearty laugh of disbelief.

In 2006, my wife and I attended a spiritual weekend retreat led by a local car dealership owner "turned" Presbyterian pastor. At the time, I found his story confusing but mysteriously convicting. Attending church seemed different after that weekend. It was more a time of faith and spiritual exploration than of being a responsible parent. This season of seeking was followed by months-long medical mission trips to Kenya accompanied by my family.

On the 2010 mission trip, I became critically ill. I had had a long history of acute bouts of abdominal distention that always resolved within a few hours. An extensive medical workup over several years had been largely negative.

Ironically, under the care of a general surgeon in the small, rural, mission hospital in Africa that I had traveled to serve, I finally received the definitive cure for a diagnosis that had eluded many specialists in the United States. After major abdominal surgery, including having two feet of my colon resected, I awakened to cows mooing and chickens clucking. By God's grace, I made a full recovery at Tenwek Hospital. However, one month later, as I resumed my work as a neonatologist at home, I was dumbfounded by the discrepancy in the faith support my family and I had received during my health crisis in Africa and the faith support my colleagues and I were routinely offering the families here in the United States. I felt compelled to better understand the intersection of faith and medicine.

In 2013, I became a full-time seminarian and a part-time physician. Duke Divinity is where I met Matt Floding and the residents of Friendship House Durham, as well as the writings of Jean Vanier and the Apostle Paul. An email was circulated to all the incoming first-year divinity students that detailed a new living opportunity at the Friendship House. At my wife's request, I called the Friendship House director, Matt Floding, for details. What Matt described to me was foreign but intriguing. Friendship House is an intentional living community of young adults with I/DD and graduate students. The concept holds that the residents or "Friends" with disabilities grow in their independent and interdependent living skills, secure jobs, and participate fully in the life and ministry of the church. Meanwhile, the graduate students attend academic classes while also being formed in this residential opportunity with their roommates with disabilities. Specifically, in the seminarian context, students gain a deeper appreciation for all people and develop a practical understanding of how to integrate people with disabilities into the church. I remained a bit wary, but I signed on.

After settling into Friendship House, I attended a local, daytime, disability ministry celebration. What I experienced is almost indescribable. Everyone was dancing, singing, hugging, and eating. They were loving on each other. Their joy was irresistible—it was contagious. Moreover, it was disarming. There was no need for pretense; I could be myself. It was unexpected. There I met the other Friendship House residents, including one of my new housemates, Alex. Immediately from the time of our introduction, I knew from his outward appearance that Alex had Trisomy 21 or Down Syndrome. As a NICU physician who routinely cares for infants with Down Syndrome and counsels their parents regarding long-term outcomes, I felt my usual sense of misgiving and sympathy for someone with a "poor outcome." Our initial conversation was brief and awkward, mostly because of my biased assumptions.

A few days later, Alex and I met again on the campus bus. Alex was sitting in the front of the tandem bus, which pivots in the center as it rounds a turn. He spotted me sitting near the part of the bus that actually pivots. Lifting his arm to wave and calling out my name, he walked back to where I was sitting and sat down beside me. Feeling self-conscious from all the attention he had garnered in his move, I asked how his day had gone. He relayed that he was returning home from his job at the Divinity School library where he shelves books. Eyeing how the floor in front us swiveled as the bus turned, Alex stood up and moved to the center of the swiveling floor and began to "surf" with each turn. His initial giggle evolved into a raucous laugh. While I was suppressing my urge to ask Alex to sit down and not create a greater spectacle than he already had, the bus started on the straightaway and the surfing stopped. Alex returned to his seat beside me. I was temporarily relieved. Then abruptly, Alex began to bury his head in my chest while laughing hysterically. Red-faced, I unconsciously surveyed the facial expressions of the bus riders from front to back. The "normal" bus riders were staring at Alex and now me with tired, blank faces. Strangely, I felt a deep sense of joy in Alex's behavior. My previous sense of misgiving and sympathy was now redirected to all the seemingly joyless "normal" bus riders. Before getting off the bus Alex said to me, "I am excited you are living at Friendship House. We will become good friends." We had only just met, but Alex had already begun to shatter my medical and social lens for individuals living with I/DD.

Friendship House Durham profoundly shaped my call. As a physician, I am tempted to refer to this intentional living community as a living laboratory that complemented my academic work. But the truth is, the residents, both the Friends and the students, deeply altered my value system. In the book *Living Gently in a Violent World: The Prophetic Witness of Weakness*, Jean Vanier, the founder of the L'Arche communities, writes, "Jesus came to change a world in which those at the top have privilege, power, prestige and money while those at the bottom are seen as useless. Jesus came to create a body."[1] Vanier is rewriting the letter that Paul wrote to the Corinthians in the first century. Paul presents a radical position of urging more privileged members of the community to respect and value the indispensable contributions of those members who seem to be weak. Paul points out that the apparent weakness of the subordinate class has no relationship to their real value and necessity to the body. As Vanier points out, this concept is at the heart of our faith: this is what it means to be the church. Although separated by two thousand years, both the Apostle Paul and Jean Vanier are calling for those we hide away, those deemed dispensable, to be placed front and center. This is the *reality* of Christ's love for the body, the entire body, the church. To get there, we've got to rely on the Holy Spirit. As Jeff McSwain proclaims in *Movements of Grace*, "Only the Spirit can open our eyes to [this truth] . . . and until we come to a saving knowledge of this truth, we will live in disorientation."[2]

The term *Christian* carries heavy baggage these days. But as someone who has been trying to follow Jesus since 2006, the guideposts have been more than Scripture. They have been more than creeds, confessions, and polity. For me, they have been a mixture of new relationships formed and old ones remade as my hometown community adapted the Friendship House model to Friends living with health-care professional students. While my journey has certainly been disappointing at times, it has been revelatory at others. But the joy, the privilege, is being with my Friends and pressing forward to the next surprise.

QUESTIONS FOR REFLECTION

1. Bivocational pastors are especially beholden to this truth: if things are going really well at work, then things are at risk on the home front; and the converse. Time and money are finite resources. What are the non-negotiables that will allow you to not only maintain the status quo but also flourish in each setting?
2. Your nonprofit will have a mission statement. One of the Friendship House supporters advised me, "Do not despair. Keep telling the story of Friendship House because you will often be surprised by those who do and those who do not respond to the vision." Does your nonprofit have a mission/vision statement that you truly believe, that is, a narrative that you can repeatedly share with others?
3. Nonprofits are predominately faith-based or secular. They routinely partner with other faith-based and secular groups. What are the potential pros and cons of working for and partnering with faith-based and secular nonprofits?

Jarena's Daughter

Faye Taylor

I recently sat in on a panel of women in ministry discussing the life and ministry of the Reverend Jarena Lee, the first woman licensed to preach in the African Methodist Episcopal (AME) Church. As women ordained in the AME Church, we affectionately call ourselves *Jarena's Daughters*.

As a young woman attending church, it never entered my consciousness that I would be anything other than a lay person who loved God, loved worship, and loved working as part of ministries in the church. I was raised in the Baptist tradition in the southern part of our country where there was no provision for women in ordained ministry. I was content with being a lay leader.

That contentment stayed with me through my young adult years and well into my early forties. By then I had relocated to New York City and become a part of the AME Church. It was in the AME Church where I saw, for the first time, ordained women in leadership as pastors and assistant pastors. Still, there was no tug at my heart to be more than someone who volunteered easily for anything that needed to be accomplished as a lay person.

I believed I would live out my life being a good "church member," lending my organizational skills to the Christian education ministry. However, that began to change. I had no dramatic call experience. My call was subtle—a "knowing" that I could not ignore. The more involved I was with ministry opportunities, the less satisfied I felt. So, I increased my involvement, thinking I needed to do more to feel satisfaction.

Finally, I agreed to attend a seminar facilitated by my pastor, whom I respected deeply, along with his wife, the assistant pastor. These seminars were offered periodically for anyone desiring direction and guidance on being in God's will. During that seminar, the puzzle pieces came together, revealing a picture I was not expecting. I left the seminar, sat in my car, and cried, overwhelmed by the realization that God was summoning me to ordained ministry.

Long ago, I began a regular practice of journaling my thoughts. After that seminar, I filled pages and pages, pouring out my doubts, fears, and misgivings about the path that lay ahead. Part of my trepidation had to do with my denominational requirement to attend seminary and attend the denomination's training institute. After all, I was married, a stepmother, a grandmother, employed full-time, and in my mid-forties. Going back to school was not a part of my career path. Yet, I knew if I were to fulfill God's plan for me, I would have to do it. I made a bargain with God: If I answered this call and enrolled in seminary, I would expect God to make sure that I would do it well. I did not want to be mediocre! Such arrogance! It makes me smile when I reflect on it now.

Off I went to seminary, trepidation and all. It was while in school at New Brunswick Theological Seminary that I discovered my gifts for ministry and found a community that was supportive and nurturing. I discovered I had a voice that God could use in God's kingdom.

I worked full-time and attended classes in the evening. I began at a very slow pace, thinking I would never really complete this ninety-six-credit master of divinity degree. Nor did I think when I finally did graduate that I would enter pastoral ministry. I would concentrate on Christian education, that is, until I was assigned to my supervised ministry site (what is now known as field education).

My site was in a small congregation whose pastor was female, and she quickly became a mentor. As I worked through the goals of my covenant, I experienced such joy in working in a parish. My home church had a membership of four thousand. My field education site had a membership of fewer than fifty. Yet, it was the connection that I made with the members, on an intimate level, that opened me up to pastoral ministry. The times of theological reflection with my supervisor were transformative. She was not just an able mentor, but she was a woman in ministry, in leadership in her denomination, and comfortable with who she was. Under her supervision, I gained a new perspective on parish ministry and saw it as a possibility in my future.

When I reflect on that time, I realize that all God desired was a willingness on my part to walk in the path designed for me. When I said "yes" to parish ministry, God provided the opportunity. Within a month of graduation from seminary and receiving my ordination as an itinerant elder in the AME Church, I was appointed to pastor a congregation in upstate New York while I still lived and worked full-time in New York City. It is a four-hour round-trip commute to the church, but is the greatest joy of my life to serve the members of St. Mark's Chapel AME Church.

I was working full-time and serving the members of St. Mark's when God impressed upon me to return to school in a doctor of ministry program in pastoral care and counseling. God does have a sense of humor! How, I asked, am I going to add one more thing to my already stretched life? Not to mention that the school to which I applied and was accepted was in Madison, New Jersey, an hour away from my home and job. Something had to change.

During my time of prayer and reflection, I asked God what I could eliminate. The answer was my job! It took a tremendous leap of faith to leave a job that I loved and held for twenty-four years. So, about midway through my doctoral program, I left my job to continue the program while serving my congregation. Still needing some income, I answered an ad posted by my previous seminary, New Brunswick, for a part-time recruiter for students. That position gave me the opportunity to assist prospective students in discerning call and preparing for theological education.

Upon graduation from my doctoral program and through a series of events that made it possible, I accepted the position of director of field education for New Brunswick Seminary. That was seven years ago.

My journey has taken me from the pew to the pulpit to the academy. Additionally, I now oversee several churches in my denomination. There is an intersectionality in my calling. The privilege of traveling alongside students in their preparation for ministry has enriched my life. Serving a church keeps me in touch with congregational care and concerns. My administrative and organization skills provide the tools for overseeing my churches.

When I reflect on where I am now, I am grateful for my journey and look forward to what is to come. I am Jarena's daughter, and her legacy lives on in me and other women who answer the call. God does make the way.

QUESTIONS FOR REFLECTION

1. God called Samuel's name several times before Eli helped him to understand it was the voice of God. Who might be your Eli? How have you discerned God's voice?
2. What may have been your reluctance to heed God's call to ordained ministry?
3. How do you understand the intersectionality of your ministry call with the other areas of your life?

Cobbling a Mosaic in Vocation

Rebecca Jeney Park-Hearn

Bivocation is an apt term and descriptive of the vocational trajectory I have carved out since graduating from seminary almost two decades ago. Since then, ministry has usually involved more than one setting, more than one community, and the invitation to access different aspects of my identity to say "yes" to God's invitation to minister to people and communities.

I work in two different ministry settings, one a Jesuit university and the other an ethnic local church. Currently, I am the director of contextual education and a core faculty member in the School of Theology and Ministry at Seattle University (SU), where I also teach classes in the Couples and Family Therapy Program. Located in a thriving urban environment, SU provides ample opportunity for students to envision and practice their professional identities as aspiring therapists, ministers, chaplains, and community organizers. As a teacher and administrator, my aim is to support students' efforts to interpret their contexts, with their senses open to justice and compassion.

A Japanese American local church in Seattle is another ministry context where I live out my vocation. Our church's 110+ year history includes ministry to, and with, generations of Japanese Americans, many who endured the persecution and racial profiling of Executive Order 9066, issued by Franklin D. Roosevelt in 1942, relocating thousands of Issei (first generation) and Nisei (second generation) Japanese American citizens on the west coast to concentration camps further inland. As congregational care pastor, I oversee pastoral care efforts aimed at supporting senior members living into the challenges and opportunities that accompany the aging process.

I recall my first awareness of vocation when I was in college and involved in a parachurch ministry. Many of us, being away from home for the first time, found comfort in our weekly gatherings where we worshipped and supported one another's attempts to figure out newfound autonomy and independence. It was in this ministry setting that I experienced a stirring in my spirit to minister to people. Having been raised in a pastor's family, my sense of identity was already primed toward a lifestyle and rhythm that was responsive to the physical, spiritual, and psychological needs of people. My parents immigrated to the United States in 1968, when my father enrolled in seminary to live into his vocation. It was in the Korean American immigrant churches he pastored that I witnessed firsthand families like ours navigating language barriers, class inequity, and other societal pressures that obstructed pathways to job security, educational opportunities, and life beyond surviving.

Fast forward through college, three different seminaries, and important formative educational experiences (e.g., field education, chaplaincy, pastoral psychotherapy), where I learned about just, responsible, theologically informed, and culturally attuned pastoral care and ministry. The particularities of Korean American culture in the local church context set into motion and also fueled my compassion for families facing the challenges of immigration, acculturation, discrimination, mental illness, addictions, and class disparity, while at the same time shaped how I understood a personal sense of vocation.

Because I am a second-generation Korean American woman, my worldview informed how I envisioned myself living out vocation and what I thought was possible and "right." By the time I got to seminary, the theological assumptions I held directed me toward a seminary quandary: how can I graduate with a master of divinity degree without taking a preaching class? I believed that women were relegated to nontraditional ministry roles that precluded ordained positions reserved for male preachers. Needless to say, and despite seminary classes, this assumption about gender persisted and I sought different paths to live out my vocation. How, as a woman, could I minister and address systemic and structural inequities? How, as a woman, was I to find meaningful employment that paid a living wage and where I could live into my vocation? At the time, I wasn't bothered that my vocational discernment was circuitous and required that I try on many ministry hats to find *the* correct fit. It didn't occur to me then that my limited and culture-specific views about women in ministry steered me away from a more direct ministry path. I also didn't know that each year spent exploring was another year I didn't have to establish myself and to have the stability I wanted to settle down and to start a family. I have done some serious soul searching about what I have lost, and the costs incurred because I am a woman called to ministry.

Questions that stemmed from the intersection of gender and ministry set me on a course to explore different paths. While I have doubted myself and my calling and have been frustrated in the quest for *the* "right" opportunity and in the "right" amount of time, this searching has afforded me the privilege of experiencing hospital chaplaincy, seminary administration, graduate theological education, pastoral counseling, and now, teaching and local church ministry on my circuitous route. Today, I'm convinced that my bivocational identity in the church as an ordained minister and in the academy are enlivened and have depth *because of* the numerous ministry paths I've traversed. Learning from different ministry settings, for example, supports my teaching and pastoring as I draw upon clinical work with former clients and hospital ministry experiences with individuals and families facing terminal diagnoses and the death of loved ones.

It was only after my father passed away that I heard about his amazement that in my twenties I was a hospital chaplain. I think he was intrigued that I could journey and connect with patients and families facing the hardships of health crises, illness, death, and loss. Like this, ministries on my circuitous path have been a series of invitations to dig deep and to draw upon courage I didn't know I had.

Looking back from the vantage point of today and a few years of life experience, I have a greater appreciation for all the particularities of my social location and identity—gender, ethnicity, and immigration, for instance, and how these have necessarily shaped the trajectory and expression of vocation. All these have required that I stretch my imagination and push myself to embody distinctive ways to live into vocation that have exceeded my expectations. The desire to minister, however, set in me by way of the Korean American immigrant church, has been the constant thread in my ministerial identity over the years.

I have been pleasantly surprised to learn that it's possible to experience and to frame vocation as fluid, dynamic, and evolving. Much like the opinion that there isn't *one* soul mate out there, I believe the same can be said about vocation. Perhaps it is that we can find fulfillment and meaning on varied roads because there is more than one way to respond purposefully to the needs of the world. This is a breath of fresh air! Multiple experiences combine into a mosaic of ministry, where different colors and patterns touch upon, highlight, and accentuate the features of the entire work of the art of vocation.

Living into varied expressions of vocation has made bivocational ministry possible for me. It is deeply gratifying and also demands time and considerable emotional investment. Ministering to more than one community requires the engagement of context-specific skills and practices that involve body, mind, and spirit. The arc of my vocational life has been nontraditional, and I have piecemealed my version of living into vocation. Each ministry and community with whom I have learned coalesce into a solid repository of experience and wisdom that will continue to nurture the next steps of my journey. While I don't know how my vocational path will continue to unfold, I trust that the flow of vocation and a community's call will continue to find one other.

QUESTIONS FOR REFLECTION

1. In what ways does your identity and social location show up in your vocational discernment?
2. What memories do you connect with your vocational formation journey?

Conclusion

Matthew Floding and Kristina Lizardy-Hajbi

Our hope is that you have seen glimpses of your own story reflected in some of these narratives, as well as encouraging possibilities for ministry that God might be nudging you to pursue. In other words, we pray that *Explore* has sparked your theological imagination!

Some of the memoirs focused on individual paths to current vocational calls, and others spent more time detailing the joys and challenges of those calls. A variety of traditions were represented by our contributors: African Methodist Episcopal, Catholic, Baptist, Christian Church (Disciples of Christ), Episcopalian, Lutheran, Mennonite, Methodist, Presbyterian, Reformed, and United Church of Christ. They received their MDivs from a range of seminaries and theological schools across the United States. Some have just begun their ministry work, and others are seasoned ministers. Young adults, middlers, and retirees shared their stories. We worked to center the voices of women, LGBTQI+ individuals, and people of color, especially Black and Brown voices, as part of our commitments to racial justice.

And yet, these stories represent only a small fraction of the deep and wide array of traditions, racial and ethnic identities, generations, and backgrounds represented in ministry today, much less those who are enrolled in seminary today. Moreover, there are ministry roles and settings beyond the scope of this text (and beyond the scope of our imaginations) that cry out for the creation of new stories of call and purpose. In the selection of only three memoirs for such broad areas of ministry (also knowing that some narratives could have been situated in multiple ministry areas within this book), we knew that we were just skimming the surface of a very rich, deep well. Any one of these ministry areas alone could fill volumes!

With the ever-increasing diversity of students comes the reshaping of ministry for new times and places. Regardless of where you are on the discernment journey on which all of us are traveling, may you be ever attentive to the Spirit-breathed stirrings within you and the communities around you in order to bring forth the gifts of service that only *you* can embody in the world.

Notes

INTRODUCTION

1. According to the ATS 2017 Workforce Mapping Survey, "While 41% of students served in fairly easy-to-categorize ministry roles within congregations, the remaining 59% served in a wide array of ministry settings with very diverse responsibilities." Source: Jo Ann Deasy, "Where Are Graduates Serving? New Insights from the Educational Models Alums Workforce Survey," *Colloquy Online*, April 2018, 2.

1. A COMMUNITY SAID YES

1. *Evangelical Lutheran Worship* (Minneapolis: Augsburg Fortress, 2006), 228.
2. Matt Bloom, *Flourishing in Ministry: How to Cultivate Clergy Well-Being* (Lanham, MD: Rowman & Littlefield, 2019).
3. Bloom, *Flourishing in Ministry*, 103.
4. Bloom, *Flourishing in Ministry*, 56.
5. Bloom, *Flourishing in Ministry*, 57.
6. Bloom, *Flourishing in Ministry*, 57.
7. Parker J. Palmer, *Let Your Life Speak: Listening for the Voice of Vocation* (San Francisco: Jossey-Bass, 2000), 9.

2. CALLINGS SHAPED BY PURPOSE

1. Stephen Lewis, Matthew Wesley Williams, and Dori Grinenko Baker, *Another Way: Living and Leading Change on Purpose* (Saint Louis: Chalice Press, 2020), 85.
2. Lewis, Williams, and Baker, *Another Way*, 83.
3. Loida I. Martell, "My GPS Does Not Work in Puerto Rico (2011)," in *The Wiley Blackwell Reader in Practical Theology*, ed. Bonnie J. Miller-McLemore (Hoboken, NJ: Wiley, 2019), 73.

3. WHAT ARE PASTORS FOR?

1. Sorry, attempting to beg out of the ministerial vocation by pleading, "I'm not the best person in the world," or "I've got these personal problems," or "I'm just not _____ [fill in the blank]" won't work. Read some of the many vocation stories in scripture and you will find that God is a sucker for losers when it comes to summoning people to do God's work. Known only to God are the reasons why God summons none-too-talented, untrained, often inept people like us to not only be disciples but also lead disciples.

2. The external, divine authorization that's at the heart of the pastoral vocation can be a source of great freedom and empowerment for pastors. When somebody says to you, "You're not the best preacher we've ever heard," or "You have the wrong personality to be a pastor," you can retort, "Take it up with the Lord. My being a pastor was God's idea of a good time, not mine."

3. Choosing you doesn't mean that God has chosen you for special blessing and others are rejected. It just means that you have been chosen for a role, a function, a task, a special service, not a higher status. God blesses others through you so that they may be a blessing to the world. As Jesus told his disciples, "You didn't choose me, I chose you." Why? "So that you go and bear fruit" (John 15:16).

6. A CALLING WORTHY OF MY LIFE

1. Frederick Buechner, *The Clown in the Belfry: Writings on Faith and Fiction* (San Francisco: HarperSanFrancisco, 1992), 96–97.

2. "'The Best Life': Eugene Peterson on Pastoral Ministry," interview by David Wood, *Christian Century*, March 13, 2002, https://www.christiancentury.org/article/2002-03/best-life.

3. C. S. Lewis, *The Problem of Pain* (1940; repr., San Francisco: HarperSanFrancisco, 2001), 91.

7. CHAPLAINCY: MINISTRY THAT FERMENTS AND SEASONS

1. Judith V. Jordan, *Relational-Cultural Therapy* (Washington, DC: American Psychological Association, 2017), 51.

2. Jordan, *Relational-Cultural Therapy*, 25.

3. "Absolutely Clear," *All Poetry*, accessed January 1, 2022, https://allpoetry.com/Absolutely-Clear.

10. A CALL TO SERVE

1. Vashti Murphy McKenzie, *Not Without a Struggle: Leadership Development for African American Women in Ministry* (Cleveland: Pilgrim Press, 1996).
2. Elise M. Edwards, "'Do the Work Your Soul Must Have': In Remembrance of Rev. Dr. Katie Geneva Cannon," August 19, 2018, https://feminismandreligion.com/2018/08/19/do-the-work-your-soul-must-have-in-remembrance-of-rev-dr-katie-geneva-cannon-by-elise-m-edwards/.

11. A CALLING TO THE ACADEMY

1. Yvonne Delk, "God's Yes Was Louder than My No," in *The Irresistible Urge to Preach: A Collection of African American "Call" Stories*, ed. William H. Meyers (Eugene, OR: Wipf and Stock, 1991), 92.

15. PARTICIPATING IN GOD'S WIDE WELCOME: THE MINISTRY OF CAMPS, CONFERENCE, AND RETREAT CENTERS

1. See the work of Retreat Center Collaboration, a network of conference and retreat center leaders committed to racial equity initiatives, land legacies, and other forms of social justice: https://www.retreatcentercollaboration.org.
2. For example, the Evangelical Lutheran Church in America (ELCA) has 135 camps and retreat centers spread across the United States and Puerto Rico. One hundred fifty similar centers affiliate with the Presbyterian Church (USA), and more than four hundred retreat centers identify as Roman Catholic.
3. Dorothy Bass, "Placing Christian Formation," Robert Jones Lectures, Austin Seminary, 2006.
4. Theresa Latini, "Leadership Formation in and as Retreat," Louisville Institute Pastoral Studies Project, 2020–2021.

16. IT STARTED WITH TREES

1. Wendell Berry, "Sabbath Poem (Untitled)," *This Day: Collected and New Sabbath Poems* (Berkeley: Counterpoint Press, 2014).
2. Frederick Buechner, *Wishful Thinking: A Theological ABC* (New York: Harper & Row, 1973), 95.

19. A CALLING TO CAMPUS

1. Annie Dillard, *The Writing Life* (New York: HarperCollins, 1989), 32.
2. The final line of Georges Bernanos's classic novel, *The Diary of a Country Priest* (Boston: DaCapo Press, 2001).
3. Gerhard Manley Hopkins, *The Poems of Gerhard Manley Hopkins*, ed. W. H. Gardner and N. H. Mackenzie, 4th ed. (Oxford: Oxford University Press, 1970), 66.

20. DOING CAMPUS MINISTRY LATINAMENTE

1. William Shakespeare, *Hamlet*, 1.3.78–82.

23. SO, YOU'RE THE BISHOP

1. Max De Pree, *Leadership Is an Art* (New York: Currency, 2004).

26. THE INWARD AND OUTWARD JOURNEY OF MINISTRY

1. Reinhold Neibuhr, *Moral Man and Immoral Society: A Study in Ethics and Politics* (New York: Charles Scribner's Sons, 1932).

27. THE COMMUNION TABLE AS VOCATIONAL PATHWAY IN NONPROFIT LEADERSHIP

1. See, for example, Marcus Hill, "The Food Desert: A Thing of the Past?," June 24, 2016, https://medium.com/@ForsythFood/the-food-desert-a-thing-of-the-past-f262254a8a9.

31. SPIRITUAL ENTREPRENEURSHIP

1. "Entrepreneur," Oxford Languages, accessed September 22, 2021, https://languages.oup.com/google-dictionary-en/.
2. United Nations, Department of Economic and Social Affairs, "The 17 Sustainable Development Goals," accessed January 3, 2022, https://sdgs.un.org/goals.
3. Victoria Finlay, ed., *The Zug Guidelines to Faith-Consistent Investing: Faith in Finance—What Do You Do with Your Wealth to Make a Better Planet?* (Bath, UK: The Alliance of Religions and Conservation, 2017), 5–6.

4. The National Jewish Center for Learning and Leadership (CLAL), the United Church of Canada's EDGE program, the Christian Church (Disciples of Christ) Social Entrepreneurship program, and Adese are among a number of religiously affiliated spiritual entrepreneur programs all launched in North America in the twenty-first century.

5. The twentieth-century term "intrapreneur"—an inside entrepreneur, or an entrepreneur within a large firm, who uses entrepreneurial skills to work on a special idea or a project—is perhaps a better way to describe my own professional experience.

6. John Burger, "What Is the Preferential Option for the Poor?," *Aleteia*, February 4, 2013.

32. A WAY OUT OF NO WAY

1. Emily Fairchild, "An Overview of Jewish Beliefs and Traditions for Counselors" (master's thesis, James Madison University, 2010), 90.

2. Monica A. Coleman, *Making a Way Out of No Way: A Womanist Theology* (Minneapolis: Fortress Press, 2008), 17.

3. Octavia E. Butler, *Parable of the Sower* (New York: Warner, 1993), 79.

4. See "Healing the Healers II: Domestic Violence," *Odyssey Impact*, accessed December 8, 2021, https://healingthehealers.org/series-2-domestic-violence/; "Healing the Healers III: Youth Mental Health," *Odyssey Impact*, accessed December 8, 2021, https://healingthehealers.org/series-3-youth-mental-health/.

5. Seth Godin, *Tribes: We Need You to Lead Us* (USA: Portfolio, 2008), 9.

6. Godin, *Tribes*, 11.

7. Emilie M. Townes, *Breaking the Fine Rain of Death: African American Health Issues and a Womanist Ethic of Care* (Eugene, OR: Wipf & Stock, 1998), 177.

34. A THREAD YOU FOLLOW

1. *Keeping the Faith*, directed by Edward Norton (Touchstone Pictures, 2000).

2. William Stafford, *The Way It Is: New and Selected Poems* (Minneapolis: Gray Wolf Press, 1999).

35. HOLY FRIENDSHIPS: ECUMENICAL AND INTERFAITH CONNECTIONS

1. Howard Thurman, "Conversations with Howard Thurman," interview with Landrum Bolling, 1976, https://www.youtube.com/watch?v=CGX4-Wv9UD0. A corresponding holding may be found in film reel 23 of the Howard Thurman Audiovisual Collection, 1951–1982, Pitts Theological Library, Emory University, https://findingaids.library.emory.edu/documents/P-MSS394/?keywords=Landrum.

2. "The Confession of 1967—Inclusive Language Version" (Congregational Ministries Publishing, A Division of the General Assembly Council, Congregational Ministries Division, Presbyterian Church [USA], 2002), 9.42, accessed January 26, 2022, https://www.pcusa.org/site_media/media/uploads/theologyandworship/pdfs/confess67.pdf.

3. Thurman, "Conversations with Howard Thurman."

36. AN UNEXPECTED WAY

1. Michelle K. Ryan and S. Alexander Haslam, "The Glass Cliff: Exploring the Dynamics Surrounding the Appointment of Women to Precarious Leadership Positions," *Academy of Management Review* 32, no. 2 (2007): 549–72.

37. THE UNEXPECTED CALL WITHIN A CALL

1. In another interview, Huston made a similar statement on digging for water, referencing a Buddhist parable. See April Thompson, "Water From a Deeper Well: Huston Smith on Why Spirituality without Religion Isn't Enough," *The Sun*, October 2002, https://www.thesunmagazine.org/issues/322/water-from-a-deeper-well.

2. Address at the opening of the exhibit on the world's religions, Santa Clara University, March 31, 2005.

38. JUST KEEP WALKING

1. Paul Tillich, *Systematic Theology*, Vol. 1 (Chicago: University of Chicago Press, 1951), 235.

40. ON STARTING NEW THINGS WHILE THE WORLD IS BURNING

1. Tyler Sit, *Staying Awake: The Gospel for Changemakers* (St. Louis, MO: Chalice Press, 2021), 134.

42. FARM CHURCH

1. The miracle is that we are in Durham, North Carolina—the home of Duke University Medical System. Ben has been receiving world-class medical care and is doing well as of this writing.

43. INTRODUCING BIVOCATIONAL MINISTRY

1. Discussion of the following is drawn from Darryl W. Stephens, "Bivocational Ministry as the Congregation's Curriculum," in *Bivocational and Beyond: Educating for Thriving Multivocational Ministry*, ed. Darryl W. Stephens, Teaching Religion and Theology series (Books @Atla Open Press, Scholarly Editions, 2022).

2. Cynthia G. Lindner, *Varieties of Gifts: Multiplicity and the Well-Lived Pastoral Life* (Lanham, MD: Rowman & Littlefield, 2016), 4.

3. Frederick Buechner, *Wishful Thinking: A Theological ABC* (New York: Harper & Row, 1973), 95.

4. For discussion, see Jessica Young Brown, "Black and Bivocational," in *Bivocational and Beyond: Educating for Thriving Multivocational Ministry*, ed. Darryl W. Stephens, Teaching Religion and Theology series (Books @Atla Open Press, Scholarly Editions, 2022).

5. Deacons are one of three forms of ordained ministry recognized ecumenically, complementing the ministry of presbyters and bishops. See World Council of Churches, "Baptism, Eucharist and Ministry," Faith and Order Paper No. 111 (Geneva: World Council of Churches, 1982), Ministry III.A.19, https://www.oikoumene.org/resources/documents/baptism-eucharist-and-ministry-faith-and-order-paper-no-111-the-lima-text. On the diaconate, see Diakonia World Federation Executive Committee, "Diaconal Reflections: How We Experience Our Diaconal Calling in Our Diversity." (Diakonia, 1998), http://www.diakonia-world.org/files/theologiepapier98english.pdf.

44. THANK GOD FOR FRIENDS

1. Stanley Hauerwas and Jean Vanier, *Living Gently in a Violent World: The Prophetic Witness of Weakness* (Downers Grove, IL: InterVarsity Press, 2008), 74.

2. Jeff McSwain, *Movements of Grace* (Eugene, OR: Wipf and Stock, 2010), 80.

Index

ABC. *See* American Baptist Church
absence, leave of, 139
abundance, 181–82
Academy of Catholic Hispanic Theologians of the United States (ACHTUS), 89
active duty, 45
activism, 135–36
administration, 67, 94
advisors, 48–49
advocacy, 127, 136
Advocate Aurora Health, 123
African Methodist Episcopal (AME) churches, 135, 190
air force, 46
Alex, 188–89
Alliance of Baptists, 37
AME. *See* African Methodist Episcopal churches
America, 22–23
America College of Healthcare Executives, 125
American Baptist Church (ABC), 44
ancestor, 22–23
Another Way (Lewis, S., Williams, and Baker), 5–6
anti-racism, 36–37
appreciation, 100–101

L'Arche Portland, Oregon, 18

art, 90
assumption, 15, 30–31
attention: to art, 90; on God, 81; pastoring paying, 19
attorney, 173
authenticity: gifts of, 81; leadership wanting, 104; of relationship, 129
authority, 127, 202n2

Babchuck, Elan, 166
Baker, Dori Grinenko, 5–6
Bangalore, India, 96–97
Banks, Monica, 115
Barth, Karl, 63
Bass, Dorothy, 68
belief, 38–39
Berry, Wendell, 71
Beth El Synagogue, 148–50
betweenness, 5–6, 8
Bible, 25, 80, 95, 107, 136–37, 158; stories in, 7
bishops: challenges by, 101; conversations of, 99; ELCA, 124; leadership of, 99; as lesbian, 105–6; ministry directed by, 101; pastors and, 100, 124–25

bivocationality, 130, 195; abundance demonstrated by, 181–82; of deacons, 183; gifts in, 181; hierarchy overturned by, 184; of ministry, 197; names of, 182; of pastors, 190; stigma of, 182
Bloom, Matt, 3
Bolling, Landrum, 147
Bridgeman, Valerie, 130
Brite Divinity School, 161–62
Brown, Michael, Jr., 109
Brunswick Theological Seminary, 192
Buechner, Frederick, 73
burden, self-giving as, 60
business, 42, 76
Butler, Octavia, 136

call, 5, 64, 77, 127; to active duty, 45; to air force, 46; betweenness expressed in, 8; within call, 159–60; clarity of, 113, 165; to college, 84; to communities, 129; congregation established by, 175; Copeland confirming, 45; as corporeal, 21; discernment of, 27, 42; of dreams, 53, 55; at Eden Theological Seminary, 97; Elijah answering, 107–8; to episcopacy, 105; to Farm Church, 179; of God, 143; to leadership, 12, 15; during Lent, 161; love guiding, 72, 75; to ministry, 22, 38, 95, 107, 109, 129, 158; obstacle to, 46; pain shaping, 27; of pastors, 13; as planters, 169; purpose and, 6, 8, 9; to retreats, 69; to share, 155–56; to teaching, 51, 54; as thunderous, 3; without traditions, 137; of vocation, 55, 199; women answering, 193
camps, 65–69, 72, 95–96, 203n2
campus, college, 87–88, 96
cancer, 178–79
Cannon, Katie G., 40, 45, 63
CB&LF. *See* Church Building and Loan Fund

CCMM. *See* connector-creator-misfit of multiplicities
CCP. *See* chaplain candidate program
celebration, 100
centers, for retreats, 65–69, 92, 203n2
challenges, 71, 109, 159, 170, 196; by bishops, 101; character developed by, 46; culture in, 114
change, 32, 63, 187
chaos, 94, 116–17
chapel, 85
chaplain candidate program (CCP), 44
chaplains: at college, 84, 91–93; CPE compared with, 40; as directors, 88; education of, 35, 37; experience of, 30; in hospital, 197; interruption influencing, 93–94; for military, 43–44; Monica seeing, 29; names said by, 84–85; pastors as, 45; people uprising, 30–31; power of, 31; religions known by, 33; staff cared for by, 31–32; traditions known by, 33; worship led by, 85
character, 46
Chicago, Illinois, 87–88
Christ. *See* Jesus Christ
Christian Associates of Southwest Pennsylvania, 153–54, 155
Christianity, 71, 149. *See also specific topics*
Christmas, 149
Church Building and Loan Fund (CB&LF), 131
churches, 129, 132; camps for, 95–96; as communities, 26–27, 59; divorce rejected by, 174; exploration encouraged by, 2; hospital compared with, 125; of Japanese Americans, 195; justice outside, 75–76; of Korean Americans, 196; language of, 18; leadership of, 1–2, 12–13; Mennonite, 18; mission of, 11; nourishment of, 75; ordination by, 13; pastors outside, 178; planters of, 169, 183; relevance of, 134; song in,

47; Youth Sunday at, 25. *See also specific churches*
Church Innovations, 114
Church of Many Peoples, 36
Church of the Saviour, 112
clarity: of call, 113, 165; of leadership, 149; in ministry, 108; of path, 162; seminary without, 128–29
classroom, 85
clay, 79–80
clergy, 11–15
Cleveland, Ohio, 140
Cleveland, Reginald, 43
climate change, 170
clinical pastoral education (CPE), 37, 40
Coleman, Monica A., 136
collaboration, 88–89
college: call to, 84; chaplains at, 84, 91–93; God in, 57; ministry in, 7; pastors at, 12; vocation in, 195–96
colonization, 68–69
coming out, trauma of, 174
commissioned officer training (COT), 44
Communion, 118
Communion Table, 115–17
communities, 97; advocacy in, 136; call to, 129; on campus, 88; churches as, 26–27, 59; Communion Table in, 115–16; in discernment, 4, 28, 38; gifts appreciated by, 18; I/DD in, 187; to Jesus Christ, 1; A Just Harvest centering, 127; without justice, 170; leadership of, 27; listening to, 171; prayer and, 119–20; Pulse shooting impacting, 175; religions shaping, 163; starting of, 165–66; as tribe, 137; values altered by, 189; in vocation, 54, 55; worship invited by, 59
Community Covenant Church, 112
complaint, 105
complexity, 31–32
conference, of ministry, 65–69
Conference of Bishops, 124

confirmation, 1, 60
congregation: call establishing, 175; leadership of, 99–100; membership built by, 177–78; staff with, 102
connector-creator-misfit of multiplicities (CCMM), 8
conservatism, 61–62
constructing solidarity, 36
conversations, 99, 101
Copeland, Claudette Anderson, 45
Corner House, 119–20
Cosby, Gordon, 112
COT. *See* commissioned officer training
cotidiano. See daily lived experience
Council of Churches of the Pittsburgh Area. *See* Christian Associates of Southwest Pennsylvania
COVID-19 pandemic, 175, 179
CPE. *See* clinical pastoral education
cultural immersion, 107
culture, 107, 114
curiosity: with Farm Church, 178; about religions, 157; traditions contrasted with, 130

daily lived experience (*cotidiano*), 88–89
daughter, 32
deacons, 183, 207n5
Delk, Yvonne, 47
denominations, 113–14, 148
Denver, Colorado, 135, 162
De Pree, Max, 100
Dillard, Annie, 84
directors: administration by, 67; of CB&LF, 131; chaplains as, 88; of Interfaith Alliance of Colorado, 163; land recognized by, 67; mission communicated by, 66; reflection by, 81; as women, 153–54
discernment, 3; betweenness influencing, 5; of call, 27, 42; by communities, 4, 28, 38; God in, 21; imagination enlarged by, ix–x;

path of, 97; in questions, 47–48; by students, 47–48
discipline, 14
diversity, ix; of denominations, 148; ministry shaped by, 199–200; of students, 201n1
divorce, 26, 174
Dobson, James, 63
Down Syndrome, 188–89
dreams, 53, 55, 77
Duke Divinity School, 120

ecumenism, 154
Eden Theological Seminary, 97
education, 35, 37, 40, 87, 89
ELCA. *See* Evangelical Lutheran Church in America
election, 62
electronic medical record (EMR), 31
Elijah (biblical figure), 107–8
Ellison-Jones Convocation, 43
El Salvador, 173
EMR. *See* electronic medical record
entrepreneurs: faith of, 132; "intrapreneur" compared with, 204n5; leadership as, 133; spirituality guiding, 131–33, 204n4; theology on, 133
episcopacy, 105
equity, 118
eurocentrism, 64
Evangelical Lutheran Church in America (ELCA), 123–24
evangelicals, 61–62
exclusion, 66, 89
Executive Order 9066, 195
expectations, 3
experience, 108; of chaplains, 30; daily lived, 88–89; God shaping, 79; identity shaped by, 97; of interruption, 38; of learning, 149; of preparation, 50; for self, 147; vocation led to by, 92

exploration, 3, 47–48; churches encouraging, 2; of religions, 159–60; vocation through, 6

faith, 108; confirmation of, 1; of entrepreneurs, 132; God and, 72; land shaping, 69; with politics, 111; questions challenging, 159; religions encountered by, 158–59; science contrasted with, 30; support in, 187–88; teaching growing, 33
families: belief influenced by, 38–39; change in, 187; ecumenism of, 154; God in, 25; hospitality committed to by, 120; immigration challenging, 196; of mother, 131–32; religions in, 30, 103
Farm Church, 177–80
farmer, 19, 140, 177
farms, 92, 141–42
FCAB. *See* Franklinton Center at Bricks
feeling, 157–58
Ferguson, Missouri, 109
field, 76–77
First Christian Church, 115
fish, 181
Floding, Matt, 188
Florida, 62
Flourishing in Ministry (Bloom), 3
Floyd, George, 171
Focus on the Family, 63
food, 118, 139–40, 141
forestry, vocation as, 71
fragility, 18
framing, 117–18
Franklinton Center at Bricks (FCAB), 76–77
Friendship House, 188, 190
fundamentalism, 63–64

gayness, 36
gender, 196–97
Gibson, Ardella, 40
gifts, 141–42; of authenticity, 81; in bivocationality, 181; communities

appreciating, 18; imagination and, ix; of mentor, 170; pastors giving, 2; Proverbs 18:16 on, 136–37
Glide Memorial, 105
Global Christian Forum, 114
Goatley, Dean, 47, 51
God, 120–21; attention on, 81; call of, 143; in college, 57; in discernment, 21; experience shaped by, 79; faith and, 72; in families, 25; healing by, 171; in hospitality, 69; Ignatius on, 79; to Jeremiah, 132; listening for, 81, 119, 161; ministry guided by, 190; priest compared with, 17; reconciliation longed for by, 144–45; role chosen by, 202n3; Thurman on, 150; "yes" to, 107–9. *See also* Jesus Christ; Spirit
Godin, Seth, 137
Gordon, Jennifer, 173–74
gospel services (GS), 45
Gould Champ, Patricia A., 43
Greybur, Daniel, 148
GS. *See* gospel services
guests, 67

Hafiz (poet), 33
Hamlet (Shakespeare), 89
Haslam, Alexander, 154–55
Hatfield, Mark O., 112
Hauerwas, Stanley, 57
healing, 171
health, 163
health-care, 125
Heart of the Rockies Christian Church, 161
hierarchy, 184
Hofstra University, 173
Holy Spirit. *See* Spirit
Hope College, 111
Hopkins, Gerard Manley, 85–86
hospital, 125, 197
hospitality: families committing to, 120; God in, 69; in ministry, 65–66

I/DD. *See* intellectual and developmental disabilities
identity, 97
Ignatius, 79, 80
Iliff School of Theology, 7
illness, 187–88
imagination, 19, 42, 143, 170; clay in, 79–80; discernment enlarging, ix–x; gifts and, ix; of pastors, 33; in prayer, 81; questions opening, 79; stories sparking, 199; vocation influenced by, 79
immigration, 173, 196
Incarnation Fund (program), 171
Iniguez, Carmen, 175
insula (housing), 83
integrity, 147, 150, 163
intellectual and developmental disabilities (I/DD), 187
Interdenominational Theological Center, 135
Interfaith Alliance of Colorado, 163
interruption, 38, 93–94
"intrapreneur," 204n5
irony, 92
Israel, 83, 162

Jakes, T. D., 45
Japanese Americans, 195
Jeremiah (biblical figure), 132
Jeremiah 18, 80
Jeremiah 29:7, 158
Jesus Christ: clergy chosen by, 11–12, 14–15; Communion Table guided by, 117; communities to, 1; grit of, 140; justice and, 75; in orthodox triangle, 83; Peter implored by, 184; stories told by, 140–41; "yes" to, 1
job, bivocationality of, 182
John (biblical figure), 22
John 20, 95, 97
Johnston-Krase, Ben, 177–79, 206n1
Jones, Sam, 131–32
Jordan, June, 92
journaling, 192

joy, 1; in Alex, 189; service as, 14; of Spirit, 57; of teaching, 55
Judaism, 149

A Just Harvest, 127, 129

justice, 37, 77; outside churches, 75–76; communities without, 170; Jesus Christ and, 75; social, 36

Keeping the Faith (movie), 143
Kentucky, 62
King, Martin Luther, Jr., 77
1 Kings, 107
knowledge, 166–67
Korean Americans, 54–55, 196
Küng, Hans, 159–60

land, 67–68
language: of churches, 18; John employing, 22; spirituality before, 35–36
Lassen National Park, 104
latinamente, 88
leadership: authenticity wanted by, 104; of bishops, 99; call to, 12, 15; of churches, 1–2, 12–13; clarity of, 149; colonization acknowledged by, 68–69; of communities, 27; of congregation, 99–100; as entrepreneurs, 133; of Farm Church, 179; framing in, 117–18; in healthcare, 125; by ministry, 14; of nonprofits, 117–18; by pastors, 11, 13; reality defined by, 101; women in, 135, 154–55, 190
Leadership Is an Art (De Pree), 100
learning, 49–50, 149
leave of absence, 139
Lee, Jarena, 190
Lent, 161
lesbians, 105–6
Let Your Life Speak (Palmer), 3
Lewis, C. S., 28
Lewis, John, 100

Lewis, Stephen, 5–6
LGBTQ people, 36, 104–6
liberalism, 63–64
limits, 167
listening, 81, 119, 161, 171
Living Gently in a Violent World (Vanier), 189
location, 48–49, 52
love: call guided by, 72, 75; integrity with, 147, 150; reincarnation of, 72–73; of tress, 71

Making a Way out of No Way (Coleman), 136
Mandziuk, Natalie, x
marriage, 105
Marshall, Willie, 43
Martell, Loida I., 8
McKane, Hilary, x
McKenzie, Vashti, 45
McSwain, Jeff, 189
mentors, 71–72, 170–71, 192
Mepkin Abbey, 120–21
Meyer, Ray, 26
military, 43–44
Ministerio Latino, 175
ministry, 15; absence from, 139; bishops directing, 101; bivocationality of, 197; business of, 42; call to, 22, 38, 95, 107, 109, 129, 158; at camps, 65–69, 72; on campus, 87; celebration by, 100; clarity in, 108; collaboration by, 88–89; in college, 7; complaint against, 105; of conference, 65–69; covocational ministry, 183; deacons in, 207n5; diversity shaping, 199–200; in education, 87; without exclusion, 66; of food, 141; gender intersected with by, 196–97; God guiding, 190; hospitality in, 65–66; land stewarded by, 68; leadership by, 14; LGBTQ people and, 104; marketplace, 183; multiplicity in, 182; organization compared with, 127; outdoor, 66, 68;

partially funded, 182; part-time, 183; pastoral care, 123; of presence, 141; reflection by, 3–4; reincarnation of, 72–73; resources sustaining, 34; of retreats, 65–69; sacramentality of, 142; skills of, 181; surprises in, 157; traditions and, 196; as vocation, 47, 103; "yes" to, 131, 192
mission: advocacy in, 127; of churches, 11; directors communicating, 66; of Friendship House, 190
mission trip, 107, 187–88
mobile food pantry, 118
Monica, 29, 32
morality, 170
Moral Man and Immoral Society (Niebuhr), 111
mother, 131–32
Mount Olivet Conference & Retreat Center, 65–67
Movements of Grace (McSwain), 189
Mulder, Ed, 113
Müller, Max, 159–60
multiplicity, 8, 182
multivocationality, 182

names, 84–85, 182
needs, of neighborhood, 141
neighbors, 139–41, 148
nets, 181
Network, Glean, 166
New City Church, 171
New Communion of the Triad, 115–17
Newsom, Gavin, 105
Niebuhr, Reinhold, 111
nonprofits, 117–18, 136, 190
nourishment, 75
novelty, 87–88
nurture, 54–55

O'Conner, Elizabeth, 112
openness, 46
ordination, 13, 174–75
organization: complexity of, 31–32; good done by, 132; ministry compared with, 127. *See also specific organization*
orthodox triangle, 83
others, 60

Pacific School of Religion, 105, 174
pain, 26–28
Palestine, 162
Palmer, Parker, 3
Parable of the Sower (Butler), 136
parents, 6
Passover, 149
pastors, 187; attention paid by, 19; authority of, 202n2; bishops and, 100, 124–25; bivocationality of, 190; call of, 13; change in, 63; as chaplains, 45; outside churches, 178; at college, 12; in Denver, 162; expectations of, 3; farmer compared with, 19, 140, 177; fragility of, 18; gift given by, 2; imagination of, 33; with job, 182; in Kentucky, 62; leadership by, 11, 13; as mentor, 192; ordination encouraged by, 174–75; part-time, 130; path of, 173; sacramentality of, 139; before seminary, 108; women as, 43, 103
path, 3, 161; clarity of, 162; of discernment, 97; journaling of, 192; of pastors, 173; questions on, 108, 163; of vocation, 50, 79
Patterson, LeRoy "Pat," 111
Paul (apostle), 188, 189

The Peaceable Kingdom (Hauerwas), 57

people: chaplains surprised by, 30–31; knowledge of, 166; priest apart from, 17
Perez, Karla, 175
Peter (biblical figure), 184
Peterson, Eugene, 27
physician, 187
planters, church, 169, 183
Plato, 57

Poetry for the People Program, 92
politics: of denominations, 113–14; faith with, 111; seminary postponing, 62
poorness, 61
power, 31
prayer: communities and, 119–20; imagination in, 81; reflection and, 193; spirituality grown by, 80
preparation, 49–51
Presbyterian Church (USA) Confession of 1967, 147
Prescott, Kent, 26
presence, 141
priest, 17
privilege, 169–71
problem, solutions to, 166
profession, vocation compared to, 53
professors, 47–51
Proverbs 18:16, 136–37
pulpit, 45–46
purpose, 5–6, 8–9

questions, 30, 43, 80–81, 103; discernment in, 47–48; faith challenged by, 159; imagination opened by, 79; openness demonstrated by, 46; on path, 108, 163; of privilege, 169; for reflection, 4, 9, 15, 19, 23, 28, 34, 38, 42, 46, 51, 55, 60, 64, 69, 73, 77, 82, 86, 90, 94, 98, 102, 106, 110, 126, 130, 134, 137, 142, 145, 151, 156, 160, 164, 167, 172, 176, 180, 184–85, 190, 193, 198

racism, 35–37, 53–54, 76–77
reality, 100–101
Reality Ministries, 120
realtors, 61
reconciliation, 144–45
reflection, 19; by CCMM, 8; by directors, 81; by ministry, 3–4; on pain, 28; prayer and, 193; questions for, 4, 9, 34, 38, 42, 46, 51, 55, 60, 64, 69, 73, 77, 82, 86, 90, 94, 98, 102, 106, 114, 118, 122, 126, 130, 134, 137, 142, 145, 151, 156, 160, 164, 167, 172, 176, 180, 184–85, 190, 193, 198; service renewed by, x
Reformed Church in America, 113
reincarnation, 72–73
Relational Cultural Theory, 29
relationships, authentic, 129
relevance, 134
religions, 29; chaplains knowing, 33; communities shaped by, 163; curiosity about, 157; exploration of, 159–60; faith encountering, 158–59; in families, 30, 103; Müller on, 159–60. *See also specific religions*
representation, 48–49
resources, 34
retreats: call to, 69; centers for, 65–69, 92, 203n2; Ignatius and, 80; ministry of, 65–69; with neighbors, 148; values of, 66
Robertson, Pat, 61
role, God choosing, 202n3
Roman Catholic Diocese of Pittsburgh, 154
Rome, 22–23
Ryan, Michelle K., 154–55

sacramentality, 139, 142
Sager, Steve, 149
Samuel DeWitt Proctor School of Theology, 43
Sankofa CPE Center, 40–41
Santos, Raymond, 171
School of Theology and Ministry, at Seattle University, 195
science, 30
SCOS. *See* Summer Communities of Service
Segres, Richard "Buck," 44
self, 147
seminary, 59, 157; without clarity, 128–29; in Israel, 83; pastors before, 108; politics postponed by, 62; stories

at, 143; students at, 123. *See also specific seminary*
service, x, 14
sexuality, 38
Shakespeare, William, 89
share, call to, 155–56
shooting, 149, 175
sin, 13
Sit, Tyler, 170–71
skills, 181
Smith, Huston, 159
Sojourners (communities), 112, 114
solution, 166
song, in churches, 47
Spirit: joy of, 57; in teaching, 60; unfolding by, 91
spiritual care visit, 29, 31–32
spirituality: entrepreneurs guided by, 131–33, 204n4; before language, 35–36; prayer growing, 80
staff, 31–32, 102
Stafford, William, 144
starting, 167
starting, communities of, 165–66
Staying Awake (Sit), 170–71
Stephen Ministries, 124
stigma, 182
stories: in Bible, 7; imagination sparked by, 199; Jesus Christ telling, 140–41; at seminary, 143; of vocation, 202n1
students, x; discernment by, 47–48; diversity of, 201n1; location shaping, 52; professors questioned by, 47–48, 51; at seminary, 123
success, 61
Summer Communities of Service (SCOS), 97
support: in faith, 187–88; for Farm Church, 178; knowledge of, 167
surprises, 157
sustainability, 167
Sweet Honey in the Rock (singing group), 38
synagogue, 83. *See also specific synagogue*

talking, 32
teaching, 57; call to, 51, 54; faith grown by, 33; guests shaping, 67; joy of, 55
team, 166
tentmaking, 183
theology: Communion Table centralized by, 116; on entrepreneurs, 133; Latinx, 90; in nonprofits, 117
thread, vocation as, 144
Thurman, Howard Washington, 23, 147, 150
Torah, 149–50
traditions, 43; call without, 137; chaplains knowing, 33; curiosity contrasted with, 130; ministry and, 196; Reformed, 147, 151
trauma, 171, 174
Tree of Life Synagogue, 149
trees, 71
tribe, 137
Tribes (Godin), 137
Trinity Avenue Presbyterian Church, 148–50
Trinity Christian College, 57
turning points, 158–59

UCC. *See* United Church of Christ
UMC. *See* United Methodist Church
unfolding, 91, 92
United Church of Christ (UCC), 7, 77, 97, 123, 131, 153–54, 174
United Methodist Church (UMC), 103, 105, 139
United Nations Sustainable Development Goals, 132
United Theological College, 96–97
UpCycle Farm, 139–41

urbanity, Cleveland of, 140

values, 66, 189
Vanier, Jean, 188, 189
Vietnam War, 111
vocation: call of, 5, 199; in college, 195–96; communities in, 54, 55;

experience leading to, 92; through exploration, 6; forestry as, 71; imagination influencing, 79; location influencing, 49; ministry as, 47, 103; path of, 50, 79; profession differentiated from, 53; stories of, 202n1; as thread, 144. *See also* bivocationality

"The Way It Is" (Stafford), 144

WCC. *See* World Council of Churches
Western Theological Seminary, 113
White, Ken, 103
whiteness, 62
Williams, Matthew Wesley, 5–6
Willimon, William, 15
Winston-Salem, North Carolina, 118
WomanPreach, 130
women, 95; of AME churches, 190; call answered by, 193; directors as, 153–54; as Korean Americans, 196; in leadership, 135, 154–55, 190; as pastors, 43, 103; as priest, 17; in pulpit, 45–46

Workplace Project, 173–74
World Council of Churches (WCC), 113

The World's Religions (Smith), 159

worship, 59, 83, 85

The Writing Life (Dillard), 84

Yale University, 89
YASC. *See* Young Adult Service Communities
"yes": cost of, 104; to God, 107–9; to Jesus Christ, 1; to ministry, 131, 192
Young Adult Service Communities (YASC), 97
Youth Sunday, at church, 25

About the Contributors

Elivette Mendez Angulo is a God-loving woman of faith. She is a Christian pastor ordained in the United Church of Christ. A graduate of Andover Newton Theological School with a master (mistress) of divinity degree with a concentration in interfaith dialogue, Elly has served as co-pastor and teacher of Manantial de Gracia "Spring of Grace" UCC in Connecticut. She currently serves as the program manager and interim executive director of the Franklinton Center at Bricks in Whitakers, North Carolina, where she uses her love of storytelling to welcome social justice activists to confer, retreat, fellowship, and act.

The Rev. Liddy Barlow has served as executive minister of Christian Associates of Southwest Pennsylvania since 2014. She grew up in New Hampshire and earned her master of divinity degree at Andover Newton Theological School, then located in greater Boston (now Andover Newton Seminary at Yale Divinity School). Liddy is a lifelong member of the United Church of Christ and has served local churches, regional boards and committees, and national working groups, including the *Manual on Ministry* and *Manual on Church* revision teams. She lives in Pittsburgh with her husband Greg and their children, Pippa and Edmund.

Rev. Traci Blackmon is associate general minister of justice and local church ministries for the United Church of Christ. As a public theologian, Rev. Blackmon's voice is featured on many local, national, and international platforms spanning the breadth of the White House to the Carter Center to the Vatican, as well as several documentaries and print publications. Rev. Blackmon earned a bachelor of science degree in nursing from Birmingham-Southern College and a master of divinity degree from Eden Theological Seminary. She currently serves as pastor in residence for Eden Theological Seminary in Webster Groves, Missouri.

Mary Schaller Blaufuss serves as vice president for advancement at Eden Theological Seminary, St. Louis, Missouri. Her formal education includes an MDiv from Eden Seminary, a BA from Westminster College, and a PhD from Princeton Theological Seminary. Mary has served as a local church pastor, a seminary teacher at the United Theological College, Bangalore, India through Global Ministries, and as a UCC national staff team leader. She has authored two books and multiple chapters and articles on mission history and theology of the United Church of Christ and the ecumenical church.

The Rev. Dr. Michael Bos is senior minister of Marble Collegiate Church in New York City. He also serves as chaplain of the Collegiate School, where he teaches Islam. He has written two books with coauthor Dr. William Sachs: *A Church Beyond Belief: The Search for Belonging and the Religious Future* and *Fragmented Lives: Finding Faith in an Age of Uncertainty*. He received his BS in psychology from Grand Valley State University, MDiv from Western Theological Seminary, and DMin from Duke University Divinity School. He was a pastor at a megachurch in Michigan, started a church in Texas, and developed an interfaith study center in Oman. Through his interfaith work he developed programs with institutions such as Princeton Theological Seminary, the Center for Interfaith Reconciliation, and the US State Department. Working with the US Embassy and government of Oman, he helped establish a first-of-its-kind program on religious diplomacy in the Middle East for the top chaplains in the US armed services. For his work in bringing together Christians, Muslims, and Hindus in Oman to aid low-income workers, he received the US Ambassador's Award for Community Service.

The Reverend Allen Brimer has served the church professionally for over twenty-five years as a missionary, administrator, chaplain, program director, pastor, church planter, professor, and farmer. He is a graduate of McCormick Theological Seminary in Chicago and the University of Tennessee–Knoxville. He is the father of two remarkable sons, Benjamin (twenty) and Eli (fourteen). Allen is currently the pastor of the Church of Reconciliation in Chapel Hill, North Carolina, a historic and ornery band of flaming-haired prophets committed to race equity, peacemaking, and justice.

Rev. Dr. Danielle J. Buhuro is executive director of Sankofa CPE Center, LLC (https://www.sankofacpe.com/), which offers innovative online clinical pastoral education programming with a unique social justice orientation. Dr. Buhuro is passionate about issues of race, gender, and sexuality. She is author of *Spiritual Care in An Age of #BlackLivesMatter: Examining the Spiritual and Prophetic Needs of African Americans Living in A Violent America*. Dr.

Buhuro attended Chicago Theological Seminary, where she earned the master of divinity and doctor of ministry degrees respectively.

Rev. Kent Busman is a 1993 graduate of New Brunswick Theological Seminary, New Jersey, having also attended Western and Fuller Seminaries part-time while working various jobs. In the pre–distance learning environment, there were four years of long drives, late classes, and sleeping at highway rest stops in order to continue working the next day. Kent is still serving his first call as executive director of Fowler Camp and Retreat Center in the Adirondack Mountains. The camp is jointly affiliated with both the Reformed Church in America (RCA) and the United Church of Christ (UCC).

Scott Cameron is a 2016 graduate of Duke Divinity School. During his first year of seminary, he lived in Friendship House Durham, which actively shaped his call. In a previous life, he graduated from UNC Medical School and completed an internship, residency, and fellowship in neonatology at Johns Hopkins. He currently lives in his hometown, Fayetteville, North Carolina, working as a NICU physician, is ordained, and volunteers as a Presbyterian (PCUSA) chaplain at Friendship House Fayetteville. He and his family live immediately adjacent to Friendship House Fayetteville. Together, they enjoy the rhythm of this intentional community: eat, pray, and celebrate.

A Wisconsin native, **Reverend Dr. Katie Crowe** is a graduate of Berry College (BA), Princeton Theological Seminary (MDiv) and Pittsburgh Theological Seminary (DMin), and an ordained minister in the Presbyterian Church (USA). She served as associate minister for service and mission at First Presbyterian Church in Charlotte, North Carolina, for eight years prior to moving to Durham, North Carolina, where she has served as senior pastor of Trinity Avenue Presbyterian Church since 2012.

Rev. Dr. Chris S. Davies grew up in Connecticut, lives in Cleveland, and is a wandering Irish Rover at heart. She loves faith deeply and is committed to finding ways to bring spiritual innovation into the world past this generation and into those to follow, through clear leadership development and deep relationship building. Chris is a millennial leader, a queer femme, an urban beekeeper, and a lover of community. Chris attended Smith College for her undergraduate work and Andover Newton Theological School for both master of divinity and doctor of ministry degrees, focusing on queering proclamation. She is an ordained minister in the United Church of Christ.

Reverend Tawana Davis, PhD, was born in Harlem, New York, and raised there by her late parents Edward Eugene and Rose Lee Davis.

Tawana completed her undergraduate studies at State University of New York–Empire State with a bachelor of science degree in human resources management. Dr. Davis later received a master of divinity degree at Turner Theological Seminary at the Interdenominational Theological Center in Atlanta, Georgia, and master of arts in leadership and change and doctor of philosophy in leadership and change degrees at Antioch University Graduate School of Leadership and Change. Rev. Dr. Davis is the cofounder of Soul 2 Soul Sisters, a Womanist-centered, faith-based, racial justice nonprofit organization.

Rev. Dr. Tammerie Day is associate director of clinical pastoral education at UNC Hospitals, and an ACPE certified educator. Tammerie earned an MDiv from Brite Divinity School and a PhD in religious studies from SMU; she has taught theology and religious studies in seminary, university, and congregational settings, authored several books and numerous articles, and is a frequent presenter on social justice and spiritual care at state and national gatherings.

Tammerie is married to Mary E. Hill and is the parent of Harper and Chandler Spires; she loves running, kayaking with her dog Roadie, and cooking and eating with everybody else.

Dr. Miguel A. De La Torre's academic pursuit is social ethics within contemporary US thought, specifically how religion affects race, class, and gender oppression. Since obtaining his PhD in 1999, he has authored hundreds of articles and published forty-one books (six winning national awards). An ordained Southern Baptist, he received his MDiv from the Southern Baptist Theological Seminary in Louisville, Kentucky. He presently serves as professor of Social Ethics and Latinx Studies at the Iliff School of Theology in Denver, Colorado. A Fulbright scholar, he served as the 2012 president of the Society of Christian Ethics and is the recipient of both the 2020 AAR Excellence in Teaching Award and the 2021 Martin E. Marty Public Understanding of Religion Award.

Rev. Dr. Eddie De León, CMF, a Latino pastoral theologian and minister, is assistant professor of pastoral ministry and preaching at the Catholic Theological Union (CTU) in Chicago, where he has served as chair of the Spirituality and Pastoral Ministry department. His more recent research and travels focus on the study of art with particular appreciation for its relevance for ministry. While he has collaborated with archeologists in Pompeii, Italy, and has researched the cave of Lascaux in France, his great love is street art. His joy for art is second to his love for the church. He holds a master of divinity degree from CTU and a doctor of ministry degree in preaching from the Aquinas Institute. ¡Adelante!

The Reverend Doctor Patrick Garnet Duggan was ordained to the Christian ministry in 1989 and obtained full ministerial standing in the United Church of Christ in 1995. He earned the bachelor of arts degree from Harvard University (1980) and the master of divinity (1993) and the doctor of ministry (2013) degrees, both from New York Theological Seminary. A bivocational pastor, Duggan has served as senior pastor of the Congregational Church of South Hempstead/United Church of Christ since 1995, and as executive director of the United Church of Christ Church Building and Loan Fund (CB&LF) since 2012.

Matthew Floding is general editor and contributor to Rowman & Littlefield's Explorations in Theological Field Education series and coeditor of the journal *Reflective Practice: Formation and Supervision in Ministry*. He formerly served as director of ministerial formation at Duke Divinity School. He is one of the founders of Friendship House, a residential opportunity for graduate students in which persons of all abilities live in intentional community formed around eating together, praying together, and celebrating life together. He earned an MDiv at McCormick Theological Seminary in Chicago and a DMin at Western Theological Seminary in Holland, Michigan. Matt lives in Minneapolis, Minnesota.

Melissa Florer-Bixler is the pastor of Raleigh Mennonite Church and is a founding member of L'Arche North Carolina. A graduate of Princeton Seminary and Duke University, she is the author of two books. Her writing can be found in numerous publications including *Christian Century*, *Image Journal*, and *Sojourners Magazine*.

David Emmanuel Goatley is associate dean for academic and vocational formation, Ruth W. and A. Morris Williams Jr. Research Professor of Theology and Christian Ministry, and director of the Office of Black Church Studies at Duke Divinity School. He is a constructive theologian whose scholarship and practice lies at the intersection of missiology, Black theology, and leadership strategy. He is ordained in the National Baptist Convention, USA, and serves in leadership capacities with the NAACP, Lott Carey Baptist Foreign Mission Society, the Baptist World Alliance, and the World Council of Churches.

Rev. Wesley Granberg-Michaelson served as general secretary of the Reformed Church in America from 1994 to 2011. He is a graduate of Hope College and Western Theological Seminary. Earlier he served as legislative assistant to US Senator Mark O. Hatfield, and as the associate editor of *Sojourners Magazine*. Wes is known globally for his ecumenical leadership. Presently he serves on the boards of Sojourners, Church Innovations, and the

Global Christian Forum. His tenth and most recent book is *Without Oars: Casting Off into a Life of Pilgrimage*. Wes and his wife Kaarin live in Santa Fe, New Mexico, where he enjoys fly fishing.

David Harrison is a graduate of Wake Forest School of Divinity, the pastor of First Christian Church in Winston-Salem, North Carolina, and executive director of New Communion of the Triad.

Rev. Dr. Mariah Hayden (she/her) is a graduate (MDiv) of the Iliff School of Theology in Denver, Colorado. She received a doctor of ministry degree from the Methodist Theological School in Ohio, focusing on food justice and faith formation in their ecology and justice ministry specialization. As a United Methodist elder, her ministry has taken her to Colorado, Minnesota, Ohio, and Maine. She is passionate about sharing with churches how to create food-based ministry programs that cultivate a just food system and address systemic inequities.

Rev. James Hazelwood serves as the bishop of the New England Synod, ELCA Lutheran. Prior to this office, he served as a parish pastor for twenty-five years in Brooklyn, New York, and Charlestown, Rhode Island. He holds an MDiv from Pacific Lutheran Seminary with studies at Union Theological Seminary in New York. His DMin is from Fuller Theological Seminary, Pasadena, California. He is the author of *Everyday Spirituality: Discover a Life of Hope, Meaning & Peace*, and the forthcoming *Weird Wisdom: Why the Second Half of Life is the Better Half*. He blogs regularly at https://www.jameshazelwood.net/.

Rev. Amanda Henderson is the director of the Institute for Religion, Politics, and Culture at Iliff School of Theology. The institute performs research on the ways religious histories inform political perspectives and shares that information to educate public leaders for transformative action. Before launching the institute, Amanda served for seven years as executive director of the Interfaith Alliance of Colorado, bringing people from different religious traditions together for political action. Amanda is ordained with the Christian Church (Disciples of Christ), author of *Holy Chaos: Creating Connections in Divisive Times*, and is pursuing a PhD in religion and politics at the University of Denver.

Kate Holbrook is a practitioner of contemplative and embodied spiritual practices who values their capacity for helping us stay grounded. She has been an interfaith college chaplain since 2006 and is an MDiv/MA graduate of the Pacific School of Religion. A teacher of Wisdom Healing Qigong, she is passionate about finding creative ways for people, especially young adults, to bring their heads and hearts together to engage meaningfully in community and in the world. Ritual is important to her as is working with families and individuals in crisis, including during times of death. She is ordained in the PC(USA) and rooted in the Quaker tradition. She lives in Colorado.

Christine J. Hong is associate professor of educational ministry and the director of the Doctor of Educational Ministry Program at Columbia Theological Seminary in Decatur, Georgia. She earned her MDiv and ThM at Princeton Theological Seminary. Her research includes anti-colonial and decolonial religious and interreligious education. She is a PC(USA) clergyperson. Hong authored two monographs: *Youth, Identity, and Gender in the Korean American Church*, and *Decolonial Futures: Intercultural and Interreligious Intelligence for Theological Education* from Lexington Press.

Trygve Johnson is the Hinga-Boersma Dean of the Chapel and vice president at Hope College. Ordained in the Reformed Church in America, he earned his MDiv from Western Theological Seminary in Holland, Michigan and holds a PhD in theology from the University of St. Andrew. He is the author of *The Preacher as Liturgical Artist*.

Rev. Dr. Brian Keepers is an ordained pastor in the Reformed Church in America. He graduated from Northwestern College (Orange City, Iowa) with a bachelor of arts, then went on to receive his master of divinity and doctor of ministry degrees from Western Theological Seminary (Holland, Michigan). He currently serves as the lead pastor of Trinity Reformed Church in Orange City, Iowa. Brian is married to Tammy; they have two daughters and one granddaughter.

Nathan Kirkpatrick is an Episcopal priest who serves as one of the principal consultants at Saison Consulting, a Durham, North Carolina–based consulting firm. He has almost two decades of experience working with the leaders of organizations and congregations on issues of change leadership, strategic visioning, conflict, innovation, and sustainability. He serves as an adjunct faculty member for the Lake Institute on Faith & Giving and has been a facilitator for the Center for Courage & Renewal since 2007. When not working, he is an avid photographer, wine connoisseur, amateur chef, and aspiring cyclist.

William H. Lamar IV is pastor of Metropolitan African Methodist Episcopal Church in Washington, DC. He serves alongside a people committed to worship, liberation, and service. To that end, Lamar writes, organizes the community for justice, and strives to confront the external and internal forces that seek to inhibit human flourishing and shared abundance. Acknowledging and embracing the strange call to ordained ministry has been his blessing and burden since 1994.

The Reverend Theresa F. Latini, PhD, is the executive director of Mount Olivet Conference & Retreat Center (Farmington, Minnesota). Ordained in the Presbyterian Church (USA), she received her MDiv and PhD degrees from Princeton Theological Seminary. She previously served as a pastor and seminary professor and administrator. She is the author of *The Church and the Crisis of Community: A Practical Theology of Small-Group Ministry* (2009) and coauthor of *Transforming Church Conflict: Compassionate Leadership in Action* (2011).

greg little is a husband to Janice and father to JoyAna and Elias, and he has a home at Corner House in Durham, North Carolina. He received an MDiv from Duke Divinity School and currently works as director of residential life at Reality Ministries, a nonprofit committed to sharing Christ's love through making room for friendships between people with and without disabilities.

Kristina Lizardy-Hajbi is director of the office of professional formation and assistant professor of leadership and formation at Iliff School of Theology. She is an ordained minister in the United Church of Christ and received her MDiv from Iliff and PhD from the University of Colorado in Educational Leadership, Research, and Policy. Kristina's previous ministry roles span the areas of undergraduate multicultural student affairs, hospital chaplaincy, congregational and young adult faith formation, and denominational leadership.

Karen Oliveto was born on Good Friday and raised in Babylon, on New York's Long Island. She holds a master of divinity degree from Pacific School of Religion and a doctor of philosophy degree from Drew University. She is the author of several books, including *Our Strangely Warmed Hearts: Coming Out Into God's Call* (2018) and *Together at the Table: Diversity Without Division in the United Methodist Church* (2018). She is the first openly LGBTQ bishop in the United Methodist Church, serving as the spiritual leader of the Mountain Sky Conference.

Rev. Dr. Marilyn Pagán-Banks (she/her/ella) is a queer womanist minister, healer, writer, and lifelong co-learner committed to the liberation of oppressed and colonized peoples, building power, and creating community. She currently serves as executive director of A Just Harvest, pastor at San Lucas UCC, and adjunct professor at McCormick Theological Seminary and Garrett Evangelical Theological Seminary. Rev. Pagán-Banks received her master of divinity degree from McCormick Theological Seminary and her doctor of ministry degree from Chicago Theological Seminary, where she has twice been named Hispanic Scholar. She is a joyful contributor to the newly released book *Words of Her Mouth: Psalms for the Struggle*. Rev. Pagán-Banks lives in Chicago with her spouse and loves laughing and dancing with her beautiful Black grandchildren.

Jeney Park-Hearn is director of contextual education and lecturer in the School of Theology and Ministry and in the Couples and Family Therapy Program at Seattle University. She is also congregational care pastor at Blaine Memorial United Methodist Church, a Japanese American faith community with a 118-year history in Seattle. Her academic and ministry interests are where spiritual formation, psychology, and theology meet to enrich the lives of individuals and communities. Jeney lives with her family in the suburbs of Seattle.

Rev. Rhina Ramos is an ordained United Church of Christ minister leading a Spanish-speaking congregation open to the LGTBQI Latinx community. Rhina is also the national coordinator for Encuentros Latinx at the United Church of Christ national office promoting LGBTQI inclusion in faith communities as well as Latinxs in traditional white congregations. Rhina was born in El Salvador and emigrated to the United States at age fourteen in 1983. She graduated from Hofstra University Law School in 1995 and was a labor attorney for five years, recouping thousands of dollars in unpaid wages for immigrant workers. In 2003, she obtained a master of divinity degree from the Pacific School of Religion. In her free time, she loves long walks and listening to sappy romantic music in Spanish.

Rev. Kathie Bender Schwich is chief spiritual officer of Aurora Advocate Health, overseeing the system's chaplaincy, clinical pastoral education, faith outreach, ethics, environmental sustainability, physician and team member well-being, and trauma recovery programs. Ordained in the Evangelical Lutheran Church in America, she holds degrees from the University of Michigan and Saginaw Valley State University, and a master of divinity degree from Luther Seminary in St. Paul, Minnesota. She is a graduate of the Harvard Kennedy School's Executive Leadership program, holds graduate certificates in health-care management and patient experience leadership, and is a fellow in the American College of Healthcare Executives.

Chaplain, Lieutenant Colonel Ruth Naomi Segres is deputy chief of plans and program for the Chief of Chaplains Office, United States Air Force. She earned her doctor of ministry and master of divinity degrees from the Samuel Dewitt Proctor School of Theology, Virginia Union University. She earned master of military science and master of strategic studies degrees from Air University and a bachelor of science from Saint Augustine's University, and did postdoctoral studies at Oxford University, United Kingdom. She is ordained by the American Baptist Churches, USA, a member of Delta Sigma Theta Sorority, Inc., and author of the book *Commanded to Live: Moving Beyond the Pain*.

John Senior is ordained teaching elder in the Presbyterian Church (USA) and assistant dean of vocational formation and director of the art of ministry program at Wake Forest University School of Divinity in Winston-Salem, North Carolina.

Megan Shepherd serves as the program director of Notre Dame Vision in the McGrath Institute for Church Life at the University of Notre Dame. She also serves as a certified spiritual director in Ignatian Spirituality for the campus community and directs silent retreats through campus ministry. Megan received a bachelor of science degree in pre-professional studies and theology and a master of divinity degree from the University of Notre Dame. She has spent more than twenty years working with young people in parish, high school, and national settings.

Tyler Ho-Yin Sit is the pastor and church planter of New City Church, a community in Minneapolis led mostly by queer people of color. Sit is the author of *Staying Awake: The Gospel for Changemakers*, and cofounder of Intersect: A Co-Planting Network. He is a second-generation Chinese American, trained community organizer, and United Methodist pastor. Sit has been featured in the *New York Times*, City Lab, Minnesota Public Radio, and more. See https://www.tylersit.com/.

Keith Starkenburg received his MDiv from Western Theological Seminary in Holland, Michigan, in 2002. He also took a number of courses at Calvin Theological Seminary in Grand Rapids, Michigan, before transferring to Western. He spent most of his youth in Rapid City, South Dakota, just outside of the Black Hills. He's married to Becky Starkenburg, who has also spent more than a couple of decades serving the Triune God in the academy as a student life administrator. They have three children, one of whom is about to start college.

Darryl W. Stephens teaches at Lancaster Theological Seminary and is an ordained deacon in the United Methodist Church. He is a graduate of Rice

University (BA), Perkins School of Theology (MDiv), and Emory University (PhD). As a Christian social ethicist, his research focuses on the church and social change, particularly relating to issues of gender, sexuality, and moral witness. A prolific author and editor, his books include *Professional Sexual Ethics: A Holistic Ministry Approach*, *Out of Exodus: A Journey of Open and Affirming Ministry*, and *Bivocational and Beyond: Educating for Thriving Multivocational Ministry*. He also maintains the blog http://www.ethicsconsidered.com/.

Faye Banks Taylor holds a bachelor's degree in sociology from Virginia Commonwealth University in Richmond, Virginia, a master of divinity degree from the New Brunswick Theological Seminary in New Brunswick, New Jersey, and the doctor of ministry degree, with a concentration in pastoral care and counseling, from the Theological School at Drew University in Madison, New Jersey. She is currently the director of field education for New Brunswick Seminary and the director of the school's site in New York City. She remains the pastor of St. Mark's Chapel AME Church and is a presiding elder in the western New York Conference of the AME Church.

William Willimon is a bishop in the United Methodist Church. He served as the dean of Duke Chapel and professor of Christian ministry at Duke University for twenty years. He returned to Duke after serving as the bishop of the North Alabama Conference from 2004 to 2012. Willimon is the author of seventy books and in 2017 he published *Who Lynched Willie Earle? Confronting Racism through Preaching*.

Nancy Wood is the manager of spiritual care at the University of Vermont Medical Center. She earned her MDiv at Harvard Divinity School and is a United Church of Christ minister, an ACPE certified educator, a mother, a spouse, and a huge fan of musical theater.

www.ingramcontent.com/pod-product-compliance
Lightning Source LLC
Chambersburg PA
CBHW021756230426
43669CB00006B/98